SECOND EDITION

FINDING THE **HEART** OF THE NATION

The journey of the Uluru Statement from the Heart continues

THOMAS MAYOR

Hardie Grant

EXPLORE

This second edition published in 2022 by Hardie Grant Explore, an imprint of Hardie Grant Publishing.

Hardie Grant Explore (Melbourne)
Wurundjeri Country
Building 1, 658 Church Street
Richmond, Victoria 3121

Hardie Grant Explore (Sydney)
Gadigal Country
Level 7, 45 Jones Street
Ultimo, NSW 2007

www.hardiegrant.com/au/explore

Photo insert credits (*from left to right, top to bottom where more than one image appears on a page*): page 1 Jimmy Widders Hunt/Commonwealth; 2–3, 5 Copyright image of the Uluṟu Statement canvas © Anangu Uwankaraku Punu Aboriginal Corporation/Copyright Agency 2022; 4 Clive Scollay; 6 (a) & (b) Jimmy Widders Hunt/Commonwealth; 7 (a) Mathew Lynn, (b) supplied by Thomas Mayor; 8 (a) & (b) Torres Strait Regional Authority.

A catalogue record for this book is available from the National Library of Australia

Hardie Grant acknowledges the Traditional Owners of the Country on which we work, the Wurundjeri People of the Kulin Nation and the Gadigal People of the Eora Nation, and recognises their continuing connection to the land, waters and culture. We pay our respects to their Elders past and present.

Finding the Heart of the Nation 2nd edition
ISBN 9781741178210

10 9 8 7 6 5 4 3 2 1

Publisher
Melissa Kayser
Project editor
Amanda Louey
Editor
Bernadette Foley
Proofreader
Ella Woods
Design
Tristan Schultz, Relative Creative
Typesetting
Mike Kuszla
Production coordinator
Simone Wall

Colour reproduction by Splitting Image Colour Studio

Printed in Australia by Griffin Press, an Accredited ISO AS/NZS 14001 Environmental Management System printer

I dedicate this book to the next generation, with the hope that they will benefit from what we do in ours.

♡

THE ULU_RU STATEMENT FROM THE HEART

We, gathered at the 2017 National Constitutional Convention, coming from all points of the southern sky, make this statement from the heart:

Our Aboriginal and Torres Strait Islander tribes were the first sovereign Nations of the Australian continent and its adjacent islands, and possessed it under our own laws and customs. This our ancestors did, according to the reckoning of our culture, from the Creation, according to the common law from 'time immemorial', and according to science more than 60,000 years ago.

This sovereignty *is a spiritual notion: the ancestral tie between the land, or 'mother nature', and the Aboriginal and Torres Strait Islander peoples who were born therefrom, remain attached thereto, and must one day return thither to be united with our ancestors. This link is the basis of the ownership of the soil, or better, of sovereignty.* It has never been ceded or extinguished, and co-exists with the sovereignty of the Crown.

How could it be otherwise? That peoples possessed a land for sixty millennia and this sacred link disappears from world history in merely the last two hundred years?

With substantive constitutional change and structural reform, we believe this ancient sovereignty can shine through as a fuller expression of Australia's nationhood.

Proportionally, we are the most incarcerated people on the planet. We are not an innately criminal people. Our children are aliened from their families at unprecedented rates. This cannot be because we have no love for them. And our youth languish in detention in obscene numbers. They should be our hope for the future.

These dimensions of our crisis tell plainly the structural nature of our problem. *This is the torment of our powerlessness.*

We seek constitutional reforms to empower our people and take *a rightful place* in our own country. When we have power over our destiny our children will flourish. They will walk in two worlds and their culture will be a gift to their country.

We call for the establishment of a First Nations Voice enshrined in the Constitution.

Makarrata is the culmination of our agenda: *the coming together after a struggle*. It captures our aspirations for a fair and truthful relationship with the people of Australia and a better future for our children based on justice and self-determination.

We seek a Makarrata Commission to supervise a process of agreement-making between governments and First Nations and truth-telling about our history.

In 1967 we were counted, in 2017 we seek to be heard. We leave base camp and start our trek across this vast country. We invite you to walk with us in a movement of the Australian people for a better future.

CONTENTS

INTRODUCTION TO THE SECOND EDITION

This edition of *Finding the Heart of the Nation* comes at a crucial time. Australians have elected a new prime minister, Anthony Albanese, who has demonstrated a capacity to listen to First Nations people. With Minister for Indigenous Australians, Linda Burney, and Special Emissary for Reconciliation and Implementation of the Uluṟu Statement from the Heart, Pat Dodson, the Prime Minister has made the commitment to hold a First Nations Voice referendum, just as my people invited the federal government to do in 2017.

The referendum to enshrine a First Nations Voice is imminent.

This book is important to the success of the Uluṟu Statement from the Heart and the referendum. In addition to the 'Voices' chapters, which are a collection of stories full of hopes and dreams, of joy and heartbreak, and of problems and solutions, in this edition I offer you practical information. I want you to be both inspired and informed. I want you to help me find other Australians who will join us on this journey.

Our campaign to find the heart of the nation has entered a new phase and we are calling you to join us.

Thomas Mayor

'You will hear us tonight and we will be singing to our ancestors, who are your ancestors too. We will be singing to them to remind them that we are here, maintaining our connection to them, for their appreciation. And we do this not just for us, but for all of us.'

~ Djawa Yunupingu

AN INVITATION TO LISTEN

The Uluru Statement from the Heart was conceived from the collective experiences of Aboriginal and Torres Strait Islander peoples from all points of the southern sky. From an unprecedented process of dialogue and consensus building, it was forged from more than two centuries of hardship and struggle. It gives hope to a nation born from many nations, that we may find our collective heart.

The eloquent words of the Uluru Statement make an affirmation that the first sovereign nations of the Australian continent and its adjacent islands have never ceded sovereignty – not when first colonised by the British and not with the enactment of the Australian Constitution in 1901. The words remind us that colonisation did not extinguish the sacred link that no other civilisation on earth can claim – that the Aboriginal and Torres Strait Islander peoples are born from, remain attached to, and will return to be united with ancestors stretching back an amazing 60,000 years. At the same time, the Uluru Statement acknowledges the sovereignty that we all share, as citizens of the nation we now call Australia.

In haunting prose and with First Nations Voices that sing as a chorus, the Uluru Statement decries the scale of our crisis – disproportionate incarceration, children aliened from their families, young people languishing in detention – the awful effects of intergenerational trauma and systemic powerlessness writ large in the official statistics of Australia. It should be obvious that the dimensions of our crisis are not due to an inability to love and care for our own. But sadly, it seems it hasn't been obvious in this country where there is still a toxic inertia that forms part of the 'great Australian silence'. In the Uluṟu Statement, First Nations people did more than lament our present and our past; it wasn't created to only stir empathy. On 26 May 2017, through the Uluṟu Statement, Aboriginal and Torres Strait Islander peoples gifted all Australians with their vision – a roadmap to find the heart of the nation.

The Uluṟu Statement from the Heart was made through a process that imbued it with unprecedented cultural authority. Further, it carries the name of a sacred place and was given its name – Uluṟu – from those Elders of the Mutitjulu community who are its cultural guardians. They gave the name to the Statement because they want its proposals to succeed.

The Uluṟu Statement makes three very important proposals that will be transformative. They are in sequence: first, for a First Nations Voice enshrined in the Constitution; second, for a Makarrata Commission to supervise agreement making, or treaties; and, third, to oversee a process of truth-telling for the nation.

The establishment of a First Nations Voice enshrined in the Constitution is the priority reform – indeed it is now an urgent reform – because, unlike other racial or ethnic groups, laws and policies are being made by governments specifically about us, without us, and too often to our detriment. A Voice is the first reform because it will start to address this political disempowerment, setting us on the path for the future reforms of Treaty and Truth.

We invite you to walk with us in a movement of the Australian people for a better future.

Uluṟu Statement from the Heart

When we gifted Australia with the Uluṟu Statement from the Heart, we struggled to be heard. The federal government almost immediately dismissed it, and there was no money for a campaign. With the support of First Nations Elders and my union, the Maritime Union of Australia, I decided to travel the country with the canvas on which the Uluṟu Statement is written. I showed the artwork, the signatures and the words to thousands of people. I shared what I had heard, seen and felt at Uluṟu with small crowds in remote places, such as ancient meeting grounds at Yule River in the Pilbara, and dense urban centres. With other passionate Indigenous change-makers, I took the Uluṟu Statement to the people, and we started a peoples' movement.

In June 2018, after twelve months on the road with the Uluṟu Statement canvas, I realised I had a compelling story to tell. I had met many Aboriginal and Torres Strait Islander people who had unique stories and perspectives that I thought should be heard. I floated the idea of telling our stories with my friend, Professor Marcia Langton, who had just written the book *Welcome to Country*. Marcia immediately encouraged me to start writing. So I did.

In these pages, you will find my story along with the stories of Aboriginal and Torres Strait Islander people from a variety of backgrounds and age groups, and from all around the country. Our stories are of struggle and hope. We tell of their people's challenges and achievements. Most importantly, we will give you reason to walk with us.

Kunturu Kulini

(Heart Listening)

RACHEL PERKINS

Rachel Perkins is an Arrernte and Kalkadoon woman and a master storyteller through the art of film-making. She maintains her connection to her Country in the heart of Australia, especially now that it is the place where her family spread the ashes of her father, the legendary Indigenous Rights campaigner, Charlie Perkins.

I first met Rachel during the making of the Uluru Statement from the Heart. Since Uluru, we've campaigned together to see the aspirations of the Uluru Statement become a reality. In that time, I found that she is one of the hardest workers I have ever met, and one of the humblest.

I heard Rachel speak about the Uluru Statement artwork at the launch of the 'Heart Listening' art exhibition in Sydney in November 2018. It was an exhibition inspired by the Uluru Statement campaign, and it marked the launch of a week of action. She told a story about the practical work she had done to assist the creation of the amazing artwork on the Statement canvas. She told the story as she introduced Rene Kulitja, the lead artist.

Rachel and I have edited the introduction she gave to Rene and the other artists at the launch.

Here it is.

It's fitting that the Uluṟu Statement from the Heart is bordered by Tjukurrpa (the lore, law, 'Dreaming', song lines) relating to the place of Uluṟu, where we had our convention. Rene led that design, which includes all of the Tjukurrpa that lead into that very sacred area.

Painting our petitions and statements is a tradition that started with the Yirrkala Bark Petitions, painted by the Yolŋu People in 1963. When their Country was being taken over by Nabalco for bauxite mining, they put a petition to the federal government. They painted around the borders of that petition their expression of their connection to their land, and they wrote to the Parliament saying, 'This is our land, this is our law, here are the symbols that are the expression of our connection to the country.' We also had the Barunga Statement that was painted in 1988, which requested a treaty and that Galarrwuy Yunupingu and Wenten Rubuntja presented to the government. But the aspirations of the Barunga Statement were not realised.

The Uluṟu Statement from the Heart follows that tradition of art expressing people's connection to the land through their Dreaming. The one thing we have learnt is not to give these statements to the government. They haven't earned the respect to receive them. When they rise to the aspirations in the Uluṟu Statement, then it may be given to them.

We're very proud to have the ladies paint around the Uluṟu Statement from the Heart. But I want to tell you a little about how the Statement artwork came to get done, because it was a bit of a funny story. So I was at the convention, as a delegate from Alice Springs. It was the second last day and I was sitting with Noel Pearson, who was one of the Referendum Council members who organised the convention. He said, 'We need to do something like the Barunga Statement, we need some physical expression of what comes from the delegates.'

I said, 'Right, I'll ring my friend Clive Schollay, who works just down the road at the Maruku Art Centre. I'll ring him up and I'll see what he can do.' This was at about seven o'clock at night. I rang and said, 'I need a painting to put the Statement on and we need it by ten o'clock tomorrow morning for the press conference.' The art centre was about to close and I said, 'I'll come in an hour.' So I drove over there and I said, 'What have you got?' We pulled out a couple of paintings, and none of them suited it because they weren't the Dreaming from that place. But we brought some paintings back to the resort where we were all meeting, and we looked at them.

We went, 'Oh, maybe this one.'

'Maybe that one.'

'No, it doesn't quite work.'

Eventually, after considering lots of paintings we agreed: 'What we should do is just get a big roll of canvas', because the tradition is for the Yirrkala Bark Petitions and the Barunga Statement that people sign the work. 'We'll get the canvas and everybody can sign it, and we'll paint on it later.' That way, all the Dreamings of Uluru could be painted on it, and it would be created for this purpose. Then we would be doing it the right way.

The painting wasn't ready for the media but we did have the signatures of all the delegates on the canvas. Rene and all the artists painted the canvas afterwards. It happened in a very short space of time.

It's a wonderful, beautiful painting and I'm so proud we did it that way, even though it was pretty stressful at the time. So, the canvas exists now, and we are waiting for the time when our government will rise to the occasion and agree to the aspirations of the Uluru Statement. The Tjukurrpa that is expressed on the canvas is part of Australian history and law, and it's still not being recognised.

Dreaming Together

RENE KULITJA

Rene Kulitja was the lead artist in the group of artists who painted the Uluru Statement from the Heart canvas. She, along with Charmaine Kulitja, Happy Reid and Christine Brumby imbued the painting with great cultural significance and power. They did their work at Maruku Arts, where Rene is a director, in the small community of Mutitjulu, close to Uluru.

Rene speaks several languages including Pitjantjatjara and English. She is an Anangu law woman, an Elder, connected to her land through ceremony, spirit and her very being. Her people in the dry Central Desert were some of the last to feel the impact of white settlement in Australia.

Rene was born in 1958 at the remote Ernabella Mission, situated in the north-west of South Australia and established by Dr Duguid (pronounced Do-Good) in 1937. He was a medical doctor who could see that the increased settler and dingo-hunting traffic endangered the people in the Pitjantjatjara region, so he set up a Presbyterian mission after gaining financial support from the South Australian Government. Unlike other missions, the staff at Ernabella sought to show the pathway to God through hard work and without interfering with the practice of culture and language. Furthermore, all the staff were expected to learn the Pitjantjatjara language. Growing up on the mission, Rene was able to learn about her culture from her parents and the Elders.

Rene was at the closing ceremony of the Uluru First Nations Constitutional Convention when the Uluru Statement from the Heart was read for the first time after it was endorsed. At the ceremony, young Anangu men performed the Emu Dreaming Dance and Rene proudly sang for them. Rene loves to sing. She is a member of the Central Australian Aboriginal Women's Choir, which is the subject of the documentary, *The Song Keepers*.

When I caught up with Rene, we were far from her home in the sacred heart of the country. She and some other Central Desert artists were in Sydney to launch a Maruku Arts exhibition inspired by the Uluru Statement from the Heart's travels around Australia. The exhibition was aptly titled 'Heart Listening', or in Pitjantjatjara, 'Kunturu Kulini'. It was also the launching point for the 'Put it to the People' week of action. It was organised to influence the federal government's bipartisan Joint Select Committee on Constitutional Recognition that was due to release their final report that month, on 30 November 2018. We wanted the Committee to be aware that there was a groundswell of support for a First Nations Voice referendum.

At a cafe in Surry Hills, Sydney, during a break in the artists' schedule, I sat at a rickety table on the footpath with Rene Kulitja and Aunty Yuka Trigger, the most senior Elder in the group of artists. Maruku Arts General Manager Clive Scollay, a fluent speaker of Pitjantjatjara, and emerging Pitjantjatjara speaker, Saha Jones, were on hand to translate.

During our meeting, Rene talked to me about the meaning of the artwork, starting with these words: 'A long time ago, our grandfathers and grandmothers on their Country, they walked from water to water, looking after families, and they told us this story. They have passed away now, and we're lucky. We have the story. The walking is important to the story.'

On the bottom left-hand corner of the Uluru Statement from the Heart, Rene has written 'Uluru-Ku Tjukurrpa'. This translates as: 'The traditional stories of Uluru'. 'Tjukurrpa' cannot fully be described in English. Through story and song lines, Tjukurrpa tells the Anangu people about the creation of Country. It tells of the law, religion and moral system for the people who belong to Country. You may have heard it described as the 'Dreamtime' or 'Creation Stories', but neither of those names does justice to the full meaning of Tjukurrpa.

When I asked Rene to explain what the painting symbolises, she said in her quiet and precise manner, 'Uluru-Ku Tjukurrpa – Uluru Story. It is the story for everyone.' For emphasis she repeated '*everyone*' and went on, 'The Uluru-Ku Tjukurrpa connects everyone, like the Uluru Statement.'

I didn't have the Uluru Statement canvas with me and before I could bring a photo of it up on my phone, Rene had opened my notepad and had begun to draw the convergence of song lines, the Tjukurrpa-Ku Uluru, exactly as it is on the Uluru Statement canvas.

Section by section, she sketched out the Tjukurrpa and explained the story as she drew.

'Tjukurrpa came from north, west, south, east, and teaching all the families so they know. Uluru is that shared place where all of those stories meet,' she said. 'You can see the tracks of "Mala", the Rufous Hare Wallaby people. The track of the rufous hare wallaby shows that the Mala came from the north.

'From the south-west came the men of the Liru, the poisonous snake people. Kuniya, the carpet snake who was pregnant and about to lay her eggs, she came from the east. The Kuniya and Liru clashed.

'Kurpalynga, the desert dingo dog, came from the west.

'Together, the Mala and the Kurpalynga left Uluru to the south.

'In the middle [of the painting], where the Uluru Statement is, that is where Uluru is. The Uluru Statement is where all of our different stories come together.'

As Rene talked about the Tjukurrpa song line and the animals associated with it, she also gave the names of the various families who look after each of the Tjukurrpa, including the artists who, significantly, are from each of the different song lines. Rene described the stories associated with each Tjukurrpa, relating them to the markings, the crevices and the cracks in the rock. She explained how each detail is meaningful to Anangu life and culture.

As I listened to Rene, unfortunately struggling to hear and interpret her words while we sat by the busy street, I realised that I could never do the interconnecting stories justice in these few pages. I have only been able to summarise them. The cultural centre at the Uluru-Kata Tjuta National Park has exhibits that explain the stories in far greater detail, and the best way to learn these stories is to go to Uluru with an Anangu guide, as I did. If you are respectful, you will find that the Anangu people are both welcoming and generous.

I have little doubt that in any other nation, the citizens would celebrate these wonderful Anangu stories. These, and many other First Nations stories are integral to our national history – they are the heartbeat of the country. We should enshrine them, not silence them. The Uluru Statement and the stories that made it are as epic and as significant as Homer's *Iliad* and *The Odyssey*. The stories, the Tjukurrpa, are truly as marvellous and as powerful in their telling, humanity and spirit as any of the greatest dramas by Euripides and Shakespeare, among others, and older than all of them put together.

FIRST NATIONS REGIONAL DIALOGUES

HOBART, 9–11 DECEMBER 2016

BROOME, 10–12 FEBRUARY 2017

DUBBO, 17–19 FEBRUARY 2017

DARWIN, 22–24 FEBRUARY 2017

PERTH, 3–5 MARCH 2017

SYDNEY, 10–12 MARCH 2017

MELBOURNE, 17–19 MARCH 2017

CAIRNS, 24–26 MARCH 2017

ROSS RIVER, 31 MARCH–2 APRIL 2017

ADELAIDE, 7–9 APRIL 2017

BRISBANE, 21–23 APRIL 2017

TORRES STRAIT, 5–7 MAY 2017

CANBERRA, 10 MAY 2017

NATIONAL CONSTITUTIONAL CONVENTION, WELCOME TO COUNTRY CEREMONY, MUTITJULU, 23 MAY 2017

NATIONAL CONSTITUTIONAL CONVENTION, ULURU MEETING PLACE, YULARA, 24–26 MAY 2017

FROM ALL PARTS OF THE SOUTHERN SKY

When you cast your eyes over the signatures surrounding the Uluṟu Statement canvas, imagine you are looking up at the southern sky. The southern sky is both endless space and countless stars. From the brightest to the faintest, the stars are distant, yet they are linked in an intricate tapestry displaying the stories and lessons from our forebears. The stories of the First Nations of Australia, written in the sky, are the most ancient in the world. They have been guiding us for over 60,000 years. The southern sky embodies our collective wisdom. When we gathered at Uluṟu for the culmination of the constitutional dialogues, we carried our wisdom from all parts of the country. We were Aboriginal and Torres Strait Islanders from many First Nations and from distant places, and we came together to guide generations to come.

It is the names on the canvas and the countless others unseen behind them that truly make the Uluṟu Statement from the Heart. Our hopes and aspirations could not have been conveyed in such a powerful way if it weren't for the hard work of many people to advance the rights of Aboriginal and Torres Strait Islander peoples. We have long taken action to be included, self-determining and respected as a sovereign people who have been terribly wronged.

We have worked to claim our rightful place in our own country, but, we have been denied.

Now, our perseverance has led to an opportunity to change the founding document of Australia, the Constitution.

At Federation in 1901, Aboriginal and Torres Strait Islander peoples were excluded from the Constitution. The forefathers of Australia believed we were a dying race, and their policies and actions were designed to expedite their belief. In more recent times, Australia's conscience has begun to stir. It has stirred because of our courage and activism. We have pushed our agenda for land rights and self-determination. Substantive constitutional recognition – a form of recognition that empowers us – has been an important goal for many decades.

From 2007, a symbolic form of constitutional recognition has been promised with bipartisan support. It began with Prime Minister John Howard's proposal to add a preamble to the Constitution, merely recognising that we exist. The bipartisanship has been welcomed by First Nations leaders, though the key difference between us is that the Indigenous peoples desire more than symbolism. We desire a strong form of constitutional recognition, such as enshrining a First Nations representative body, or Voice.

In 2015, 39 Aboriginal and Torres Strait Islander leaders called for a crisis meeting with Prime Minister Tony Abbott and Opposition Leader Bill Shorten. Since John Howard had repealed the legislation that established the Aboriginal and Torres Strait Islander Commission (ATSIC) – destroying an effective national representative body elected by First Nations people – rates of Indigenous incarceration, deaths in custody and child removal were on the rise.

The leaders met at Kirribilli House, and from the meeting came the Kirribilli Statement. The Statement, written by Indigenous leaders, called for the continuation of bipartisan support for constitutional recognition, and that the recognition be in the form of 'substantive changes to the Australian Constitution', not merely symbolic change. They stated that constitutional recognition 'must lay the foundation for the fair treatment of Aboriginal and Torres Strait Islander peoples into the future'.

To avoid the process stalling, the Indigenous leaders proposed that a referendum council be established for 'an ongoing dialogue between Aboriginal and Torres Strait Islander people and the government and parliament, based on the significant work already completed, to negotiate on the content of the question to be put to referendum'.

The Indigenous leaders also called for the resources required to provide useful information to Aboriginal and Torres Strait Islander communities to enable informed decision making, and to engage 'over the coming months with Aboriginal and Torres Strait Islander peoples about the acceptability of the proposed question for constitutional recognition'.

With bipartisanship, the Referendum Council was established. The Council took the question of constitutional recognition to the people who will be recognised.

On the Referendum Council, the Indigenous members were: Ms Dalassa Yorkston, Mr Noel Pearson, Professor Megan Davis, Ms Tanya Hosch, Mr Pat Dodson (before becoming a Senator), Dr Galarrwuy Yunupingu AM, Mr Mick Gooda and Mr Stan Grant. The non-Indigenous members were Ms Kristina Keneally, Mr Murray Gleeson AC, Mr Michael Rose AM, Ms Natasha Stott Despoja AM, Mr Andrew Demetriou and Ms Amanda Vanstone AO. The Council's co-chairs were Professor Pat Anderson AO (Aunty Pat) and Mr Mark Leibler AC.

The Indigenous members of the Council seized the opportunity to give First Nations people the rare opportunity to reach a consensus on how we wish to be recognised and empowered.

In the coming chapters that tell my story, I will describe the consensus building process from my point of view as a participant. But first, we should acknowledge how we got there.

Acknowledging Elders past and present

As well as the many people who helped to create the Uluṟu Statement from the Heart, we must acknowledge the ancestors, the heroes of the resistance, and the leaders of recent times.

Ancestors

Our ancestors, throughout millennia, forged intricate systems of law and culture that provided peace and stability for our people. In the time before the beautiful fabric of our existence was torn apart by colonisation, First Nations people developed agriculture and aquaculture, they were the first humans to mill flour and bake bread, they had granaries and food preservation techniques, and they had complex social systems that maintained order and strong strains of DNA. Our ancestors had reliable ways to record their achievements and pass knowledge on to generation after generation. Our song lines connected generations across time and First Nations across the expanse of the continent. They achieved these feats while living in harmony with each other and without harming the land. Much of this can be learnt from reading Bruce Pascoe's book *Dark Emu*. He learnt a good deal of it from reading the early explorers and settlers' diaries. But we don't need books, anthropologists, and explorers' journals to tell us what abundant lives our advanced societies enjoyed. The knowledge has been passed on through the generations and be can be heard in our Voices today. There is much to thank First Nations ancestors for, and there is much Australia must cease to ignore.

Heroes of the resistance

The songs in praise of the heroes of the resistance largely remain unsung. Our lands were never ceded in the brutal frontier wars. The warriors in those struggles must be remembered. One of these warriors was Pemulwuy, who bravely defended his Darug Nation lands in the late eighteenth century. He was a Bidgigal man, thought to be a 'clever man' with spiritual powers, who led a hundred warriors in the 'Battle of Parramatta'. The club-footed leader terrorised the invaders. When he was shot dead in 1802, his head was severed and sent to Sir Joseph Banks in England, another for the Englishman's collection.

Noongar leader and resistance fighter Yagan did not accept injustice. In 1831, when a Noongar boy was killed by a servant who was shooting at Noongar people caught harvesting potatoes, Yagan retaliated. In accordance with Noongar law, he killed another servant. Yagan was imprisoned but escaped. When he was caught again, he was spared the death sentence, but was ambushed by two white men in 1883. Yagan's head was severed and sent to the Liverpool Museum in England.

Aboriginal women were leaders in the resistance. Tarenorerer was born in Tasmania at the beginning of the nineteenth century. Escaping sealers who had bought her, she returned to her homelands, gathered up her people and trained them in guerrilla warfare. Eventually, she was abducted by sealers again, though they did not know who she was. When her identity was discovered, the elated 'Protector of Aborigines', Augustus George Robinson, kept her imprisoned in isolation so that she couldn't spark a revolt. She died of influenza in 1830, cold and lonely.

These are but a few examples of heroes I've learnt about. They fought bravely during the frontier wars. I will not be telling their stories, but I encourage you to seek them out and learn. If you are non-Indigenous, imagine if it were your homeland that was being taken and they were your kin, because that is what they are for us – our ancestors and kin protecting the land and their people. Their stories should be told and respected.

Leaders and activists

Finally, there are the leaders and activists of recent times. Respect is due to the people who lead from the front – on the streets in dissent, caring for Country, healing our wounded, or wielding the tools of two worlds for progress. Many different types of action culminated in the opportunity for more than a thousand Aboriginal and Torres Strait Islanders to be heard in the regional dialogues and the Uluru Convention. Collectively, we are the authors of the Uluru Statement from the Heart.

Before I tell you about some of my own story, I want to clearly say that it is one among countless other stories and perspectives that are as important as mine. I use my own experiences as a way to bring others' stories together, and to communicate the profound importance of the gift of the Uluru Statement from the Heart.

My story is a short one. It is a small part. I appreciate and have learnt from all those people I've mentioned so far and from the people I spoke to in the interviews for this book. I pay my respects to them and their Elders, past and present.

My Journey

THOMAS MAYOR

My father, Celestino Mayor, left the Torres Strait Islands for the Northern Territory two days after his seventeenth birthday. His goal was to work hard and earn enough money to buy a boat when he returned to the islands. Instead, he fell in love with my mum, Liz Thomas, and settled down on the land of the Larrakia people, Darwin.

Dad's first language was Islander Kriol; a mixture of English, Torres Strait and Asian languages. My mum tells me that when she first met Dad, her friends thought he didn't speak English. By the time I was old enough to notice, Dad spoke English like anyone else.

As I was growing up, I yearned to learn more about my Torres Strait Islander heritage, and I was frustrated when I'd ask my dad a question about it and he wouldn't say much. It took a long time for me to understand why. I thought perhaps it was because Dad expected us to get on with doing well at school and not think about anything else. He had come to Darwin, thousands of kilometres from his island home. He needed to learn to communicate, to fit in. We had to too.

Torres Strait Islanders are well known for working hard. Dad was no exception. He strived to build a better life for us, and always sent part of his income back to Grandma on Thursday Island.

A hard worker. A hard man. I have never met anyone who has worked with Dad who hasn't marvelled at his work ethic. He never complained about his ailments or struggles. But at times he was harsh toward me, his eldest child and only boy. Maybe this contributed to my quiet nature. Nevertheless, I couldn't have asked for a better father. Yes, he was a hard man, but he was also loving and had a heart of gold. Dad taught me good morals and values and gave me a solid grounding, and I will always admire him.

My mother dedicated her life to my two younger sisters, Tanya and Leonie, and me, and she stayed at home to care for us and other children whose parents worked. She had a tough upbringing. Her mother was killed in a car accident when my mum and her younger sister were only toddlers. A drunk driver ran the young family off the road. My mum's tragic loss meant that she, being the eldest, had to take on a great responsibility from a young age. Grandad, a Polish World War II refugee and a brilliant engineer, was very much a European male from that era. By the time Mum was six, she was cooking and cleaning for the household. In those days, it was unusual for a single father to raise two little girls on his own. Keeping the family together was a precarious task as they were always under the eye of the authorities.

I was also a single father for two years. When I broke up with my first partner, my kids were only four, six and seven years old. However, I was lucky. I had my two sisters and my mum to help me. At my eldest daughter's twenty-first birthday, we made sure to thank my mum. She not only kept her own family together as a child, but later she helped me do the same. She kept us together until I met Melanie, my beautiful wife, who became an instant mother not long after her twentieth birthday. My first three children, three of five, still call Melanie 'Mum'.

When I was a boy, my mum cared for four little girls every day, in addition to my two sisters. In the mornings and afternoons, it was my job to collect the gaggle of little girls, six in total. They would follow me to and from school as I rode on my big blue mountain bike, all in their school uniforms on their tiny bikes. I imagine I looked like an ugly, brown Kermit the Frog with a messy afro leading a long line of cute little muppets.

As my sisters and I have grown up, we've stayed close. We have a family tradition that started when I first left home at eighteen. Every Sunday, without fail, our family gets together, mostly at my mum and dad's house for breakfast or dinner. Coming together to cook a feast is part of Torres Strait Islander culture. So, true to our heritage, we cook up a feast and enjoy mocking each other's cooking skills. Cooking is something the men in my family love to do as much as the women. Whenever there is a wedding, funeral, or any excuse for a large gathering of family and friends, we relish the work we do together: hunting, preparing the food and cooking for everyone.

I vividly remember the first time I went hunting as a boy. I can still hear Dad saying, 'Thomas, Thomas, Thomas. Wake up, we're going hunting.' We had packed the dinghy the night before; the wap (harpoon), water, spare rope, anchor, and everything else we needed for a safe and successful hunt, were all carefully stowed in 4.2 metres of aluminium hull. We set off to sea well before sunrise.

Going out at night or before dawn in a dinghy is humbling, especially when you are young and heading out for the first time. You feel so small and insignificant, though at the same time, proud – like you are following the footsteps of your ancestors.

Our voyage would often start at night, and with no light and no GPS to guide us, we would use the glow of the city of Darwin behind us to find our general bearings until we reached the Vernon Islands, Mantiyupwi – Tiwi Country – where we would hunt. As we moved further away from civilisation, our senses would sharpen. The stars would shine brighter, guiding our way forward, and in the sea the glow of the bioluminescent plankton marked our wake. Even today, surrounded by this magnificence, breathing in the cool, fresh, salty air, there's nothing that can make me feel more alive.

Learning to hunt, navigate and survive at sea was a bonding experience with my dad. It also made me feel connected to the Torres Strait. While on a shallow reef off Darwin, standing on the bow of a dinghy, scanning for signs of our prey, there is little separating me from what people are doing on the islands more than 1000 kilometres away. This connection for an Islander raised on the mainland, makes me more of a Torres Strait Islander than any of my many other heritages.

I now feel lucky that Dad taught me how to provide my family with our traditional food.

It's hard to describe how my spirit is roused when I hear the music of the Torres Strait. The deep reverberating *thrum* of the warup (drum), the rhythmic tapping of the bamboo, and the beautiful, almost wailing hymns of the women lifting their voices together with the deep, proud voices of the island men. This combination of sounds, the unique island harmony, connects me to a time before mine, before I was born, before the first Europeans. The Islanders thought the Europeans were Markai – the spirits of the dead – when they sailed through the Torres Strait intent on claiming a false *Terra Nullius*.

In my teenage years, I was lucky enough to practice and perform traditional island dancing with other local Torres Strait Island boys who were growing up in Darwin. Our teachers, Uncle Tawi and Aunty Yvonne Nona, Uncle Yaru and Aunty Serena Tom, Aunty Marie McCleod, Uncle Duluwa David, Uncle Charlie Tapau and Uncle Torres Namoa, made sure we shared the island dancing with our Aboriginal mates. We were a young crew that practiced dance together during the week and played rugby together on the weekend. Wayne Kurnorth, a Larrakia man, is one of the boys I grew up with and I interviewed him for this book. When we spoke, he reflected on the sadness he feels for his loss of Larrakia culture. He hasn't been able to learn about the dances of his own ancestors. By comparison, again, I was lucky.

Aboriginal and Torres Strait Islander people have a standard way to get to know a fellow Black fella when we meet. We say, 'Who's your mob?' I've always known I'm a Torres Strait Islander and that my mum's father was a Polish refugee. It wasn't until later in my life that I began to learn about my broader family tree. To say that my heritage has many layers is an understatement. My Torres Strait Islands heritage is from Waiben (Thursday Island), Muralag (Prince of Wales Island), Badugal (Badu Island), Erub (Darnley Island), and Gerber (Two-Brother Island). The totem we identify with is Kaigas (shovel-nose shark).

My dad is also descended from his Philippine and Dayak great-grandfathers, who were both married to Torres Strait Islanders. There is Barbadian, Dutch, and Chinese ancestry in those lines as well. On my mother's side, I have Polish, Jewish and English ancestry.

While my mob could be from every corner of the earth, if you wanted me to tell you who I am in one sentence, I would say: I am a Torres Strait Islander born and raised on Larrakia land, who loves family above all, and who has been following my heart to do what is right.

My early years were very much about Rugby League. In Darwin, there was only one Rugby League ground – Richardson Park. It was like a second home to me. I would be there every weekend, watching every grade of our beloved Brothers Rugby League Club play, or roaming around and getting up to all kinds of mischief until late at night, waiting for Dad to finish the post-game revelry. We would pass the time collecting tadpoles, teasing the caretaker's vicious dog, sliding down the hills on empty beer cartons, and of course, playing our own little games of footy on the field at half-time.

I started playing Rugby League when I was about eleven years old, and I think the game toughened me up. And I needed toughening up. Embarrassingly, I'd step out of the way of any player who ran towards me. I don't think I was a shrinking violet, really, but on the field, I was scared. My mum said they had no choice but to put me in an older age group, so at first, the other boys were bigger. I was incredibly skinny. Skin and bone, tall and lanky. So skinny I was often teased. I thought the other boys were stronger, and most of them had been playing for longer than I had.

It was at the end of the under-13 season that something snapped in my mind, sparking a fire that has burned ever since. We were undefeated that year, all the way up until the Grand Final. Somehow, I was the last with the ball that night as the full-time siren blew. I hadn't contributed anything decent to the game. I hadn't contributed anything to any game at all, other than to pat the opposition on the back as they ran through my wing. I'd like to say that the fire spontaneously combusted, and with sudden determination I ran 80 meters to score the winning try. But no. Instead, I ran as hard as I could, yelling at the top of my voice something along the lines of, 'Not losing without a fight!'

Such sudden heroics from the 'bony decoration' on the wing would've taken the other players by surprise.

I got nowhere. I was tackled almost immediately. We lost the game, humiliated. We'd been undefeated all season, then lost the only game that counted, the grand final. A cruel team mate mocked me afterwards, but I wasn't laughing. The fire had started to burn and I couldn't wait for the next season.

The following year I excelled. The determination that I have carried into adulthood started on the field. I would tackle my heart out and run at the biggest guys all the way through the game. My bony frame didn't matter, I had found my own heart.

I played on until I was thirty-one, representing the Territory several times and captaining the club that I stayed with for all my years, Brothers Rugby League Club. As far as Rugby League goes, playing at the top level in Darwin isn't much compared to the big boys in the National Rugby League (NRL). But playing with great mates, putting my body on the line week in, week out, and supporting the club that I loved were years that I will always cherish and that I still dream about. In 2004 we won a first-grade premiership, my one and only. After that, I could retire from the game happy. I met Melanie in 2006, we married in 2008, and Rugby League started to become a chore. I looked to a life without playing footy. I looked to a new challenge at work. After sixteen years as a wharfie, I'd became a full-time official of the MUA, the Maritime Union of Australia.

When I finished year 12, I sat an aptitude test in a basketball stadium full of other graduates. The tests were part of the application process for government traineeships. I won the one I wanted – a maritime traineeship.

For the next two years, I was able to work across many sections of the industry – for the Port Authority in port maintenance, administration, security, and on the pilot boats. I was also sent out to work at the navy base and for Customs. On the wharf, I spent time as a shipping agent and in stevedoring, loading and unloading cargo from ships. The traineeship gave me valuable experience. I loved it. And I had my first lessons in workplace politics amongst the colourful characters around the port.

Of all the places I worked at the port, I enjoyed stevedoring (the occupation of wharfie) the most. There was a great variety of work for Darwin wharfies, and I relished being outdoors. I liked to get my hands dirty, to sweat and work hard, and most of all, to operate the massive cranes and fork-lifts. The other appeal of the wharf was the freedom. I noticed that the workers on the wharf had a high degree of self-respect and comradery, unlike the situation in other workplaces. We wouldn't take risks with our health. We wouldn't be pushed around. And if pushed, we would stop working and only resume when decency was restored. I liked that. I was learning about the leverage of unity.

In a port such as Darwin, there are three categories of employment: casual, guaranteed wage earner (GWE), and permanent. I was a GWE, which meant that I was only guaranteed two days of work per week. I shared a house with my partner, Makezha, her sister and some friends, so we could afford to get by. Also, with the great employment conditions – thanks to the well unionised history of waterside work – I would earn a good wage.

By the time I turned twenty, our first daughter was born, and nine months later the next daughter was on her way. So, with a young family, I did everything I could to maximise my chances to get work. I would never knock it back (within the rules of the union), because I knew that being available would be vital to getting a permanent job. And that was my goal. I was determined to be a permanent wharfie.

For all my efforts to get a permanent job, I knew that they were rare. It took wharfies generations of disputation and strikes to gain the right to job security. Stevedore companies have always wanted completely casualised workforces. They relished the old 'bull system', where wharf labourers were forced to hustle and fight to win a ticket to work each day. I worked hard, but the real reason I got a permanent job was because of the strength of the union.

It was the united efforts of trade unionists and the community that got me and my workmates through the most significant industrial dispute in many decades – the 1998 Patricks dispute. In the dark of night on 7 April, balaclava-clad mercenaries marched onto the Patricks wharves. They climbed from small rubber zodiacs up onto the wharf apron. These men were menacing, armed with batons and Rottweiler dogs that gnashed their teeth at the end of lightly held leashes. It was an ambush, orchestrated by the Howard government and Patricks' boss, Chris Corrigan. Their hired muscle physically dragged 1400 workers from their workplaces and locked them out of their livelihoods.

As daylight broke in Darwin, I was driving my not so trusty old Mitsubishi L300 to work. When I approached the wharf, listening to the radio, the news report gave me the bad news – all wharfies had been locked out.

Fortunately for us in Darwin, we were not yet fully owned by Patricks. The union decided that we must continue to work where we could. We wanted the community on side. People remembered the union's long history of supporting social justice struggles and community advancement. They recognised this injustice against us, so they supported us. Throughout the country, masses of citizens eventually joined the workers on the picket lines on Patricks' wharves, helping in our fight to get our jobs back.

After a four-month struggle, Justice North of the Federal Court ruled in favour of the MUA. Through the win in the court, and profound acts of national and international solidarity, we'd won the war to keep our jobs. Prime Minister John Howard, Industrial Relations Minister Peter Reith and Patricks' Managing Director, Chris Corrigan, had failed to de-unionise the waterside workers.

There were scenes of jubilation and tears of joy when the wharfies marched triumphantly back through the gates at Patricks' wharves around the country. Livelihoods for hundreds of families were restored, though many of those families didn't survive the stress of the long lock-out. Some workers had nervous breakdowns and were never the same again. Some took their own lives.

As the wharfies down south marched back through the gates, past the scowling security guards who had locked them out, the Darwin wharfies went on strike for just one more day. Many old workers were retiring as part of a deal to put the dispute behind us, but the boss wanted to make their permanent jobs casual. The old wharfies wouldn't cop that, so we fought another brief battle and won. That was how I got a permanent job on the wharf.

The union taught me that we are custodians of our jobs. We must always strive to defend the rights that we have won as workers and improve the conditions of employment for the next generation. After 1998, I walked that talk by becoming the workplace delegate. I owed it to those old fellas who fought so hard for permanent jobs and good conditions, and I owed it to the next generation of wharfies. But it was a tough time to do so.

When Patricks replaced the old wharfies, most of the new employees thanked the company for the great work conditions, not the union that had just fought to defend them. Some had never been in a union. As one lone delegate in a small workforce that mostly comprised of men twice my age, it took me many years of perseverance to change this mindset. A mindset that not only put at risk the conditions that had been won by the elders, but worse, it was a mindset that made the wharf an unsafe place to work.

I learnt a lot in those years. To bring those guys from weak individualism to structured collective strength took many tough battles, not just with the bosses but sometimes with my fellow workers. From wins and losses, trial and error, moments of loneliness to amazing solidarity, eventually the unity on the Darwin waterfront was strong once more – though the struggle continues. Unity can be hard work, and the employers' divisive tactics never stop.

When I was nineteen, Dad and I went to the local pub for a beer together. We sat mostly in silence, as we tended to do. There was some banter; Dad always mocked me (with a laugh, not seriously) for choosing to be a 'bludging' wharfie. He had studied to become a refrigeration mechanic at the age of 38, no easy task with his very limited education, and he'd hoped that I'd become an electrician so we could start a business together. I explained that I was happy as a wharfie. I liked the work, and I was learning to drive the massive cranes.

I was enjoying this rare man-to-man conversation when Dad asked, 'Why don't you travel the world?' He said, 'I would've gone to see the world if I could have at your age.' But I was in love with my first partner, just like he had been in love with Mum when he was my age. Travel wasn't on our radar at all.

'I'm not interested in travelling, Dad. I don't want to go anywhere; I just want to start a family.'

I can't remember his response. Perhaps there was a slight shake of the head and a little laugh. He wasn't laughing a few months later when I told him my girlfriend was pregnant. But he got over it. He had to. Nine months after my first daughter, Shayla, was born, my next daughter, Tiah, was on her way.

Although I told Dad I wasn't interested in travel, several years later, with my third child, Celestino, added to the family, I set off on my first trip overseas. I didn't have much notice, and barely had enough time to get a passport. I was to travel to the USA, to Tacoma in Washington State, with Paddy Crumlin, the National Secretary of the MUA. Paddy's good friend and longshoreman (that is what they call a wharfie in the USA), Willie Adams, had invited Paddy to attend a Black History and Labour Conference he had organised. Willie is a great man who has recently become the International President of the International Longshore and Warehouse Union, which covers longshoremen on the East Coast of the USA, Canada and Panama.

I was nervous about the trip. I never expected to be travelling overseas. The United States is a long way from Darwin, and it wasn't too long since the 9/11 terror attacks. I was to fly out at 0000 hours, so after saying goodnight to my partner and kids, I had a few beers with my mates at the local before going to the airport. I was quite unsure of myself when I handed over my passport at check-in. The woman looked at my itinerary and frowned. 'Sir, do you realise you are 24 hours late for your flight?'

My heart sunk – 0000 meant the day before. There I was, representing my port, my people and my union, and I had stuffed up at the first point of travel.

The kind woman behind the counter said, 'You can still go. It turns out your flight to the US from Sydney isn't until late this afternoon, so you will still connect!'

Oh, happy days! Off I go to the US of A!

The Black History and Labour Conference was a celebration that I will never forget. I saw beat boxing, different types of poetry, tap dancing, wonderful performances and art that I had never seen or appreciated before as an uncouth Darwin lad. I heard powerful speeches from Malcolm X's daughter, Betty Shabazz, Martin Luther

King's daughter, Yolanda King, and the renowned orator, the Reverend Al Sharpton.

Paddy, who was one of the only white people in the theatre that day, had the unenviable task of speaking after Reverend Sharpton. But if anyone can follow the powerful oratory skills of the Reverend Al Sharpton, it is Paddy Crumlin. With Australian swagger and a style that is only Paddy's, he nailed the speech and received raucous applause. When I reflected on why it was so well received, I think it was because Paddy told the audience about the continuing struggle for justice by Indigenous people in Australia. He made the point that where workers are united and strong, equality and fairness should also be forged for people of colour.

That trip was an inspiration to a quiet, young Torres Strait Islander from the land of the Larrakia. Inspiring enough to make me want to do more for my workmates and my mob.

During the smoko break one day, I got a call from a couple of comrades, Garry Keane and Glen Williams. Glen was the union organiser in Darwin and he was interested in moving south to run as Northern New South Wales Branch Secretary. Garry was one of the most senior officials in the MUA, and together they were working on Glen's exit strategy. They looked to me to take his place. It was an exciting prospect. A chance to step up and challenge myself.

The first thing I did, once I had wrestled with myself in my mind and decided that yes, I was capable enough to do this, was email my wife Mel. Following a brief explanation of what had just transpired, I made a list of pros and cons for her consideration. I must admit that in the many years that I have been an official of the union, the pros for Mel have rarely transpired. It meant a hefty pay cut, and I knew, from observing MUA union officials, that the job would be high stress and many more hours of work than I was used to doing on the wharf. Throughout it all, Mel's support never waivers.

I became a successful organiser, soon doubling the membership of the branch. Over time, I also became more involved in community and social justice struggles; continuing our union's long tradition to do more than fight for our wages and conditions alone.

I helped start a First Nations union member network; I organised rallies in 2014, in response to the Western Australian Liberal government's underhanded attempts to close Aboriginal communities by cutting services; I also helped organise a rally in response to the disgraceful treatment of youth at the Don Dale Detention Centre. Using the organising skills I'd learnt on the wharf, I encouraged people to come out onto the streets of Darwin to be heard, and I was proud to see so many people standing up and being counted. But with each action on the streets, I felt that something was missing. I started to wonder, Surely, we can do better? Not only by more people coming out onto the streets, but by stopping governments from making bad decisions. I realised that our actions were reactive and our proposals for solutions were barely heard, or were inconsistent in their message and aims. Also, I noticed that our actions tended to peak early and peter out with the weariness of time. With only some success or none at all, we'd need to fight against the next bad decision. We were stuck in a cycle of activism that was changing far too little, far too slowly.

The timing for this realisation was good, because I was about to be invited to a First Nations' dialogue on constitutional recognition.

JOINING THE ROAD TO ULURU

My life was full to the brim in 2016. I was the elected leader of the Northern Territory Branch of the MUA, looking after 500 wharfies and seafarers. They were difficult times for maritime workers. A downturn in vessel visits to the port provided the opening for the stevedore employers to attack job security arrangements. And seafarers were struggling to find work as Australian flagged ships were being replaced by foreign 'flags of convenience'. Also, I was still organising around local Indigenous issues, such as helping establish an Indigenous union and political organisation. So, when I was contacted by the Darwin Regional Dialogue co-chair, Gurindji woman, Josie Crawshaw, and asked if I would join the team of five work-group leaders for the Darwin Constitutional Dialogue, I hesitated because my life was already hectic.

But I couldn't resist, as I was looking for a way to empower First Nations people. After consulting with national officials of the MUA, Ian Bray and Will Tracey, I accepted the invitation. I was soon on a plane to Melbourne to participate in a trial dialogue on constitutional recognition.

Have you ever walked into a room of living legends; people you've read about but never expect to meet? As I stepped in to the hotel lobby in Melbourne, I immediately saw the familiar faces of high-profile Indigenous leaders, and I felt simultaneously conspicuous and invisible. After I checked in, I looked around for someone I knew, and saw the smiling face of seafarer and respected Elder, Kuku Yalanji man Uncle Terry O'Shane.

Uncle Terry introduced me to Aunty Pat Anderson and Kaylene Malthouse. The group of friends, sitting together at a table in the lobby, were having a good laugh, catching up on old times. They showed a genuine interest in who I was, and when I mentioned I was an official of the MUA, Aunty Pat and Kaylene's faces brightened. They looked at me like a comrade and commented on how the unions have been very important for our struggle. This was the first time I had rubbed shoulders with such great leaders in our movement. I felt welcome from that point on, and I was looking forward to what was to come.

At the trial dialogue, I learnt that twelve regional constitutional dialogues would be held covering the entire continent and adjacent islands. Canberra was added later. For each dialogue, the local leaders would invite up to a hundred participants using a formula of: 60 per cent Traditional Owners from First Nations within the region, 20 per cent Indigenous people from Indigenous organisations, and 20 per cent key Indigenous individuals who were actively engaged in Indigenous issues. At every dialogue and in all the workshops, we would have the support of experts in constitutional law and human rights who could answer questions immediately. Importantly, each dialogue would elect delegates to attend the culmination of the dialogues, one big national constitutional convention in the heart of the country at Uluru.

On the first day, after Aunty Pat had welcomed all the participants to the trial dialogue, we watched a 25-minute film narrated by Arrernte and Kalkadoon director Rachel Perkins. The film took the participants through many key moments from our history of struggle, survival and resurgence. It was a roller coaster of emotion that prepared us with lessons from the past. Professor Megan Davis took the podium next. She led us through a presentation about our political system, the Constitution, and the nuances of the systems of law. She explained everything clearly and I came to realise that the Australian Constitution is like a rule book for the nation.

Inspired by the presentations, I asked the Elders if there had ever been an opportunity like this before. In my mind, these well-structured, well-informed dialogues towards a chance to form a collective national position that we could campaign for was an exercise in building the power required for major positive change.

The Elders said there hadn't been an opportunity like this before. This was a unique opportunity for Aboriginal and Torres Strait Islander people. Unprecedented in Australian history since colonisation. The Elders said it was perhaps the greatest hope we would have for a national consensus position on big-picture reform in any of our lifetimes.

At the Darwin Regional Dialogue were many people I had known my entire life – through footy and work, as well as friends and family. Truth-telling was the hot topic on the first day. The participants wanted the truth of our history to be recognised and for our non-Indigenous neighbours to know and understand the reasons why our circumstances today are in crises in so many cases.

The participants in the dialogues were always especially emotional on the first day. People needed to vent their frustrations and anger. They spoke of their sadness for a sibling or child who had taken their own life; in some cases children as young as ten. They spoke of the ignorance and acts of blatant racism in their home community – by authorities and by their neighbours – and they wanted this to change.

I didn't say much in the Darwin dialogue. Although, when a debate arose about whether or not we should be talking about the politics to achieve our desired outcomes, I had to speak up. 'How can we not get political?' I said. 'Everything is politics. If we come to a consensus at Uluru, we will need to get political to win our proposed reforms.'

I missed the last session of the Darwin Regional Dialogue. An enterprise-bargaining meeting scheduled for that day couldn't be moved and it was a crucial time in a long negotiation. In the break between bargaining sessions, I returned a phone call from my friend Wayne Kurnorth, who was at the dialogue. He asked if I would accept a nomination to be on the Darwin region delegation to the Uluru First Nations Constitutional Convention. He explained that I should have the support required and, further, that Darwin Elder Uncle Jack Ah-Kit would speak to my nomination. I said yes. I was elected.

A CONSTITUTIONAL
MOMENT AT ULURU

I've never considered myself a spiritual person. On the flight to Uluru, I wasn't praying to a god to bless us with a powerful consensus. I didn't meditate in the hope of finding a solution to our problems. On the short flight from Darwin to Uluru, I read the Australian Constitution.

I read it from beginning to end. It wasn't hard to read. Our Constitution provides structure and rules; it is how power is shared. As a workplace delegate, I had learnt to understand the nuances of words in agreements and legislation. Every word could make or break our livelihoods.

Once we all arrived at Uluru, we went to the Welcome to Country ceremony at Mutitjulu, a tiny community of only around 300 people. Mutitjulu is surrounded by a sea of red dirt and sparse desert flora, and it is literally situated in the late afternoon shadow of Uluru. The majestic rock watches over Mutitjulu, omnipresent.

I heard the sound of excited greetings as friends from long ago were catching up – those Elders who had marched the streets together in the 1970s, '80s and '90s; some who had started the first Aboriginal legal services and Aboriginal medical centres together. We doubled the size of the community when we arrived. We were the largest national convention of Indigenous representatives ever to be held, and we'd come from all parts of the country.

In the presence of Uluṟu, a higher level of spirituality is always present, and a respectful hush blanketed the excitement as the Chair of the Mutitjulu Community Aboriginal Corporation and head of the Uluṟu family, Sammy Wilson, took the microphone. In line with the law of the ancient land, he acknowledged the Elders and ancestors. He spoke of the legacy that has not died for millennia, the Tjukurrpa (traditional law), and welcomed us under their law and custom.

Djunga Djunga Yunupingu, a Gumatj Traditional Owner from Arnhem Land, responded to the welcome first. He brought word from the Gumatj's most senior Dilak (leader), Dr Galarrwuy Yunupingu. The message was one of respect for a community that bore the brunt of Prime Minister Howard's damaging and politically driven Intervention policy.

He said, 'The fire that we have brought you in our ceremony has the energy and the power to show who we are and where we come from … You've done the nation the greatest service by standing strong in Uluṟu.

'The fire was lit by our ancestors and is kept alive through song and dance. This gives us power and we seek to give that power to you. We Aboriginal and Torres Strait Islander peoples were linked throughout the country by song lines and kinship and are honoured to be in the presence of the greatest rock of all, Uluṟu, our heart and the heart of our nation.'

Dr Yunupingu's message was also a call to action for everyone who had come to Uluṟu for the historic gathering. He was asking all of us to be strong through the difficult discussions to come.

Next came a dance telling the stories of the constellations in the southern sky. Convention delegate and Mualgal (Moa Island) woman Gargu Kanai introduced the Baidam (shark) Constellation Dance – a dance brought from the Torres Strait to the Central Desert to guide our discussion.

The inma (ceremonial gathering) took us from ancient Arnhem Land to the salty blue seas of the Torres Strait, and then back to the Traditional Owners to complete the Welcoming Ceremony. A row of Anangu men entered the circle with plumes of red dust rising from their agile feet. Their bodies shaded red with the earth, they moved in unison, performing the Kuniya (woma python) Liru (poison snake) Dance. A dance significant to Uluru Tjukurrpa. As they performed, we witnessed the sun increasing in amber intensity before it melted in to the darkening red desert behind them. The rock, Uluru, displayed infinite hues of dark red to purple, to blue. As the young men born from that Country completed the ceremony, the veil of night settled over the desert, the rock and us.

The welcome ceremony at Mutitjulu was the spiritual highlight of my life. We all felt the tensions building and we sensed that a storm was coming. But with the warm welcome at Mutitjulu, with the fire passed on to us by the Yolŋu, and the Baidam constellation in the southern sky guiding us, we had the power we needed to get through to the destination we were hoping for.

During my journey with the Uluru Statement from the Heart, I always informed the audience about some opposing views that First Nations people have about constitutional recognition, because frustratingly, some Australians have a strange expectation that Aboriginal and Torres Strait Islander peoples will be homogenous.

We are not homogenous, we are similar but different, like all humans.

The participants at the dialogues and the Uluru First Nations Constitutional Convention came from communities spread throughout a country that covers 7692 million square kilometres of land. We were deliberating on reforming the founding document of a modern nation, the Australian Constitution. The rule book for all Australians, no less. The rule book that has allowed efforts to remove or diminish our existence.

We are a collective of around 800,000 Indigenous people and we will always have different views. Our hope to reach a consensus was optimistic, especially if you consider that when Indigenous people gather, we bring with us the effects of colonisation, racism and inequality – intergenerational trauma both physical and mental. To varying levels, the wounds are still weeping; the wounds are angry and raw. Our internal conflict is part of our journey, though it doesn't diminish our hope.

In the time that I had leading up to the convention, I wanted to speak to as many of my Indigenous comrades as possible, especially those who were touting the coming convention as a government conspiracy. I travelled to the First Nations Tent Embassy in Canberra just the week before I flew to Uluru.

Established in 1972, the tent embassy is a welcoming place. The uncles and aunties I sat with talked about our issues and gave me their perspective on what had happened at the dialogues they'd attended. One of the brothers I spoke to was a delegate from the Dubbo dialogue. He would soon be travelling to Uluru in a convoy with others from the tent embassy. They planned to go there to protest.

I explored the dissenting positions, and I said that the convention would be us, all Aboriginal and Torres Strait Islander people, not the government. I encouraged open minds and a preparedness to passionately debate our different positions with the many other delegates from around the country. We agreed that the process wasn't perfect, but what process is? When I left, we were all smiling. The brother who I would sit with on the first day of the Uluru Convention walked me to the roadside, we shook hands and embraced as brothers do. I felt hopeful.

In that week I also contacted others who were prominent in protesting against the work of the Referendum Council. In each of those conversations, the results were similar. I would introduce myself as a Torres Strait Islander born on Larrakia land. A fellow activist and delegate for Uluru. Of course, there was a degree of wariness, but as fellow delegates soon to attend the historic convention, we discussed what was to come. I felt movement. Calm, logical exploration of the reasons for their opposition seemed to move us toward the same conclusion – that Uluru was an opportunity that could not be wasted – and I thought, Yes, we can do this!

That positivity didn't last long at Uluru. I'd soon understand the importance of the gifts at the Welcoming Ceremony: the fire from the Yolŋu and the stars from the Torres Strait Islanders.

In the opening plenary discussion, one participant announced that he was there to say no to anything anyone else said. On the second day that same person led a walk-out of almost twenty participants. A media scrum was there waiting, hungry for the tasty morsels of controversy. When I learnt that they would walk, I approached one of the most outspoken amongst them – a person who I'd had a very good discussion with over the phone in the lead-up to the convention. I tried pressing with a calm, comradely demeanour that there was no conspiracy here. I mentioned that our varying views have been shared and heard, both in the plenary and in each of the workshops. I reminded the person that there was no interference from government. They stayed a while longer, then walked and proceeded to tell the world their voices had been silenced inside. The irony is the twenty who walked out were heard far more than the rest of the 250 First Nations delegates who remained and continued our collective work.

To speak about the conflict at Uluru is vitally important because it happened, and conflict is a normal part of collective decision making. The nature of consensus making is that the outcome is never *everything* that *everyone* wants. The conflict, on the second day of the Uluru First Nations Constitutional Convention, made what happened next all the more wonderful and profound.

On the final morning of the convention, around 250 delegates gathered. We had trudged through the quagmire of low morale after the small but loud walk-out the day before. But we hadn't given up. We completed the workshops and the deliberations. We came to the final plenary unsure but hopeful for a united resolution.

That final morning I was to deliver the strategic sequencing of reforms that had been synthesised from the dialogues and the final workshops at Uluru. Our most urgent reform would be the establishment of a First Nations Voice enshrined in the Constitution, followed by legislating a Makarrata Commission to supervise a process of truth-telling to the nation and agreement making, or treaties, between governments and First Nations.

With the documents in hand and hastily made notes, I soon found myself on the stage looking in to the eyes of 250 of my people. A massive Aboriginal flag on my right. A massive Torres Strait Islander flag on my left. I was extremely nervous. Here were my peers and many Elders who had been fighting this struggle their whole lives. I knew that if I stuffed it up, I would add to the low morale that hung over us from the day before, diminishing the chances of a consensus. I knew what I had to do. I spoke from the heart. I sought to inspire solidarity.

First, I spoke to the power-point presentation. I guided the convention through the sequence of reforms. In summary – negotiations towards a referendum bill; a national campaign to a successful referendum; First Nations-led development of the Voice Body; the development of a Makarrata Commission; and finally, the Voice and Makarrata Commission delivering a Voice and fairness for our people. I talked about how a united Voice of First Nations will be vital for treaty making in the states and territories and truth-telling for the nation.

I concluded by speaking about my background in the union movement. I talked about organising to build power and how this was our opportunity to break the cycle of reactive advocacy – a way of influencing decisions that will affect us before they are made. These are the notes I wrote to myself in the short time I had to prepare for that session:

> *I came here to listen, consider. If we understand that this is an opportunity to seize a moment that can give the power for change, we must grab it with both hands.*
> *A decision here is POWER.*
> *Indecisiveness will be death …*
> *We cannot go back into the wilderness of uncertainty, to the insanity of repeatedly doing what hasn't worked.*

Ultimately, my speech was a plea to come together on the reforms we wanted, and then to go out there and fight for them. I wrote: *We need a people's movement!*

Delivering that speech was a highlight of my life. But what happened next was far greater. What happened next was what constitutional experts call a 'constitutional moment'. No written words or oratory can do it justice.

My legs were shaking as Professor Megan Davis stepped up to the podium to read the Uluṟu Statement from the Heart for the very first time. Some of the delegates and the Referendum Council team had been up all night, working on the Statement – the culmination of our peoples' collective work. My adrenaline was pumping. My memory of the last words is vivid. Professor Megan Davis delivered them with strength and passion.

'In 1967 we were counted, in 2017 we seek to be heard, we leave base camp and start our trek across this vast country. We invite you to walk with us in a movement of the Australian People for a better future.'

What happened next was like a late afternoon Darwin downpour. The storm that was brewing approached. The room was still and tense. The air was thick with uncomfortable expectation. We listened, we waited, we heard it coming, and it swept over us – relief. Heavy, overwhelming relief. It was like we had waited endless months for the heavens to open. And when the heavens finally parted, the rains that came forth were our tears of joy and hope.

As we wept together, young and old, I looked around the room and saw those who had been in passionate debate with each other over the course of the convention embracing and tenderly wiping the tears from each other's eyes. I saw the wrinkled faces of the Elders dawning with bright, beaming smiles. It was like watching long-lost loved ones finding each other again.

It was an unforgettable moment. A political feat that should be celebrated forever.

The Uluṟu Statement from the Heart was endorsed with standing acclamation and raucous celebration.

The rest of that morning was a haze. The regions met to discuss the work ahead – we knew the Uluṟu Statement proposals would need to overcome both apathy and opposition. We had to organise to win.

Late that night, we were all on cloud nine. I joined jubilant celebrations that went into the early hours of the morning. Leo Ah Kee, from Thursday Island, among others, played many an old tune on the guitar while we sang along at the tops of our voices. Our spirit was awoken on that day, it was imbued in the Ulu<u>r</u>u Statement from the Heart.

VOICE, TREATY, TRUTH

There are many ways our people understand the importance of the changes proposed in the Uluṟu Statement from the Heart. In the 'Voices' section of this book, we will share some of these ways. Before we get there, I will briefly describe why these reforms are important and address some questions that often arise.

As you learn more about the Uluṟu Statement, I want you to understand that the reforms are achievable. Our Elders achieved the changes we benefit from today because they believed the world could be better – they had the courage to hope. Now it is our turn. If the world as it is today is not the world we want to leave for our children, then we had better find hope too. Though, hope on its own is not enough.

Hope with a sound plan – a plan made with an understanding of the world as it is and with an eye to the lessons from the past – will give us the power to succeed.

What is constitutional recognition?

Put simply, the Constitution is the rule book of the nation. It is the highest of written laws that determine how all other laws are made and by whom – the state or federal parliaments. As the foundational document for the Australian Federation, or as some describe it, as the birth certificate of our modern nation, above all other laws and decrees, the Constitution defines who we are as Australians.

The Constitution of the Australian Federation came to be after negotiations between the colonies of Queensland, New South Wales, Victoria, Tasmania, South Australia and Western Australia in the late nineteenth century. The colonies were represented by white males – there were no women or Indigenous peoples.

The forefathers of our Federation excluded First Nations people because they believed we were a dying race. When the Constitution was agreed between the colonies, and accepted by the white population, it explicitly did not count First Nations people as citizens. We had no right to vote in elections. We were Voiceless.

The very first policy of the Australian Federation was the White Australia Policy. The Australian governments we were excluded from didn't just continue to believe we would die out, they actively pursued that end.

We haven't died out though. We are still here. The sentiment of parlimentarians and the Australian people has shifted. Who today would say that First Nations people – a people and a culture that has lived and flourished on and with this country for tens of thousands of years – should not be included in Australia's Constitution? Australia's forefathers may have denied this, and did so violently. But today, Australia can be different.

For our 'young' nation to mature, constitutional recognition is vital. It is a matter for all of us – a chance to redefine our Australian identity and to right a wrong from the past. When Australia embraces the longest continuing culture on the planet as what constitutes us – the building blocks in our national DNA – we will share a unique identity in the world; an identity we can all be proud of.

This is the gift First Nations people are offering in the Uluru Statement from the Heart. It is truly a generous offer.

How does a referendum work?

The Constitution cannot be changed by the Parliament alone. The Parliament must ask the Australian people if they support the change they propose. This constitutional question, put to the people, is called a referendum. For Australia to go to a referendum, the Federal Parliament must first pass a referendum bill. This bill includes the question the Australian people will be asked, and the amendment to be made should the answer be 'Yes'.

If there are parliamentarians who oppose the referendum, they may choose to run a 'No' case. In the lead-up to the day of the referendum, voters will receive the arguments for the 'Yes' and 'No' vote. The government may or may not choose to fund the 'Yes' and 'No' case. If government funding is provided, it must be equal for both campaigns.

For a referendum to succeed, a majority of voters in a majority of states must vote 'Yes' (four out of six states), and a majority of voters must vote 'Yes' across the states and territories overall.

Some people argue that a precondition for a successful referendum is bipartisanship from the major parties. However, experts say there is no precondition for referendum because the circumstances of referenda are always different. The last successful referendum was in 1977; it amended the retirement age for High Court judges.

The most successful referendum was in 1967, when over 90 per cent of Australians voted 'Yes' to counting First Nations people as citizens in the national census, and to providing the federal government the power to make special laws about Indigenous peoples.

What do we mean by Voice?

The Uluru Statement from the Heart calls for a substantive form of constitutional recognition:

We call for the establishment of a First Nations Voice enshrined in the Constitution.

A First Nations Voice is a First Nations representative body with a constitutional guarantee that it may provide advice to the Parliament. Our people decided that the political power to influence decisions made about us – decisions that affect our health, our livelihoods, our wellbeing and justice – is the most important step to progress our interests and it is how we wish to be recognised in the Constitution.

Australia committed to establishing a Voice over a decade ago. As a nation, we ratified the United Nations Declaration on the Rights of Indigenous Peoples (UNDRIP) in 2009. Article 18 of the UNDRIP states that 'Indigenous peoples have the right to participate in decision-making in matters which would affect their rights, through representatives chosen by themselves in accordance with their own procedures, as well as to maintain and develop their own indigenous decision- making institutions'.

A Voice to Parliament will deliver on the nation's commitment to UNDRIP.

Is a Voice a third chamber in Parliament?

The proposed constitutional change will not establish a third chamber in Parliament that would have the power to veto legislation. Nor will it alter or hinder existing government processes. We understand such proposed changes would not succeed at a referendum. Claiming that this is what First Nations people want has been used as a scaremongering tactic by those who oppose Indigenous rights.

Why must we constitutionally enshrine the Voice, rather than just legislate?

Constitutional enshrinement of the Voice is important so that our Voice is guaranteed – we must protect what we build. All national First Nations representative bodies have been repealed or defunded when they have strongly challenged the decisions of Parliament, or when hostile governments have been elected.

The example that is most often recalled in this respect is the Aboriginal and Torres Strait Islander Commission. ATSIC was established in legislation by the Bob Hawke Labor government in response to the 1988 Barunga Statement's proposal for an Indigenous representative body. The John Howard Liberal National Opposition vehemently opposed its establishment. When Howard led the Coalition to government in 1996, he immediately defunded ATSIC. He shut down the representative body completely in 2005 with the support of the Labor Opposition, even though Aunty Jackie Huggins, John Hannaford and Bob Collins had just completed a wide-ranging review of the organisation. Their report made recommendations to address the challenges ATSIC was facing. But rather than working with First Nations people to improve the representative body, Howard amplified its problems and the government destroyed it.

It was easy for a hostile federal government to silence ATSIC because it had been created by an act of Parliament. Constitutional enshrinement of a Voice is different. The Constitution can only be changed by way of a referendum, not by an act of Parliament.

A successful referendum will guarantee our First Nations' Voices are in the centre of decision making. It will provide the Voice with a mandate from the Australian people that it must be respected and heard. And because it is lawfully and politically protected and empowered, it may be unapologetic in its advocacy, not sensitive to defunding and repeal.

How does a Voice help our people?

It is important to recognise what happens when our Voice is silenced. In the absence of a Voice with an ability to effectively hold politicians to account and to influence the decisions they make, they will continue to fail and harm us.

Let us look at what happened after ATSIC was repealed in 2005. In 2007, under Prime Minister Howard, we saw the Northern Territory Intervention (Northern Territory Emergency Response). The Intervention was an act of Parliament so incredibly racist, they had to suspend the *Racial Discrimination Act 1975 (Cth)*. Howard effectively announced to the entire nation that child abuse and domestic violence are Aboriginal problems. The harm the Intervention has done is covered in the stories of Wayne Kurnorth, Barbara Shaw and Sammy Wilson.

In 2015, under Prime Minister Abbott, hundreds of millions of dollars were cut from services to remote communities, leading to the Western Australian Liberal government moving to shut down Aboriginal communities. Abbott stated that the poverty in remote Aboriginal communities was a lifestyle choice, in complete ignorance of over two hundred years of dispossession, neglect and failed policies.

And still today, the annual Closing the Gap targets are dismally missed. The gap is getting wider. As the Uluṟu Statement says:

This is the torment of our powerlessness.

Without the political power a Voice provides, we will continue to slip backwards. We understand how gains made under a reasonably benevolent government can easily be lost the next time a hostile or neglectful government is elected. For example, ATSIC was building a national campaign for Treaty. When ATSIC was repealed, the Treaty campaign was set back by decades – Australia still has no treaty with First Nations people.

A Voice to Parliament is a practical reform, not merely symbolic as some have argued, because policy and legislation decisions in Canberra affect everything we struggle with: housing, justice, health, education, community infrastructure. The list goes on.

Gaining a greater ability to influence the decisions that are made about us is the most practical reform we can achieve in a democracy.

Is introducing a First Nations representative body into the Constitution racist?

Many Australians are unaware that the Federal Parliament has the explicit power to make special laws about First Nations people based on our 'race'. This is in Section 51 (xxvi) of the Constitution of Australia, known as the 'Race Power'.

Indeed, because of this power, Australia's Constitution allows the Parliament to be 'racist'. And this 'racist' power has only ever been used to make special laws about Aboriginal and Torres Strait Islander people. As ruled in the High Court's Hindmarsh Bridge case, the 'race power' may be used to the detriment of Indigenous people, not necessarily to our benefit.

While Indigenous peoples are not a 'race' different from other humans, our unique connection to Country, culture and experience of colonisation are substantive and deserving of recognition. The Uluru Statement does not propose to remove the 'race power', though. This is because some beneficial laws, such as Native Title legislation, would be jeopardised by its removal. We also do not propose to replace the word 'race' with 'Indigenous people'. Such tinkering does not empower us. We proposed a more urgent and useful amendment. We seek to establish the representative body, the First Nations Voice, to monitor the use of the 'race power' and to influence its use to benefit rather than harm us. A Voice will also hold politicians to account for the decisions they make about us.

Why are some Indigenous people not supporting a Voice to Parliament?

Surprise, surprise. Aboriginal and Torres Strait Islander people are not homogenous. We are human beings with different ideologies, beliefs and factions. There is no doubt, though, that a majority of Indigenous people support a constitutionally enshrined Voice.

First, let's remember the earlier chapters in this book that describe the Uluṟu dialogues and the National Constitutional Convention. They were the most extensive, well-informed and well-formulated constitutional dialogues our people have ever had.

Then there are the subsequent processes – the Joint Select Committee into constitutional recognition in 2018 and the Voice Co-design in 2021. Both indicated majority support for a Voice from Aboriginal and Torres Strait Islander peoples.

Finally, there has been polling. The numbers keep rising as more of our people learn about the benefits of constitutional recognition and reform. The polls reveal that over 80 per cent of Indigenous people want a First Nations Voice enshrined in the Constitution. True to our generous culture, this support is because constitutional recognition will be a unifying moment for our country.

Aren't First Nations people already equal? Instead of a First Nations Voice to Parliament, why don't Indigenous people just get elected?

Some people who oppose a First Nations Voice to Parliament argue that Indigenous people today have the right to vote and the ability to run for Parliament. They also argue that because a record number of Indigenous people were elected as members of the 47th Parliament, there is effectively an Indigenous Voice already, diminishing the need for an Aboriginal and Torres Strait Islander representative body.

These arguments ignore the fact that Indigenous candidates are not chosen by Aboriginal and Torres Strait Islander people. Nor are they accountable to them. Indigenous candidates are chosen by political parties whose preselection processes rarely involve Indigenous people. If elected, the decisions of the Indigenous member's party and the expectations of the member's electorate take precedent over the needs of Aboriginal and Torres Strait Islander people. And there is absolutely no guarantee that there will be any Indigenous people elected to be members of future parliaments.

Our democracy will be stronger with the inclusion of a First Nations Voice. Without a constitutionally guaranteed Voice to Parliament, First Nations people, as only 3 per cent of the population across these vast lands, are powerless in this democracy – hence our democracy's failure to provide equal wellbeing for Indigenous peoples since its inception. In the absence of a Voice, we Indigenous peoples are subject to the whims of parliamentarians, who we cannot effectively hold to account.

What does the Voice representative model look like?

When people talk about what the Voice will look like, they usually refer to what the composition, powers, functions and processes of the Voice will be. For example: how representatives will be elected; how representatives will assemble; what the protocols and procedures for providing the advice will be. This is the 'model'.

Only an enabling provision to establish the Voice will be constitutionally enshrined. The model, separately, will be legislated by the Parliament after the referendum. This is because the aspects of the model will need to be flexible – able to change for the continuous improvement of the Voice, and so the Voice may evolve with the needs of the people. This is a normal process called 'constitutional deferral':

the principal is established in the Constitution first; then, how the principal is enacted is determined later.

Constitutional deferral helps keep the proposed changes simple. If a referendum proposed an entire model to be inserted into the Constitution, it would be less likely to succeed. The 1999 republic referendum failed, partly, for this reason.

This referendum will only be asking people if a Voice should be established in the Constitution so there is a guarantee that, whatever the model, First Nations people's views and interests are heard when decisions are made about us.

This is an important distinction as you support the Yes campaign for a Voice. Those who oppose constitutional recognition will use the detail of the model, or the lack of detail, to confuse voters. We have already heard our opposition saying, 'If you don't know, vote no.'

We should always remind people that we are merely seeking to guarantee an Aboriginal and Torres Strait Islander Voice in the Constitution – as a principal of recognition, respect, and fairness – not a model of representation in detail.

Representative bodies are certainly nothing new in a representative democracy. The proposal for a Voice isn't new either. And shouldn't be too much to ask. First Nations have been struggling for fairly chosen representation and the right to self-determination since before Federation. This aspiration has been recorded in numerous statements and petitions, such as the 1938 Day of Mourning, the 1963 Yirrkala Bark Petitions, the 1972 Larrakia Petition, the 1988 Barunga Statement and today, the Uluru Statement from the Heart.

What will a Makarrata Commission do?

'Makarrata' is a Yolŋu word for a process of 'coming together after a struggle'. In this ancient and continuing dispute resolution process, the parties must bring truthfulness and a genuine intent to reach a settlement on how the wrongs of the past will be resolved. At the completion of this process, relations are strengthened and peace prevails. Makarrata has long been used by First Nations leaders to describe our aspirations for a settlement that improves relations and heals the wounds of the past.

It is envisioned that the Makarrata Commission would supervise, promote and assist truth-telling to the nation. It may also act as an umpire and mediator as First Nations negotiate agreements, such as treaties, with governments.

The Makarrata Commission need only be legislated. It will be separate from the Voice with no constitutional change required. To develop the best powers and functions of the Makarrata Commission, the constitutionally enshrined Voice should be established first, so First Nations representatives will be in a position to influence its development.

Why is a Voice a priority for reform?

At the First Nations dialogues in the lead up to the Uluru Convention, establishing a Voice in the Constitution was the most desired reform, closely followed by Treaty. Truth-telling was not considered an option for reform, but it was included in the Uluru Statement because in all dialogues, our people believe that truth-telling is important.

Prioritising a Voice to Parliament was formalised at the morning plenary on the final day of the Uluru Convention. I delivered the presentation that explained the logic, right before the Uluru Statement was endorsed.

Back in the regional dialogues, one of the reasons a Voice took priority over Treaty was because of the experience First Nations people had negotiating agreements with governments and corporations on Country. Agreement making is arduous and First Nations organisations are relatively resource poor. Our people have witnessed families and communities divided during agreement making, and discussed the pressing need to rebuild structures and relationships amongst First Nations people first. They talked about establishing the means to reconnect song lines. To take our time and build the strength of all First Nations so we may achieve treaty outcomes that our people will be happy with, rather than rushing to an unsatisfactory settlement.

Given treaties are being negotiated at the state and territory level, a constitutionally enshrined Voice to the Federal Parliament will be vital to negotiations at that level. The ultimate power in our Federation is held by the federal government; all state and territory laws must be consistent with federal law and the federal government controls the majority of public funds. If First Nations only engaged with state and territory governments, the claims they could make would be limited, and settlement outcomes would be vulnerable to the whims of federal government. A First Nations Voice to the Federal Parliament can negotiate a federal treaty framework, empowering all First Nations, including those most impacted by colonistaion, or without land rights or mineral wealth on their land for leverage.

Looking at what is happening in Victoria shows why it makes strategic sense to establish a Voice as a priority. In Victoria, where the treaty process has been underway for a decade, First Nations leaders chose to establish a representative body – a Voice – well before serving a log of claims and commencing negotiations. To do so was common sense. If they had tried to negotiate without a representative body, as a rabble, negotiations would inevitably fail.

Experts predict that meaningful treaties are going to take many decades to settle. A First Nations Voice will give all First Nations the ability to work together immediately, without waiting for a government to ratify a single treaty agreement – an agreement that, from the history of treaties globally, they will immediately seek to undermine.

Indigenous communities have a common urgency to address prejudice in the justice system, weaknesses in Native Title legislation, and matters related to child welfare, education, housing, culture, health and services to heal the social ills caused by over two hundred years of genocide, failed policy and neglect. If we waited decades for 'Treaty first', we would continue to lack the political power to hold Parliament to account. We would continue to fail to improve the lives of Aboriginal and Torres Strait Islander people. Treaties – satisfactory treaties – will take longer to reach.

Why not Truth-telling first?

Both Indigenous and non-Indigenous people have been truth-telling since Lieutenant James Cook first stepped ashore. The explorers' and settlers' journals record truth. In modern times, there have been countless articles, documentaries, films and reconciliation actions that have told the truth of the past and present. Some of the most significant, undeniable truth-telling has been done in royal commissions. In 1991, the final report of the Royal Commission into Aboriginal Deaths in Custody made 339 recommendations, all backed by the truth. Despite the truth being known in Parliament, key recommendations for improvements to institutions, laws and policies were ignored, still not implemented to this day. Deaths in custody, child removals and the abuse of children in detention continue.

The parliamentarians know the truth, and there is so much more truth-telling to do. What is missing is the political power of a First Nations Voice to use the truth for the benefit of all Australians. The Voice is our priority.

What will the new constitutional provision for a Voice look like?

At the Garma Festival in 2022, Prime Minister Anthony Albanese provided Australians with a draft set of words that may be inserted into the Constitution:

> *In recognition of Australia's Aboriginal and Torres Strait Islander peoples as the first peoples of Australia:*
> 1. *There shall be a body, to be called the Aboriginal and Torres Strait Islander Voice.*
> 2. *The Aboriginal and Torres Strait Islander Voice may make representations to Parliament and the executive government on matters relating to Aboriginal and Torres Strait Islander peoples.*
> 3. *The Parliament shall, subject to this Constitution, have the power to make laws with respect to the composition, functions, powers and procedures of the Aboriginal and Torres Strait Islander Voice.*

Really, this should be all the detail people need to vote Yes. The provision recognises Aboriginal and Torres Strait Islander peoples are still here, establishing a body called the Aboriginal and Torres Strait Islander Voice, while ensuring that the Voice is not a third chamber to Parliament. The model will ultimately be decided by Parliament with Aboriginal and Torres Strait Islander people, giving us the flexibility we need.

To insert the provision, the question that will be put to the Australian people may be as simple as the following, also announced by Prime Minister Albanese at the 2022 Garma Festival:

> *Do you support an alteration to the constitution that establishes an Aboriginal and Torres Strait Islander Voice?*

The answer, of course, should be, 'Yes.'

THE VOICES

Our stories about why we support a constitutionally enshrined Voice and a Makarrata Commission

When I started writing the stories in these pages, I was worried my writing wouldn't do them justice. It was difficult at first. Listening is a language in itself, I discovered. But with each interview I connected with the person and the writing became easier, because I learnt to listen.

The wonderful people I interviewed shared limitless combinations of experience and perspective. They were generous. They gave me their time and shared their aspirations.

Each of their stories is unique. Each is compelling. It is *their* voices that I have written; a collective narrative that is a mixture of sorrow, joy, anger, love and, profoundly, hope. The hope that First Nations will be heard in our own right.

Listening to the voices behind the Uluṟu Statement from the Heart has changed me, and I hope it will change you. If you stop to listen, perhaps we can change the Australian Constitution so that First Nations Voices are *always* heard. Then we can find the heart of the nation.

ON THE WAY: KATA TJUṮA

I wandered aimlessly, on my own, around the Yulara Resort. My head was still in the clouds. Only several hours earlier we had endorsed the Uluṟu Statement from the Heart; in several hours' time, 250 delegates would gather again in the community of Mutitjulu for the closing ceremony and the final formality – the cultural and spiritual endorsement of the Uluṟu Statement. I couldn't sit down and relax, the adrenalin was still rushing through my veins.

On the path ahead came John Christopherson, better known as 'Christo'. Christo is a Traditional Owner from the Coburg Peninsula in the Northern Territory and is the Deputy Chair of the Northern Land Council. He co-chaired the Darwin Regional Constitutional Dialogue. Christo is a respected activist, leader and a cool, calm and powerful speaker. In 1988, he led a procession of activists from Darwin to Sydney – by car, bus and truck – to join tens of thousands of other Indigenous and non-Indigenous Australians protesting the bi-centenary celebration of British invasion. On many occasions leading up to the Uluṟu Convention and since then, I've watched and listened to Christo, with his deep, steady voice, guide discussions toward a common goal with sage advice.

We stopped to talk and he invited me to go for a drive to Kata Tjuṯa. Other than attending the Welcoming Ceremony at the Mutitjulu community, I hadn't ventured from the resort, so I was quick to accept. I joined Christo and his partner, Trish Rigby, his daughter, Mia Christopherson, and former Australian sprinter and Kannju man, Patrick Johnson, on the 30 kilometre drive. Kata Tjuta, named by Anangu Tjukurrpa (law), means 'many heads', and I was looking forward to seeing them.

We were all on a high, laughing and recalling precious moments from the convention – moments now etched in our memories. As spontaneous as the laughter was, as one we became silent when the many heads of Kata Tjuta peered over the horizon before emerging – magnificent and monolithic. They are proud sentinels looking over Country as they have done for tens of thousands of years.

Christo pulled in and parked, and the rest of us walked along a short path to the viewing platform. I paused to marvel at the small purple and white desert flowers, so delicate yet intense against the deep red earth and the monotonous spinifex. We all took the time to feel and appreciate Country, the beauty and majesty; the moment. Christo stayed in the car. The old warrior had been fighting off cancer for some time and the struggle with his health had wearied him, but not the struggle for his people.

When I returned to the big four-wheel drive, he was sitting at the wheel. I climbed into the back seat while Christo continued staring towards the heads of Kata Tjuta. Without turning to look at me he said, 'The only thing keeping me alive is the unfinished business of constitutional reform.'

My father, John Christopherson, passed away on 18 April 2021. He was a big strong man who always worked to bring people together. He was more than a leader. Dad shaped the words of the Uluru Statement using the force of his passion, commitment and experience, and he tried to hang on to use his strength of character to help us win a First

Nations Voice referendum. I wish he was still here. I wish he was still here, especially now his old friends Linda Burney and Pat Dodson are looking after Indigenous affairs. Dad would have sat with them by now, he would be strategising on how we will win and how to ensure the nation understood they are not losing anything, instead gaining a long and rich history. He tried to hang on; I think he has, in a way. Like Kata Tjuṯa, he watches over us. The sentinel looking over our nation, guiding us to the truth. The truth that we – the Indigenous peoples on our Country – were always the heart of the nation.

Mia Christopherson

Gumatj Yolŋu, Northern Territory

DJAWA YUNUPINGU

Djawa Yunupingu is a leader of the Gumatj clan of the Yolŋu Nation. His totem is the saltwater crocodile. His people, the Yolŋu, and the Yunupingu family, have been at the forefront of the national struggle for land rights and a First Nations Voice since the 1960s. In many ways, Djawa and his brothers under the leadership of the eldest of the siblings, Galarrwuy Yunupingu, are visionaries. They led their family and many of their people from the former mission, Yirrkala, to begin a community in a place of their choosing, in their way.

Djawa is now a spokesperson for his people. He is the Deputy Chair of the Gumatj Corporation Limited and Gumatj Aboriginal Corporation, and he effectively uses his education in the ways of two worlds. He is an Elder who commands respect without demanding it. When I sat with him in his community, I could sense his wisdom, though I was also warmed by his still youthful energy.

As I travelled on the grey bitumen road toward the point of Gove Peninsula in Arnhem Land – Yolŋu land – the industrial structures of the lucrative Rio Tinto mine, stained bauxite red, emerged imposingly on the horizon. On one side of the road stood brilliant red stock piles of bauxite ore, and on the other, deep green mangroves. In fleeting moments, my eyes were drawn to narrow gaps in the thick foliage that exposed pristine white sand and flashes of blue sea. I was tempted to pull over. I wanted to flick my thongs off and feel the sand on my bare feet. But I couldn't. I was on my way to meet Djawa Yunupingu.

I had arrived on Yolŋu Country two days before heading out to Gove Peninsula. Immediately after landing, I met Djawa for a coffee in Nhulunbuy, the largest township in Arnhem Land. Sitting together in the sauna-like humidity outside the small coffee shop, we discussed a story that he had told at a conference for First Nations members of the CFMMEU (Construction, Forestry, Maritime, Mining and Energy Union). Around sixty Indigenous union members from all states and territories had gathered for the conference in Cairns on 1 May 2018 to decide what we wanted of our union. One very important decision, unanimously resolved, was that the union should continue to support the campaign for the Uluṟu Statement from the Heart. I was excited when Djawa invited me to his community, Gunyangara, so that I could interview him in the place that is central to the story he told at that conference.

Having resisted the beckoning white sand, I soon rolled in to Gunyangara and found him at the Gumatj Corporation office. We carried our chairs on to the balcony and he started to tell me the story again.

'It was in the eighties, I think, we got sick and tired of living in Yirrkala. Everything that happened around there was blamed on us. It just wasn't a good place to live in. We lived with other tribes who were looking at us closely. We wanted to get out. My brother

[Dr Galarrwuy Yunupingu] said, "Look, let's move out of here. Let's find our own place to live. Let's establish our own town." So, we looked at Gullipa, which is where the refinery is, but it was just a small area. We drove to Gunyangara, what the balanda [Yolŋu Matha word for 'white people'] call Ski Beach, where the employees of the mine would water ski. We moved there. We lived there. We told them to bugger off.'

With a sweep of his hand, Djawa drew my attention to our surroundings – the houses, the roads, the school, the children's playground and the offices for the Gumatj Aboriginal Corporation. 'We lived in tents, brother, by the way. Just on the beach over there. This was all just bush land. We'd go and shoot kangaroos, go back, cook on the open fire, and sit on the beach. We had high hopes for this community and what we could produce out of it. We started to build tin sheds for us; come hail, rain, shine. You know, we just hung on like this. What royalties we got from the mine, we saved so we could build better houses. We lobbied the government, ATSIC [Aboriginal and Torres Strait Islander Commission] in those days. They gave good housing. This was very good of ATSIC, before it was disbanded [by John Howard's federal government]. Some of the ATSIC housing is still here, though they need replacing with new homes. ATSIC was helpful. They also found ways for us to get employment.

'But there were high suicide rates, all the youth committing suicide. Not just Yirrkala had that problem. The problem followed us here too, as we built the community. Our relatives, those close to us, they started to do bad things, harming themselves. We had to do something. One day me and my brother, Balu Balu, said, "Enough is enough. We got to talk to our people, for our future, you know?"

'We got the people together, we held meetings and meetings and meetings here, and said, "Look, no more of this stringing yourself up business. That's not our culture. It came from England. We've got to focus on our well-being as well." We started to change attitudes with the strong leaders sending out a message to these people to just think before you act ... Do not argue with your wife, do not hit your wife. Whatever you're arguing about, please, make amends. If you love this woman, the woman love you, you better stop. Look after your kid.'

As I listened intently, I could feel in Djawa's voice that it had been an extremely difficult time. I couldn't imagine the heartbreak as family member after family member took their own lives. Djawa described how the hopelessness was perpetuated by an uncaring justice system.

'What happens when the parent has gone to jail, the governments, they can come and take this child anytime; that is what they do. Then, the parent loses it, does bad things. They lose their kids, and then they commit suicide.'

Djawa explained how they turned their community around with stoic leadership, care and by using the education they had gained in both the Yolŋu world and the balanda world. He said that the community's success has seen suicide rates fall significantly. Though it is still an issue that is far worse in comparison to the suicide rates in non-Indigenous communities. Indigenous people in Australia are six times more likely than non-Indigenous people to die by suicide.

'Back when we started here, we only had a cattle farm, which wasn't making money. We just put cattle there to run around. But then we done something about it. We put an abattoir in there, so we can do kills and take meat out to our outstations for countrymen when we have ceremonies. We also sell the meat in the bush stores.'

Djawa went on to talk about the many other successful Gumatj enterprises, such as a timber mill for the native Darwin Stringybark trees, a construction company, and various stores. He proudly told me there will soon be a space station on Gumatj land, sending small sub-orbital rockets into the sky, and maybe one day, into space.

With a huge smile, Djawa also explained how the Gumatj people now own a company that mines bauxite. 'We have trucks, everything here. People are surprised! Every other mine got majority balanda. But here, our young fellas are driving it. You know, like, here, we do it the other way.' Djawa's smile turned into a cheeky laugh as he said, 'Instead of the majority of workers being balanda, here the Yolŋu are the majority, about one hundred nearly. Only three balanda! We've turned it the other way around!'

Still smiling, though now with a more serious expression, he took a deep breath and said in a reverent tone of voice, 'We have come a long way in eight years, brother. Who could think that we could do all that? Only my brother [Dr Galarrwuy Yunupingu]. With us behind him. We made things happen.'

Djawa's brother, Dr Galarrwuy Yunupingu, was a key leader on the Referendum Council. In his younger days, he helped draft the Yirrkala Bark Petitions for his father and other senior Yolŋu leaders. He is a man with great authority – authority in two worlds, carrying the Yolŋu laws and customs while also having the skill and intelligence to negotiate in the white man's world. Dr Galarrwuy Yunupingu has dealt with many prime ministers, and in 2016, he wrote of his disappointment with the leaders of the balanda world:

> *All the prime ministers I have known have been friendly to me, but I mark them all hard. None of them has done what I asked, or delivered what they promised. I asked each one to be truthful and to honestly recognise the truth of history, and to reconcile that truth in a way that finds unity in the future. But they are who they are, and they were not able or not permitted to complete their task.* (*The Monthly*, July 2016. The article was included as an appendix to the Referendum Council Final Report.)

It seems Galarrwuy had hoped that Prime Minister Turnbull would be different. At his invitation, in August 2017, the prime minister and the Opposition Leader, Bill Shorten, attended the annual showcase of Yolŋu culture, the Garma Festival. Djawa explained to me that the Yolŋu Constitution, the Yolŋu law, is on display at the Garma Festival through the dances, the songs and the connecting stories they tell of the Country. How different it is to the Australian Constitution, blandly written on paper – though both are equally important. The 2017 Garma Festival was held in August, soon after the historic Uluru Statement from the Heart was endorsed in late May 2017, and the Referendum Council's final report had been released only two months before, in June 2017. Importantly, the Referendum Council recommended that the sole constitutional reform should be the one that the delegates in Uluru had determined to be the most important – a constitutionally enshrined First Nations Voice to Parliament. Two ducks were in a row, he needed to keep the balanda leaders from Canberra from straying.

At the festival's Welcoming Ceremony, I sat with an excited crowd, tightly gathered on the edge of the bush awaiting the Gumatj dancers. I have no doubt that we all felt the same spiritual energy, mixed with a hopeful anticipation that maybe, just maybe, the prime minister would announce that the proposals in the Uluru Statement from the Heart would be embraced.

I watched as the prime minister – representing the entire nation – stood up at the invitation to speak. Prime Minister Turnbull recited special Yolŋu words gifted to him by the most senior Dilak leader, Dr Galarrwuy Yunupingu. Djawa explained to me that the words were about togetherness, about Makarrata (the coming together after a struggle), and about the fire – the same fire lit at Uluru. The Yolŋu words were pronounced correctly. The audience applauded. The prime minister beamed, and with careful political speak, he indicated that he was there to listen and to act in the interest of the nation's Indigenous peoples.

Dr Yunupingu responded, 'We live in the same land. We live side by side. But not yet united. The fire is our future and I have given the fire to you [Prime Minister and Mr Shorten].'

It was easy to be hopeful, we had to be. But my hopes were dashed when I stood amongst a press of journalists and heard Mr Turnbull downplay any commitment to do what had been requested by and for First Nations people. 'I'm a prime minister that will govern for all Australians,' he said. His address to television viewers around Australia starkly contradicted what he had announced earlier. Just another prime minister who did not deliver on promises for First Nations people.

But Dr Galarrwuy Yunupingu hasn't given up, nor has his brother Djawa. His name, Yunupingu, has a Yolŋu meaning, 'The rock that stands against time'. True to his name, Dr Yunupingu helped lay the path for the Uluru Statement from the Heart to emerge. When health issues meant he was unable to travel to the Uluru Convention, Dr Yunupingu sent his brothers Djawa and Djunga Djunga with a message for the hundreds of Aboriginal and Torres Strait Islander people who had gathered at the opening ceremony.

That's where I first met Djawa and Djunga Djunga, at Uluru with their eldest brother's message – a message carried not on paper but in their spirit. They delivered it through the ancient fire dance. The dance includes the lighting of a fire, and the dancers are the fire, Djawa explained.

'When we paint ourselves up with the diamonds, black, red, yellow – this represents the fire. We brought a message from the most senior Dilak, Galarrwuy Yunupingu, that the fire would be lit in the heart of our nation, in Uluru. We danced and talked with the Anangu people there in their community at Uluru, Mutitjulu. The fire carries the concept of the Makarrata and how we would continue, with courage. We also wanted to point out that we wanted to support the people who went to Uluṟu. When you have a fire, you know when you see the sparks that fly up from it? They are us [the people], taking the message to the capital of Australia and around the nation.

'We brought the right message, Torres Strait Islander brothers and sisters, and us, from east Arnhem Land. We stood in front of that big rock, the heart of Australia. We did our bit to help send out a message that we have lit a fire that will burn bright for Australia, for all of us.'

Djawa was at the convention when the Uluṟu Statement from the Heart was read for the first time. He saw the joy and the hope and it was a source of inspiration for him.

'When the Uluṟu Statement was read for the first time, all of us in the room, we were very emotional, brother. In that moment, I could hear my brother's song in there, which is "Treaty", of course. Then, I could hear my other brother telling the concept of the Makarrata, their voices were inside me. And my very own words, "This is the way to go for a settlement, for this nation, for our nation." I was emotional, inside me, my brother singing, and again my other brother saying those words, and myself thinking about Makarrata. Thinking about all of us, really. Us, and the Torres Strait people.'

As he reminisced, I could see in his eyes that he was there again, in that large convention room with a massive Torres Strait Islands flag at one end and an Aboriginal flag at the other. Djawa sighed and with exasperation he said, 'We did the hard yards, brother. But then they dismissed it in Canberra. Why did they do that?' His face furrowed with sadness.

Djawa went on to answer his own question with his characteristic generosity and hope. 'I'm sure we just have to keep going. I have hope, brother. We stay strong, all of us. Aboriginal and Torres Strait

Islander people, we can make this happen.' He said slowly, 'If there is ever a prime minister that can deliver those words, telling us, the First Nations people, "You will be included in the Australian Constitution."' His big smile returned, 'Oh, I'd like to see that! That would be great, brother …' He laughed. 'I would die happy! Not that I'm going to die tomorrow!' We laughed together.

My mind wandered, and my heart grew heavy. I thought, Here is a man who, with his brothers, has done the hard yards, working every day to build his community and to provide opportunities for his people. He brought a message from his people to the historic culmination of regional dialogues, the Uluṟu First Nations Constitutional Convention. And again, he put in the hard yards to build a better Australia and provide opportunities for all of us by putting together a proposal to find the heart of this nation, despite broken promises and ignorant, destructive government policies. Djawa and his brother Dr Galarrwuy Yunupingu look to a shared future. They have demonstrated they can move on from the massacres that their father survived, and the truth that their father was hunted by a white man, with a lawful direction to kill him. As I left Gunyangara later that day, I felt the deepest respect for Djawa Yunupingu. A great man.

These are his words, taken from his eloquent speech at Garma 2018, where the theme was 'Truth Telling':

> *You will hear us singing tonight and we will be singing to our ancestors, who are your ancestors too. We will be singing to remind them that we are here, maintaining our connection to them, for their appreciation. And we do this not just for us, but for all of us.*

Larrakia, Northern Territory

WAYNE KURNORTH

Wayne Kurnorth is a Larrakia man with a heart the size of a football. His people are the Traditional Owners of the Darwin region, from Fog Bay in the west, Gunn Point to the north, to the vicinity of Adelaide River in the east, and down to the Manton Dam area southwards. They call themselves 'saltwater people'.

I've known Wayne since we were kids. We both played for Brothers Rugby League Club and in our teen years we performed Torres Strait Island dancing together. Wayne had to stop playing footy before the rest of us did because of a bad knee, but he helped in any way possible around the club. As an unselfish volunteer, Wayne is the type of person every team needs but often takes for granted.

Wayne brings this same dedication to his work. He was a boilermaker at a shipyard in Frances Bay, Darwin, and one of only two union members in the entire workshop. When he put up his hand to be the workplace delegate, this changed quickly. With perseverance and because of the respect the other workers had for him, the workshop became fully unionised. Thanks to that unity, the workshop forged better conditions and pay rates. Five years later, in 2017, Wayne became an organiser, employed full time by a union.

When I sat with Wayne for the interview, he had just received the highest award a union organiser could achieve – the ACTU Organiser of the Year. A well-deserved award because, while working for the Northern Territory branch of United Voice, Wayne unionised hundreds of First Nations workers from the remotest of communities to stand up against the Community Development Program (CDP).

The CDP – a remote employment and community development service – was introduced by the Indigenous Affairs Minister Nigel Scullion in 2015, under the Abbott Coalition government. The program was considered racist as it only applied to remote Aboriginal communities. It forced Aboriginal people to work three times longer for welfare payments than city-based jobseekers. For 25 hours of work per week, CDP workers were paid less than $12 per hour. The minimum wage at the time was more than $18 an hour.

Wayne explained: 'CDP workers are doing work that should be paid at award rates – I've seen a mob in Alice Springs doing tree trimming and stuff that the council would do, and the mob out Daly River way building boundary fencing. Things like that that are part of what a community needs. Really, they were being exploited by employers as cheap labour – paid nothing but welfare. It's not only a matter of pay. They also have no rights as workers. They don't get worker rights from the Fair Work Act or even protection from occupational health and safety laws. It's like a return to work for rations. They're not even getting that in cash, it's quarantined on an income management Basics Card, so it's worse.'

The program is also punitive and unforgiving. Wayne explained how although CDP workers are only a small percentage of unemployed people, they account for 'more than half the penalties across the entire welfare system'. Ultimately, the Community Development Program only serves to impoverish Indigenous people, exasperating the incredible rates of Indigenous suicide and incarceration. It is an exercise of disempowerment in remote communities. It is a program that must change. As an organiser, Wayne needed to build trust to bring the people together. He had an advantage, though, because he was already connected to those communities.

Wayne's great-grandfather, Juma Fejo, was the son of a Larrakia man named King George. Juma had eight children, six boys and Wayne's grandmother, Jone Fejo-Kurnorth, as well as one adopted child, Dot Fejo. Talking about his work in the remote communities, Wayne said, 'I have an advantage because when I go out and talk to older countrymen and countrywomen, I say who I am. They know [me], because at some stage [they] would have known one of [my grandmother's] six brothers who have gone through there working and would have stayed there for a while.

'All them brothers paved their way, and now it's sort of paving my way as well. I feel good when I hear that.'

One of the remote areas Wayne travels to as a union organiser is Nhulunbuy on the Gove Peninsula in north-east Arnhem Land. These are the lands of the Yolŋu People, who in 1963, petitioned the Australian House of Representatives with the Yirrkala Bark Petitions. The petitions were in response to the federal government's decision to excise 140 square miles of Yolŋu land for mining interests. The words of the petition, both in English and Yolŋu Matha, expressed the people's ongoing connection to and need of the land. The petitions proposed that the House of Representatives 'appoint a committee, accompanied by competent interpreters, to hear the views of the Yirrkala people before permitting the excision of this land' – a Voice to Parliament.

The Yirrkala Bark Petitions were presented to the House of Representatives by Labor politician Kim Beazley, Snr. Earlier that year, he had visited the mission at Yirrkala to personally hear the concerns of the Yolŋu people. The Federal Parliament passed Beazley's motion to establish a select committee to enquire in to the petitioners' grievances. In the committee's final report, they made twelve recommendations that included compensation, access to and protection of sacred sites, and a ten-year standing committee that would 'examine from time to time, the conditions of the Yirrkala people and the carrying out of this committee's recommendations'.

Despite the humble petitions and the efforts of the select committee, the government ignored the recommendations, unilaterally excising the land and approving the Nabalco mine. The Yolŋu people, determined to protect their land, decided to take the matter to the Northern Territory Supreme Court in the Milirrpum v Nabalco Pty Ltd case.

When the court case ended in April 1971, Justice Richard Blackburn ruled against the land claim, declaring 'there is so little resemblance between property, as our law ... understands that term, and the claims of the plaintiffs for their clans, that I must hold that these claims are not in the nature of proprietary interests'. Justice Blackburn had basically found that the Yolŋu people's 'subtle and elaborate system of social rules and customs', was 'remarkably free from the vagaries of personal whim or influence' – putting the Aboriginal form of land ownership, communal title, at odds with Australian and British law in a 'settled' colony. The mine was built.

As a result of the Yolŋu's high-profile legal tussle with the government and the mining company, and land rights protests across Australia, the next prime minister, Gough Whitlam, established the National Aboriginal Consultative Council and the 1973 Woodward Royal Commission. Its role was to determine an appropriate way to recognise Aboriginal land rights in the Northern Territory. The recommendations of the Woodward Royal Commission led to the passing of the *Aboriginal Land Rights (Northern Territory) Act 1976 (Cth)* by the Fraser Liberal government; the first land rights legislation. The Yolŋu struggle in the Northern Territory Supreme Court also paved the way for the landmark High Court case of Mabo No 2.

In the 1960s and '70s, the Yolŋu people weren't only fighting for land rights. They were fighting for survival because they were fearful of suffering the fate of Wayne's people, the Larrakia. On the 1963 Yirrkala Bark Petitions the authors wrote: *That the people of this area fear that their needs and interests will be completely ignored as they have been ignored in the past, and they fear that the fate which has overtaken the Larrakeah tribe will overtake them.*

Wayne has lived that fate. He laments the loss of Larrakia cultural practices.

'When we were young, I was glad to have the opportunity to island dance with you mob, Thomas. It was fun. Remember we'd always get told off to be serious!' We laughed as we reminisced, '"You're all going to be serious, now!" Uncle Tawie would say! It was an experience.' Wayne's laugh became a frown. 'But at the same time, it made me feel like …' He paused. 'I wish that we [Larrakia] had our ceremonies – that we could've learned our dancing and stuff like that. I mean … when I go to Nhulunbuy, Alice Springs and Groote Eylandt, places like that where culture is still strong – even the Tiwi Islands, so close to Darwin here – it's good to see. But I'm sad for what we lost. Darwin's evolved, grew over the top of our land and our people. It's no wonder the Yolŋu didn't want to suffer the same fate as us. They saw what happened to us when Darwin came along.'

Wayne said, 'I wish that my grandmother was still alive, and her brothers – to show us a lot more of what we've lost when they went. That way we would be able to hold that for now and keep it for the next generation. But we've lost that part of it.'

Wayne made me think about how my family and I are living on his land, enjoying what is ultimately the economic prosperity built from the dispossession of his family and ancestors. They have little to show for it, comparatively. The Larrakia have survived, living amongst people who don't fully grasp the truth of their fate. A fate that the Yolŋu feared.

I reflected on how, in each dialogue in the lead-up to Uluṟu, without fail, the first day was always very strong on truth-telling. Of the thirteen regional dialogues, this was especially so where the earliest and most vicious impacts of colonisation were felt. At the Darwin and Brisbane regional dialogues I heard the descendants of the massacred. I listened to their sorrow for lost songs and ceremonies. I recognised that the loss of culture was like the way an amputee describes the loss of a limb – it still feels as if the limb is there. In their minds, they feel their culture – just like a limb – was never lost.

Reflecting on the Darwin dialogue, Wayne said, 'Truth-telling and the Voice to Parliament came out really strong.

'For there to be an acceptance of what has happened, the truth should be taught in our education system. That's the only way our next generation of kids will be more accepted for who they are. You go where the kids go to school, and they're learning Greek or Indonesian. The Aboriginal language for where you live should be learnt. They should be learning our language and accepting it as part of Australia's culture.'

Talking about the federal government's dismissal of the call for a Voice to Parliament, Wayne said, 'I was expecting the dismissal from the Liberal government. Typical ignorance. The ignorance of politicians in Australia.'

But Wayne said it is changing. When we organised the rallies in the lead-up to our participation in the Darwin Constitutional Dialogue there were people like Cat Street, for example who came out onto the streets. Cat's a young, non-Indigenous health researcher who dedicated much of her time to helping us get organised. Wayne said that witnessing the increasing non-Indigenous support gives him hope.

I asked Wayne if he'd like to finish the interview with a message to the Australian people. Without hesitation, he said plainly, with the confidence of a man who had organised around 300 Indigenous union members in an award-winning effort: 'Australia needs to get with the times. A constitutionally enshrined Voice to Parliament will be good for all of us. Let's do it.'

ON THE WAY: GARMA

The politics and the manoeuvring at the Garma Festival in the Northern Territory in August of 2017 had been tumultuous. The Yolŋu people, through their most senior Dilak (person of authority), had gifted Prime Minster Malcolm Turnbull with the sacred words of the Uluṟu Statement. Mr Turnbull used the words in a speech to the crowd and the cameras. He pronounced them well.

On the final day of the festival I went fishing with Deon Mununggurr in his friend's boat. Deon is a young Yolŋu man who lives in Yirrkala and works as an Aboriginal interpreter. He is quick witted and hard working. He has welcomed and adopted many visitors to his Country.

I needed that fishing trip. The politics were depressing. And although it was a rough day at sea, in close to the little islands with their beaches of pristine white sand, the sheltered waters were crystal clear and inviting. We moored in the shallows of one of the many islands and swam across the reef, diving for crayfish. Then, we waded ashore where turtle tracks indicated there may be eggs laid nearby. We didn't find the eggs. The turtle's route was a 'dummy run', or she was just too smart for us.

The saltwater, the comradery with the small crew, and Deon's affable character cleansed me of the feelings left behind from the empty rhetoric of the prime minister. I left Garma and Yolŋu

Country on a high because I felt I knew what I had to do next. If the politicians were not compelled by our words or our plight, it was time to build a people's movement.

On my return to Darwin, I picked up the Uluṟu Statement canvas from the Darwin Museum and Art Gallery. While at the Garma Festival, I had held the canvas for the very first time. I felt its power. I realised that the wonderful Uluṟu Statement canvas was our most powerful tool. I thought that if other Australians could see it too, it would inspire the vital momentum for change that we hoped for. With the unwavering support of my union, the MUA, and the blessings of the Elders, I began my first trip with the sacred canvas and a renewed sense of purpose.

The first stop was a place that should be the most celebrated place in this nation. A place as significant as the Eureka Stockade in Ballarat, Victoria. It is the hard fought for lands of the Gurindji people in the Northern Territory. As I began the nine-hour drive to Kalkarindji, the Uluṟu Statement from the Heart artwork was next to me, rolled up inside two cardboard postal cylinders taped together.

I began my travels with excitement, but also concern. The canvas had barely been seen in public at that time. Yes, the Uluṟu Statement had been broadcast from Garma to TV screens throughout the nation, thanks to (NITV) National Indigenous Television, but this was different. I wanted to take it physically to the people so it could move them as it had moved me. I wanted to roll the canvas out and hold it up in the remotest of communities, in the homes of Elders, in offices and schools, at conferences and at forums. I knew I would do this at great risk. The canvas I would carry for months to come in many forms of transport, to many people with many perspectives was irreplaceable. I was suddenly responsible for the care of a sacred object that was vitally important to the present and the future. I was afraid.

How would the canvas be received in the broader community?

There had been much misinformation about the Uluru Statement. There would be ideologues and extremists who will leap at an opportunity to damage the canvas and our campaign.

I will need to be prepared, I thought, on that first long drive. I will need to be ready to physically protect the canvas in case of an attempt to damage or steal it. I was prepared to protect the Uluru Statement with my life.

Gurindji, Northern Territory

ROBERT ROY

When I arrived on Gurindji Country, I was warmly welcomed, and so was the Ulu̱ru Statement. I was embraced by my Gurindji friend, Rob Roy, and his colleague at the Gurindji Corporation, General Manager and Freedom Day Festival Director, Phil Smith. They were busy, running around with sweaty urgency, finishing the set up for the festival that would be kicking off in less than 24 hours. The festival, proudly named by Gurindji people as 'Freedom Day', commemorates the anniversary of the Wave Hill Walk-off.

Tired as they were, I was able to put a spring in their step. I had managed to squeeze in a fishing trip with my dad before I left Darwin, and I brought some fresh seafood with me. As Rob and Phil worked on the festival grounds in the last hour of daylight, I fried a generous batch of turtle meat, fresh fish and, of course, rice – a staple eaten with chillies at almost every meal in my household, including roasts and spaghetti. That night, we had a great feast.

With our bellies full, Rob Roy, best known as 'Double R', and I began a discussion that went until late in the night. Rob didn't attend a regional dialogue, nor was he at Uluṟu. So, I took the time to explain where the Uluṟu Statement came from, what it proposes, and why a constitutionally enshrined First Nations Voice is so important. Rob listened, asked questions and listened again. Then I listened to him as he explained the issues that his community had to deal with each day in Kalkarindji and Daguragu. We both related those problems to the systemic powerlessness of the community. The great Vincent Lingiari had stated that their struggle was to be able to 'live on our land our way'. That hope was still far from a reality.

Rob was the MC for the festival events. He is a strong public speaker with the ability to deliver a message clearly and confidently. In the morning, before the enthusiastic festival crowd gathered to mark the day with the annual walk to the strikers old camp site, Rob explained the Uluṟu Statement to the Elders in Gurindji language. The Elders then decided to make a statement of their own. Their statement was an unequivocal endorsement of the campaign to see the Uluṟu Statement proposals become a reality. Rob read it at the Freedom Day Festival opening ceremony:

> *Today on the anniversary of the Wave Hill Walk-off, we re-enacted the Walk-off that was the beginning of our struggle for land rights and fair working conditions. It was our actions that led to Prime Minister Gough Whitlam giving our Country back to us in the symbolic gesture that is celebrated today in Australian history. The call of Voice, Truth and Treaty out of Uluṟu this year was another action that we will be a part of.*
>
> *Dr Yunupingu put down a challenge to our prime minister at Garma to see the call for a Voice enacted. We join our voice with theirs with the vision of seeing a Gurindji*

speaking to Parliament, and the truth being told about our history. A settlement of our sad past can be resolved by Makarrata.

Once the festival was over, Rob and I each took a plastic chair out from the Gurindji Corporation's office, where Rob works. We found a tree that cast some shade and sat down, enjoying the warm breeze. At first, it seemed that Rob was a little nervous. Perhaps because I was too. Rob was the first person I interviewed for this book.

When we started talking, Rob told me that his totem is the witchety grub, and he explained how important song lines are to his identity as an Aboriginal person.

'We can be different clan group, family group, or skin name. These and our totem give our identity, who you are, who you can talk to, who you can't talk to. This is how our society works, like a kinship guideline. It's about being respectful. With our skin name and our totem, it represents different individual Country around Gurindji land, for different families. So, a story line is very important. We need to preserve it, we don't want to lose it. We want to continue our ceremonies. We teach our young kids their totem and dreaming. It is painted on their bodies, so they know the area, the waterhole, and all that sort of stuff. They understand this has all gone on forever, thousands of years, passed down from father to son, mother to daughter, all the way right down. Right up until today's generation.'

As a boy, Rob told me how he would listen to his parents talking about their hardships working for the white fellas on the cattle stations, before they joined a strike that is one of Australia's most celebrated – the Wave Hill Walk-off. 'We used to sit around the campfire all the time. They used to talk about it. The trouble with the way they were treated, and all that sort of stuff that caused them to take action.'

The brave and determined Wave Hill Walk-off was a significant chapter in the struggle for equal wages and land rights for First Nations people. It was a nine-year strike that began in 1966, when Gurindji leader Vincent Lingiari led around 200 of his people on the mass exodus because station owner Lord Vestey would not improve the poor working conditions. To the Gurindji people, the Country where Wave Hill Station is, is called Jimparrak. The Gurindji men, women and children walked 22 kilometres to the Victoria River, laden with all that they owned and with their babies, little children and the elderly. They made their journey in fear, looking over their shoulders. At any moment, white men could have come galloping over the horizon with guns for a slaughter. At that time, the massacres that came with the strange beasts, both cattle and white men, were in living memory.

Rob said, 'I was born after the Walk-off. My mum and dad walked with Vincent Lingiari.

'My dad's name is Younger Roy, and my mum's name is Maryanne. I'm a Gurindji man because I'm a product of them two, and I'm just so proud of them.'

I said I knew exactly what he was talking about.

'My mum was actually Mudburra, from Elliott way, but she met up with my dad at that Wave Hill Station.'

Rob's mum and dad were quite young during the long Gurindji Walk-off strike. Their first child, Rob's sister, was born before the Walk-off. Rob's mother carried her baby daughter on her hip as well as their meagre belongings when she walked with the others across the dry country, over hills and around the sparse shrubs. Despite the incredible hardship, they started a little family, and they strived to give them hope.

'I've always thought that we went on strike for self-determination as well as land rights. But we're still fighting for self-determination.

We want to take responsibility in our own ways in our own community.'

During the festival, I could see Rob was proud of his work. I asked him to tell me more about the Gurindji Aboriginal Corporation and the ongoing problems in his community.

'The Gurindji Aboriginal Corporation, we are a registered Native Title body holder. We went through thirteen years of Native Title work to have Kalkarindji recognised as our land. So, in saying that, there's a little bit of a sense of, "We got it. We won", just a small proportion of it. Now, we are doing more to this community through Gurindji Aboriginal Corporation, so we can benefit this community and help build it. I think we're doing that – slowly, slowly.

'When we formed it, we formed it with basically nothing. There was nothing in the bank balance, and slowly, slowly it just built up.

'But our communities still need better services: health, housing; that's the main thing. Overcrowding in our homes is a problem. The government need to be very serious to try and help fix that, to come out to the community, see firsthand, because a lot of them up there say, "Oh yeah, we went to this other community, and we know what the other community's like." That's wrong what they say. All communities are different, you know? Though we have got the same problems, it isn't always the same answer.'

Same problems, different answer. When I thought about this afterwards, the Uluru Statement's words came to me:

> We seek constitutional reforms to empower our people and take a rightful place in our own country. When we have power over our destiny our children will flourish, they will walk in two worlds and their culture will be a gift to their country.

Vincent Lingiari said the same in a simpler way, 'We want to live on our land our way.'

Rob Roy had told me about his mother taking him to the place where the Walk-off began, Jimparrak (Old Wave Hill Station). I didn't hesitate to say yes when he asked if I'd like to continue the interview there.

The year before, in 2017, starting out early in the morning to beat the harsh midday heat, I walked a recently established Wave Hill Walk-off Heritage trail that follows in the footsteps of the 1966 Walk-off. Beginning at the Old Wave Hill Station, it follows the same fence-line that the Gurindji people walked along when on strike. Today, at around the halfway mark, there is a structure for walkers to rest, at Junarni (Gordy Creek), where the 200 Gurindji briefly rested and dug in the dry creek bed for water. The trail then leads over a rocky hill toward the place where they settled for the wet season – a section of the Victoria River called Litanungku. The final leg of the trail takes you to the resting place of the great Vincent Lingiari at the Kalkarindji cemetery.

This time, driving, not walking, we left Kalkarindji in the afternoon. We travelled in a convoy with some politicians who joined us. Penny Wong, Malarndirri McCarthy and Warren Snowden had flown in for the day. Rob and Phil Smith led the procession of cars, with the politicians and their entourage in the middle and my family – my wife Mel and our two children, Will and Ruby, and I – not far behind. Sixteen minutes from Kalkarindji, we turned off the Buntine Highway onto the roughly corrugated, single-lane track. We passed kangaroos, cattle, donkeys and horses. We went through livestock gates and over rocky corrugations until we stopped near a huge shady Wanyarri tree. We were surrounded by arid bush and open spaces, with old relics scattered about amongst the rusted remnants of tin shacks.

I walked with Rob, side by side, with Mel and the kids not far behind. The kids loved being in the outback. As we walked, Rob reminisced on what he had heard around the campfire with his mother and father.

'I remember how amazed I was, the hardship of it. Just how cruel his [Vestey's] mob was. You know, the worst thing that anybody could ever experience. When they were telling us, we were just … well, I couldn't believe it. I would keep asking my mum over and over, "Really, did that happen?" I couldn't actually proper visualise it, you know, until now I do. So, I guess I'm proud, and I'm glad that they've been there, they've done that; that they made things better for us, you know?'

Rob pointed to where the station manager's house was. 'I remember when my mum was talking about how she was fanning those managers, and the manager's wife. Fanning them, during temperature's like this. And cooking, feeding all the white stockmen and their wives. And all we were given was flour, sugar and tea; and bones of fresh kill from a bullock. All the white stockmen and their wives, they had proper meat and everything. My mum and all the workers were just given guts and bones, and that's what they tried to live off. But they lived off the land as well, they went hunting for kangaroo, turkey, and all that sort of stuff.'

As Rob explained this to me, I didn't see anger, or even outward sadness. I saw pride.

'My mum showed me where they lived at the old station, and how my dad built the floor out of flat rocks from the river. All they had was just a few pieces of tin shed and the flat river rocks.'

Rob stared out across a fence line where two mangy looking horses slowly walked away from us. He pointed out three gnarly trees, standing alone in the paddock. 'See them ironwood. Them trees there. My mum and them old people were saying that one of those trees, only women were allowed there. Those are the birthing trees.'

We walked together toward a low, rocky hill. 'Over here is where all Gurindji, Warlpiri, all our Aboriginal mob stayed. We'll go closer. Come here, I will show you the windbreak, where they lived. Creek dry now, but in wet season, lovely and clean.

'See that stone, one big one, one little one. They used to be windbreak during the cold weather. Some family here, some family there, there.' The hill had been built up to give more shelter. Rob pointed out the remnants of structures where people lived. Through his words I could picture the scene, but the hardship would have been so great, it was unimaginable. 'My mum and dad were over there. Still see toilet pits there. Use a 44-gallon drum. While these mob were living like this, Mum would go over there, cook for them white fellas, wash their clothes, fan them.'

Though the day I was there had been hot and dry, like an oven, the night was cold. All Rob's mother and father had on nights like that to keep them warm was a windbreak, some worn-out clothes and a camp fire. In this harsh, open area, I could see the remaining stone floors of the little humpies, put together with some tin and timber. Each floor was probably less than 2 meters square.

Rob asked me to walk a little further. 'One time when I came here with my mum, she said, "I'll take you to where your father built this humpy." They had two kids but one passed away. So, there's only my sister and me. Mum pointed to a patch of rock in the distance and said, "You can go there, but I can't." She said that's where my father was. My mum stayed while I went and had a look.'

I thanked Rob for showing me a place of deep significance to him and his family. Leaving him with his thoughts, and no doubt, a mixture of heartfelt emotions, I walked back to join Mel, Will and

Ruby. The kids were excitedly chattering about a horse shoe they had found. I reminded them not to move any rocks. Mel and I were glad to have the opportunity to come to this place with a descendent of the brave Gurindji people.

Later, I turned to a topic that I knew Rob would enjoy. I asked him about the trip he took to Sydney, to doorknock the homes in the prime minister's electorate. Rob beamed and said, 'It was thrilling, knowing that Lingiari went there back in the '70s! He went to Sydney, on his journey to a great success when he won these land rights. As an experience, knowing that we went to Wentworth [a federal electorate for Sydney's eastern suburbs] … It's a pity that the prime minister wasn't there or else we could have asked him why he dismissed the Uluṟu Statement!' He smiled.

Rob happily reflected on a memorable moment at the busy Kings Cross Market in May 2018, after we celebrated and shared the Uluṟu Statement with the locals. 'Jeremy, Rosie [the two other Gurindji participants], we were sitting there and this one old white fella came up, and he said, "I remember one old fella came from Daguragu, and he came with Vincent Lingiari. His name was Captain Major." He told us how Captain Major was making a joke out of the British Lord Vestey at that time, when he was visiting. And I thought, really? And I told Rosie this story [Rosie is Vincent Lingiari's granddaughter]. I sort of nudged Rosie on the shoulder and said, "There you go. You know what you've just done today? You actually followed your grandfather's footstep, and you're here." And I tell you, she was speechless. She was, like, "Yeah, I know; can't be." That's what she said.'

Captain Major, or Lupna Giari, was a Gurindji man and union organiser who had led a lesser known walk-off in April 1966 from the Newcastle Waters cattle station. He did important work to build public support for the Gurindji strike.

I told Rob how Rosie Smiler had called me late one night, not long after she had returned to Kalkarindji after visiting Sydney. How she expressed her pride at following in her grandfather's footsteps.

'Yeah, she told me that. We were all like that, when we got to Darwin – we almost missed the plane too!' Rob laughed heartily. 'But you know, that was a good trip. Rosie was saying to me, "Well, I'm glad I did go on that. I'm glad I went to Sydney, because my grandfather was there." That's what she said. So that was a bit of an emotional time, and strong emotion, knowing that she'd done that.'

Rob was emotional himself, as he went on. 'When I made the speech in Sydney, I somehow felt that Lingiari's presence was there with us, because Rosie was there. I kind of wonder how he felt when he went down there, what was his reaction, you know? And knowing that he walked off from the station, and all of a sudden, he's down there and there's a lot of gardia [white] people there. He got a lot of support, but I wonder if he actually *found* himself there? Sometimes you've got to leave your Country to find yourself. That's how I felt.'

Rosie and Rob Roy didn't attend their region's constitutional dialogue at Ross River. Neither of them was at Uluru for the historic convention. They didn't experience what I did, with about 250 other Aboriginal and Torres Strait Islanders from around the country. But they didn't need to be there to understand what we did and why. The struggle for self-determination and the bravery to take practical steps toward living 'on our land our way' is in their blood.

As we wrapped up the interview, Rob optimistically said to me, 'Aboriginal people are not asking to live in a perfect world. All we are asking for is not to be ignored. You like a bit of a challenge in life, so being perfect would be boring. But we can make Australia a better place by learning from our history.'

ON THE WAY: JIMPARRAK

The first time I went to Gurindji Country was in 2011 for the Wave Hill Walk-off's 45th anniversary. It was a memorable celebration. That year, the great Australian singer Paul Kelly travelled from Melbourne to the anniversary celebrations to perform 'From little things big things grow'.

The song Paul Kelly and Kev Carmody wrote never fails to inspire me. Paul sings it with a style that plainly but clearly tells the story of Vincent Lingiari and his courageous people – the Walk-off, the politics, the solidarity, and the success. The small community swelled in numbers to mark the occasion. As I met the Gurindji Elders amongst a throng of gardia (white people), journalists and ever smiling politicians, I was by the side of a union man, old Brian Manning.

Brian Manning had been a wharfie and an official of the MUA, as I was. We had worked together in his last years as a waterside worker. As I sat there, I witnessed the great respect the Gurindji people had for Brian. He and his comrade waterside workers didn't hesitate to walk with the striking Aboriginal men and women. They made regular supply runs from Darwin to the strikers's camp, and worked to get the rest of the union movement and the country to join the land rights struggle. The unwavering and substantial support from the nation's waterside workers has never been forgotten on Gurindji Country.

When Brian passed away, I led the farewell service on Stokes Hill Wharf in Darwin. During the service, one by one, Gurindji people reminisced about being young men and boys cheering as an old green Bedford truck, with Brian at the wheel, limped into camp, bringing vital supplies. At the end of the service, the old Gurindji men there lined up to hug me. Old Jimmy Wavehill clasped my hand and said to me that I would always be welcome to visit Gurindji Country.

Jimmy Wavehill is a quietly spoken man, as was the great Vincent Lingiari. Jimmy was a young stockman when they walked off. On the 50th anniversary of the Walk-off, he spoke about it to the ABC news.

'One morning come, we get up, we walk to the station and tell the [owner] we're not staying, no more work for you guys, we're finished,' Jimmy said. 'We walked down the river, and the Vestey's manager came down and said I'll double the wages for you guys, you know, you mob gotta come back and work with us.

'"Sorry," Vincent said. "I'm sorry, but you couldn't think of that in the first place when we been in the job."'

The strike grew to be more than a protest against the Gurindji people's poor treatment as workers. It became an enduring struggle for land rights. 'We want to live on our land, our way,' Vincent Lingiari said.

Vincent Lingiari left his homelands for the big city. A long journey into a hive of alien people, sights and sounds. He built momentum in the campaign for land rights by gaining the support of the Australian people. More than fifty years later, his granddaughter, Rosie Smiler, has followed in his footsteps.

Gurindji, Northern Territory

ROSIE SMILER

Rosie Smiler is a teacher's assistant for years 3 and 4 at the Kalkarindji school. Her twin sister, Lisa Smiler, is also a teacher. Rosie speaks Gurindji, Walpiri and Mudburra, Gurindji Kriol, as well as English. She is a very quiet person, though. But as you will read, her actions speak louder and clearer than words from any language.

I first met Rosie in Darwin, at a conference for Indigenous union members, organised by the Australian Council of Trade Unions (ACTU). We gathered to guide the union movement on ways to support First Nations people. The conference was also a celebration of the 50th anniversary of the Wave Hill Walk-off, when 200 brave Gurindji people walked off Wave Hill Cattle Station in protest of working conditions akin to slavery.

On the conference's opening night, Rosie and I took to the stage together. Rosie, in her quiet way, spoke about how her people are still suffering from overcrowded housing. She talked about the damage the Community Development Program was doing. She explained to the audience of around 200 union members that her people had lost meaningful jobs that built the community. She said the people were left with nothing but a work for the dole system, CDP, with harsh and stringent rules. On the stage, her soft voice may have been almost inaudible, but her few words were genuine and heartfelt, and the audience listened intently.

Every time I've met Rosie it has been a similar experience. She has reluctantly stepped forward to speak for her people, and she always inspires me and the rest of her audience.

In the days before the anniversary of the Uluru Statement, 26 May 2018, Rosie and two other Gurindji people, Rob Roy and Jeremy Frith, travelled the nine hours by car to Darwin, and then flew for more than four hours from Darwin to Sydney. Their destination was the federal seat of Wentworth, in Sydney's eastern suburbs. They wanted to let the voters in Wentworth know that their member in Parliament, Malcolm Turnbull, who was also the prime minister, had seriously disrespected First Nations people. It was Rosie's first time in Sydney.

A few months later, I interviewed Rosie for the book, at the 52nd anniversary of the Wave Hill Walk-off. We leaned against a 4WD on the edge of Kalkarindji oval as a football game between the Gurindji Eagles and the Lajamanu Swans played out. From the sideline, it looked as though there were more players on the field than blades of grass. The game was a spectacle; with each burst of speed, with each deft step and bone-shaking collision, a plume of red dust would rise into the cool evening air. It wasn't the best place for an interview, but Rosie loves football. When we were in Sydney, Rosie enjoyed an opportunity to watch her favourite big city team, the Essendon Bombers, play against the Sydney Swans.

I asked Rosie how she felt going to a community action in the big city.

'When I was in Sydney – first time big city – I was nervous. I thought it was a little bit crowded. I was a bit a nervous. My mind kept saying, I gotta do it. That's why I'm here. I need to do a speech, like, say something about why I'm here in Sydney. I need to say something about my grandfather and who I am.'

We had two community actions that day. In the morning we gathered at the El Alamein Fountain in the heart of Kings Cross, and in the afternoon at Bicentennial Park. The El Alamein Fountain is a war memorial built in 1961, before the Walk-off. It commemorates a battle near the Egyptian town of El Alamein. The fountain is prominent, even during the busy weekend market – like a giant dandelion.

On the morning of the community action, I met the Gurindji delegation for breakfast. I helped ease some last-minute nerves with advice on public speaking. While they were nervous about speaking, I was nervous about whether supporters would turn up. I needn't have worried. As the time to begin drew nearer and as we laid out the Ulu_ru Statement on the pavement and set up the speakers for the band, Tripple Effect, to sing a song they wrote about the Ulu_ru Statement, a substantial crowd gathered.

After a brief discussion with police, who were concerned about the growing crowd, we began with an Acknowledgement of Country by Allan Murray, who I interview in this book, before Rosie took the mic. With the fountain spraying water in the background, and with the hustle of the markets, it was difficult to hear her quiet voice. Rosie talked about the problems at home and how we needed a stronger voice to make the government listen. The speech was brief but, as I'd witnessed before, the crowd gravitated to the shy yet brave speaker.

When the speeches were done, we handed out envelopes containing maps with highlighted streets to doorknock. Loaded up with badges and campaign materials, the ample number of supporters dispersed in to the crowd and streets. Market goers who joined our gathering lined up to pledge their support for the Uluṟu Statement from the Heart. The day was a great success. Later I heard it had tongues wagging in Canberra.

We needn't have been apprehensive, after all. I asked Rosie if she felt welcome amongst the people of the big city.

'I was happy,' she said. 'People were coming up to me, wanted a photo with me, talking to me about my grandfather and who I am.

'It's hard though, to understand English. I hear the word, but in my mind, I need to think what it means. For example, if gardia [white person] say a word like "communicate", some of us don't understand. That includes kids and old people. Even young parents here.

'When I'm at school working, I told them I want to do study. They asked me, you want to do study, do your degree. I said I don't know. I don't speak English very well because I speak my language, Gurindji Kriol. If some gardia ask me question in their hard language, I don't even know. I told my teachers, if that is how it will be, I will just stay home. I'm a shy person. I'm a minyiti person – that means "shy" in Gurindji. When I am with gardia, I can't think what they are saying. If there are too many around me talking their lingo it is really hard. But if it's just me and you it's okay.'

When we were in Sydney, Rosie made some new friends. She hung out with Mich-Elle Myers, the MUA's National Women's Officer, and went to the Bombers game under the escort of the New South Wales Construction Union President, Rita Mallia, and Wiradjuri and Wailwan lawyer, Teela Reid.

Rosie said she enjoyed visiting Sydney, but she was there because she wanted change. She said the same problems remain from two years ago when she spoke at the ACTU Conference. 'CDP [the Community Development Program] is a problem. There're not many people working in my community. They want better jobs, but they aren't getting better jobs in the community. Housing is still an issue too. Better housing is always on my mind.'

Communities such as Rosie's, throughout the country, continue to suffer a crisis in housing. There remains low or meaningless employment for the locals; but there is a thriving, predominantly non-Indigenous industry built around the social dysfunction that the constant policy failures create.

Rosie had a good idea of why nothing was changing. 'We need to have our own Voice or say. Whether in the Northern Territory or not. We need to be strong together, all Aboriginals, because what the governments are doing … they're not doing good things. I think we should go up front and talk to the government. Fight the government so they can improve what people in every community need … getting good jobs, you know? Talk to them about it. What kind of things we're not getting in our community. Sit down with them so they can get a better understanding of where we're coming from.'

She paused, then said, 'Yeah, that's the problem as I see it. They understand. But they do things their own way. They don't believe us. They don't listen to us.' Rosie said that she would be up to the challenge again. She could step up and talk to the politicians about what they need to do. 'Even though I'd never been to cities, I could sit down and talk to people. I want to see the real world, you know? Go out and talk to people. For things that have been a problem in our community, sit down and talk to them about it.'

After the community action in Wentworth, Rosie got ready to make the long journey home, but first she did some sightseeing with her new friends. We didn't have time to say much to each other before she left, but when she returned to Kalkarindji, Rosie called me with an energy in her voice that took me by surprise. Her late-night call was one of the greatest highlights of my journey with the Uluru Statement. She rang at around 9 pm; I was sitting with my feet up, relaxing, enjoying the rare familiarity of home. I sat up and asked Rosie if everything was okay. She answered with quiet but clear passion. She brought tears to my eyes as she excitedly explained how when she got home, she was suddenly overwhelmed with pride – she had followed in her grandfather's footsteps.

As the football game reached its final minutes, with the sky becoming the colours of the sand on the field, mixed with the amber hues of dusk, I finished the interview with Rosie by asking her about the ideas we had discussed in that phone conversation.

'When I got back home from Sydney, I thought, Ah! I have seen the big city, you know, like big city of lights! Well, it's time for me … I need to do something like what my grandfather did. When I was in Sydney, I'm doing something for me and my family. That's what made me so proud, you know?

'I was telling a couple of friends and family about the Uluru Statement. Firstly, to my family. We want to be strong like what our old people did. They did everything. Now we got better everything. We're living in better conditions. I want to tell the kids the stories about my grandfather and the people that he walked with, and the way it was before. Today they made us who we are. And if we are brave like my grandfather, tomorrow can be better.'

Two years after publishing the first edition of this book, Rosie and I wrote a children's book together. It tells the story of her grandfather's courage and how the Gurindji people understand the importance of constitutionally enshrining a First Nations Voice.

The Gurindji people are inviting us to walk with them again.

ON THE WAY: LOMBADINA

The road up the middle of Cape Leveque, north of Broome, cuts a swathe through the red sand and sparse bush. The beautiful scenery, topped by a brilliant blue sky, caused a flood of warm memories. My ex-partner and mother of our three children – my eldest children of five – is a Bardi woman. This is their land. When our kids were young and their mother and I were together, we would often holiday here, camping and fishing. Cape Leveque is rich with my favourite seafoods. Close by is my most loved fishing spot, a place named Oolg. On one of those camping trips, a good friend from Badu Island, Jermaine Ruben, came with us to Oolg. We dived all day, catching enough for a bountiful feed. Then we swam for hours, exploring the trapped waters at low tide. It was a heavenly day.

My destination was Lombadina, a little community near the tip of Cape Leveque. I had been there many times, but on this day, the usually quiet community was alive with activity. Four Kimberley Aboriginal organisations – the Kimberley Aboriginal Law and Culture Centre, the Kimberley Land Council, the Kimberley Language Resource Centre and Arnja – were holding their annual general meetings together, bringing hundreds of representatives from throughout the Kimberley. I soon found friends who had been at the Uluṟu Convention – Jodie Bell, Wayne Bergmann, Billy Ah Choo, Janine Dureau, Cherie Sibasado and Nolan Hunter. They were eager to see the canvas for the first time since they signed their names on it.

After having a cup of tea with the law men of the Kimberley, I was invited to speak. The large gathering listened intently as I spoke about the importance of a Voice to Parliament. Wayne concluded the session and a motion was put to endorse the Uluru Statement from the Heart. One Arm Point man Billy Ah Choo seconded it, and it was carried unanimously.

Bardi, Jawi and Yaruwu, Western Australia

NOLAN HUNTER

Nolan Hunter's Japanese and English great-grandfathers came to the north-west Kimberley region in Western Australia, to work in the pearling industry. His Japanese great-grandfather was a pearl shell diver. His English great-grandfather was a 'black birder', who kidnapped Aboriginal people to dive for pearls. Both men settled down with Aboriginal women. Nolan's Aboriginality on his mother's side is Bardi, the people on the northern tip of Cape Leveque, and Jawi, neighbouring the Bardi on the western islands of the Bonaparte Archipelago. On his father's side, he is Yaruwu, the people from the region north of Broome up to Cape Leveque.

Nolan now lives in Broome, but he had an interesting upbringing in a leprosarium in Derby, a small town to the east of Broome at the bottom of King Sound. Like most people from the coast around Broome, Nolan identifies himself as a 'saltwater' person. He told me that 'Everything we do revolves around the sea.' He also told me he loves hunting, fishing and diving. When I interviewed him, he was getting ready to go spearfishing at the Broome jetty. He was excited to tell me about his diving experiences.

'I started when I was young and I still dive today and do a lot of spear fishing. I've had a lot of close calls with different sharks … so many times!'

'You were saying you're going to the Broome jetty. Wasn't there a crocodile caught there not long ago?' I asked.

Without a hint of concern, Nolan replied, 'Yeah, yeah, well, they did shoot one up here only a couple weeks ago. He was a four-meter crocodile, hanging around near the jetty, getting too friendly with people. He was eyeing them off to eat them, I think.'

He went on, now with concern, but for the crocodile that was sizing up humans for a feed, rather than for himself. 'The rangers shot him, poor thing. I don't like it when they shoot the poor things, because that's their country, the sea, and they could either move them on or shoot them. But they do need to think about people's safety. I can understand that.'

He said, 'I've dived there when there's been crocs there, and my brother's seen some underwater up the coast and I've seen them in the water here. We just look at each other and we just come to an understanding.' Nolan explained that some of his people aren't afraid of crocodiles. He told me how the old people would speak to the crocodile, telling them not to attack.

Nolan's Aboriginal ancestors peacefully occupied the Dampier Peninsula region and adjacent islands, north of Broome, for more than 40,000 years. I say 'peacefully' with confidence. As Palawa author Bruce Pascoe has pointed out in his book *Dark Emu*, the complex social structures and the development of Aboriginal languages – in addition to an oral history that precedes the Ice Age – tell us of a continuous culture unaffected by large-scale warfare and genocidal conquest. First Nations have a model of harmonious coexistence that all humanity can learn from. A model that was only disrupted when the British arrived.

Makassan fishermen came before the British. They began seasonal visits to Nolan's ancestral home in the seventeeth century to harvest sea-cucumber, also known as trepang. Trepang was a highly valued commodity in Makassar on the island of Sulawesi, which is modern day Indonesia. Relations between the Makassans and the Aboriginal people of the north-west coast of the Kimberley were mostly peaceful. They traded, worked together, shared technology and learnt and absorbed language. There was also intermarriage. There was a markedly different impact on the Bardi, Jawi, and Yawuru people when the British people arrived.

One of the earliest recorded encounters was on 17 September 1819. British explorer Phillip Parker King observed Balanggarra Aboriginal people harvesting turtle eggs and burning vegetation on what is now called Lacrosse Island. The explorers must have thought little of the happy people they observed. The British colonisers assessed the inhabitants as hunters and gatherers; mere savages who lived from day to day; a people who did not have the capacity for agriculture. They had a Eurocentric measure of humanity, and their assessment was wilfully wrong. Today we know from many academic works and from the descendants of those Balanggarra people that they were harvesting yam on the islands of the archipelago. This was a practice that existed throughout the entire continent and its adjacent islands. Also, Aboriginal people burned the vegetation in a controlled way in accordance with their laws and customs, ensuring that the burning was beneficial, not destructive. The fire was used as a form of agriculture, and today this fact is becoming harder to ignore.

The explorers were soon followed to the Kimberley by settlers seeking their fortunes as the British colonies expanded in the late nineteenth century. According to Aboriginal oral history, they perpetrated massacres on Nolan's ancestral homelands almost immediately upon their arrival. Journal entries and government records tell us that the massacres continued across the Kimberley into the late 1920s, and there are examples of terrible brutality in the decades beyond.

With the arrival of settlers and industry came the enslavement of Aboriginal people. I think it's fair to call work for rations 'slavery'. Aboriginal people were slaves on the land, working for the cattle barons, and they became slaves on the sea when the valuable pearl shell oyster, prevalent in the pristine shallow tropical waters that belonged to Nolan's people, brought a new wave of fortune seekers. The pearl shell was in great demand before plastic; it is a hard material with pearly lustre, suitable for decorative buttons and handles. Black lives did not matter to the invading colonists in their pursuit of fortune.

Nolan Hunter is an Elder in his late fifties. When we sat down to talk, he had just returned to Broome after a year of leave without pay from his position as CEO of the Kimberley Land Council. He spent this time at Westpac in Sydney, learning agri-business and discovering how financing works. His intention was to learn what he could, so he could return and improve the economic opportunities for the people of the Kimberley.

Although he swims with crocodiles, Nolan comes across as a very practical, sensible person. In all my dealings with him since we met at the Melbourne trial constitutional dialogue in late 2016, Nolan has always been kind and helpful to me. He began the interview by telling me, with a sense of utter calm and his usual gentle demeanour, about his childhood in a leprosarium.

'We were one of the first families to go to the Aboriginal reserve in Derby. When they built housing at the Derby Aboriginal reserve, the houses were just tin boxes. There was no insulation, just tiny tin boxes. Nobody lived inside of them much, because everybody was outside on the verandah. It was too bloody hot and crowded. You did all your living and sitting outside in the cool during the day in the hot times. There were lots of health problems.

'My mother was taken off me when I was very young. They quarantined her in a leprosarium. So, in my earlier years I was shunted between grandmothers. When mum came out, I got put in the leprosarium with my brother. I was only about four or five years old. So, I was put in a leprosarium, though I had tuberculosis.'

There were many leprosaria – institutions for people with leprosy – built across the north of Australia. The Derby leprosarium, called Bungarun, was established in 1936 in response to rising numbers of Indigenous people who were becoming afflicted with health issues. Displaced from their land, they were losing their way of life, and the impact on their physical well-being was enormous and long lasting.

At that time, little was known about leprosy, also called Hanson's disease. Today, we know that it mainly affects the skin and nerves and is mildly infectious. It has varying effects on the body, from disfigurement, blindness and ulcers, to benign effects that cause little hindrance to a long and healthy life.

Bungarun had approximately 1200 Aboriginal inmates throughout its fifty years of operation. Many were misdiagnosed, found and taken by what were known as 'leper patrols', manned by police and Black trackers. The patrols would terrorise families, sometimes making surprise raids on camps to steal victims away, often in heavy linked neck chains. Many of those Aboriginal people spent their entire lives at the Derby leprosarium – 350 Indigenous people died there, and most were buried in unmarked graves. Only three white people were ever quarantined at the Derby leprosarium.

Before Bungarun was built, the Western Australian Government shipped the Kimberley Aboriginal people, who were to be quarantined, to the Northern Territory, where the Commonwealth Government had established a leprosarium on Channel Island. I fish around this island in Darwin Harbour and know it well. It is rocky, dry and baron. The island is surrounded by mangroves and is swarming with midges. Those people who went to the leprosarium near Darwin first had to endure a long trip by sea on a small vessel. They were compelled to stay below deck in cramped, unhygienic conditions. Once they arrived in the Northern Territory, they were far from their families and unsure if they would ever see them again.

'I met a lot of old people at the leprosarium that had been there since they were young, they'd been there forever,' Nolan said of Bungarun. 'Then, later on I heard that when they finally closed the leprosarium down [in 1986], they said to these people, "You can go home now." They were like, "Well, this was my home all my life." There were lots of sad stories like this. Them old people were like, "I've been here since I've been a little girl", like that. Now they're an old woman. It was really sad because that's the only home they knew. They'd been so long in quarantine.'

As Nolan spoke about the old people he loved, his voice was heavy with sadness and affection. 'A lot of the old people have passed away now, but when I was a kid in the leprosarium, they looked after me because there weren't many kids. They'd been taken from their kids, or their baby was taken away, sent to different places. There was so much love there from the old people, because lots of them didn't have children. We got special treatment. Christmases, things like that were great. So much love.'

When Nolan left the leprosarium he went to schools in Broome and Perth. He finished school in year 10, moving on, 'as a young man', to 'aimlessly seek experiences' in various jobs. When I asked him about that time, he laughed, and then said thoughtfully, 'My reflection about that is that, you know, I guess many of us start off on a similar kind of journey until you find your purpose … it's harder for kids these days in that, well, we didn't have the influence of drugs and alcohol.'

Nolan's working life began on Bardi Country, at the tip of Cape Leveque in a community named One Arm Point. The community is named after a pearler who had an accident fishing with dynamite. One Arm Point was established when the nearby Sunday Island Mission closed down. 'When everybody left the mission on Sunday Island in the 1960s, many of the Aboriginal people ended up in the scrub and on Jolugu Beach at One Arm Point there. They were digging fresh water out of the sand dunes to survive. Just carting water … There was nothing there. People were just living in their little tents and shacks, makeshift sheltering. I was there to build housing. The houses we were building were with those old panels – took ten men to lift one panel and we'd use a rivet gun to secure them in place.'

Nolan resisted working in the pearling and cattle industries where most of his family found employment. Instead, he did odd jobs, such as driving a tip truck in the Broome town shire, but he soon found his calling.

'I knew a guy by the name of Jimmy Webb, he was working for the Commonwealth. He helped me get a field officer role with the Commonwealth Government. Jimmy is now running a dance troupe that's quite popular, Wadumbah Aboriginal Dance Group. He's a Noongar fella and still a good mate of mine. Though I probably only see him every five to ten years now.

'I worked for the Commonwealth Government for around fourteen years. I had different jobs. I was running remote area operations with the old social services, the old DAA [Department of Aboriginal Affairs]. I was a project officer. I worked in the types of roles where you're out in the field visiting communities.'

As Nolan took me through the places he'd worked, he would occasionally laugh to himself. There were memories he didn't need to share and I could tell he enjoyed his work in many Aboriginal communities. 'I loved the communities in the Northern Territory; I loved the Western Desert area because I knew a lot of the fellas who came over the border from Balgo, who I went to Nulungu College with in Broome. I also would run into people that were in Bungarun, the leprosarium, when I was kid!' Nolan laughed heartily now. 'And I run in to a lot of the old people. People like some of our key Elders, like old Joe Brown, all knew me as a kid in there, when they were young men. Those old people were instrumental in setting up the Kimberley Land Council who I now work for.'

Nolan's final years working at the Commonwealth Government were served overseas. 'I headed over to Manchester in England and worked with the Australian consulate there in immigration. Then I worked in other countries doing some relief work, because Australia provided staffing resources at the Australian embassys. I also had a little bit of a chance to see other parts of the world very briefly, in places like Moscow, and shorter periods in Vienna and Switzerland.'

He explained that after a career with the Commonwealth Government, he wanted to return home, to give back to his Kimberley community.

'I came back ten and a half years ago to take up employment with the Kimberley Land Council as Deputy CEO. Since coming back from overseas I've really just put all of my focus on what I can give back to my community around all the things we deal with, whether it's engaging with governments or industry, or different stakeholders. Hopefully to try and contribute to the social and socioeconomic circumstances of Kimberley Aboriginal people.'

Now, Nolan is the CEO of the Kimberley Land Council. He said the establishment of the first ranger program is one of the great achievements of the KLC. The program employs Traditional Owners in remote communities to eradicate harmful weeds, monitor turtle and dugong stocks, and keep a watch on the coastal environment, as well as many other great initiatives to care for Country. The rangers' initiatives are valuable because they are developed from the ancient knowledge of the people who are so intimately connected to the sea and land.

Nolan explained how the celebrated outcomes of the programs came from hard work, determination, and many visits to Canberra. He also said that it can be frustrating work because government policy is inconsistent, changing from government to government, from election to election. He said it's up to the whim of the politicians who, unlike the consistency of the tides of his coastal home, are irregular and unpredictable. Nolan acknowledged one certainty though – he said that the people of the Kimberley today have opportunity because his Elders fought for it. The Kimberley Land Council was established after the Aboriginal people of the Kimberley fought with the government and an ignorant mining company in the Noonkanbah Dispute more than forty years ago.

'When you think about how the KLC started; we started out of a protest,' Nolan reflected. 'That old guard fought for our rights in the Noonkanbah Dispute, where there was a mining company who wanted to mine in a sacred land area. Everybody marched and protested and that's how the organisation was born. The unions were important in that dispute. They've been front and centre with supporting Indigenous people over the years. Not only in the Noonkanbah Dispute. The Gurindji Wave Hill Walk-off as well.'

Great things happen when our people come together, which led me to ask Nolan what he thought about his experience at Uluru.

'I think when we completed the discussions in Uluru, and we all had the information, there might have been some of us with a difference of opinion, but I think the really good thing was that people were able to put aside their differing ideas, any disagreements, and we focused on what we could agree with. Something like 95 per cent of us agreed on a Voice in the Constitution.

'Coming to that agreement was really special. We came together from this wide range of places and perspectives. It was the best we could possibly get, given the limitation on the resources to get people there and all that sort of stuff. You had a good distribution of types of key individuals, key organisations, Native Title groups – from a variety of perspectives. It's not like you can bring 3 per cent of Australia – the whole Indigenous population – to one meeting. People need to be realistic about that.

'Something that struck me as interesting was – and I realised this after Uluṟu – I came to the realisation that people weren't talking about anything new in a sense, because a Voice to make our own decisions is something our mob have been calling for this whole time. Our leaders. People like Pat Dodson, Wayne Bergman, Peter Yu. People like John Watson, Joe Brown, all the old guys. Pearly Gordon. Irene Davie. Like in that old footage that Rachel Perkins worked on for us – we've been saying to governments that they must listen to us. And to do that, we need that structure with good governance. We need that mechanism in the Constitution that governments must properly engage with. A Voice for us is a win – a win for all. Governments should have seen this as a best opportunity ever!'

I liked what Nolan had to say. He remained calm as he spoke of our collective frustrations, though his passion emphasised each word. I looked at my watch and realised we were well past the time I promised to end the interview. Nolan was eager to finish. The tide was almost right for a dive with his speargun, his favourite pastime. I said I wanted to ask him one more very important question. As always, he was accommodating. I said, 'On the matter of a First Nations Voice Referendum, what would you say to the Australian people?'

Nolan's answer was ready and certain. 'I think that we shouldn't underestimate the Australian people. You can imagine people would've been uncertain leading up to the 1967 referendum. Yet it was a resounding result. We should give a First Nations Voice referendum a real red hot go. We need to, because to win means there can be some improvement to the relationship between Australians and Indigenous people. With a Voice, we can improve the treatment of our people so that Australia can heal as a country. This country can't keep doing business the same old way, because we keep getting the same result and that's not good enough. Here in the Kimberley, we have one of the highest suicide rates in the world.

'The Uluru Statement was from the people, for the people. We shouldn't be afraid of losing a referendum on this. It's bullshit that we'll never get a chance to enshrine a First Nations Voice again. I don't believe that. We must win, and if we don't, we just try again.'

ON THE WAY: YULE RIVER

When I first travelled to Perth with the Uluṟu Statement from the Heart, my boots were still covered in the red dust of the Pilbara. I had just been to a meeting of the Pilbara tribes at the Yule River Bush Meeting, where I witnessed them establishing a representative Voice for their region. When it came time for me to present the Uluṟu Statement, it was easy to explain the importance of a nationally representative First Nations Voice. A voice in the Federal Parliament in Canberra is as important as the Western Australian State Parliament in Perth. The Uluṟu Statement was strongly endorsed.

Yule River is an ancient meeting place. The tribes have come together there for ceremony and dialogue for thousands of years. I was privileged to stay in the camp late into the evening, savouring the experience in the red dust by a campfire. I watched and listened as stories were told in dance and song – some were performed for the first time in a generation.

When I checked into the hotel near the Perth airport it was too late to find a decent meal, and I was too tired to care. The next morning when I woke up early to travel down to Whadjak Noongar Country, I could've found my jeans with my eyes closed. They were alive with the earthy smell of dirt, sweat and campfire.

Perth was the last stop in my first leg of touring with the Uluṟu Statement. In less than two months, I had been to the lands of the

Yolŋu, Gurindji, Yidindji, Warnindhilyagwa, Bardi and Marlpa, sharing the Uluru Statement from the Heart with local Aboriginal people. I had been to four capital cities, reaching hundreds of Australians from all walks of life. I was exhausted both physically and mentally.

Whadjak Ballardong Noongar, Western Australia

DAVID COLLARD

The crow is known for its intelligence and adaptability. With shiny black plumage and a sharp dark beak, the black crow carries on its wings an air of defiance and self-reliant capability.

The white cockatoo is mischievous and curious. Covered in brilliant white feathers, crowned with a proud crest, they are always conspicuous, flying as a flock, both raucously social and stubborn.

To the Noongar people, these birds are Wardong, the black crow, and Manatj, the white cockatoo. David Collard holds these birds sacred through his mother and father. Descended from his Whadjuk mother and Ballardong father, he has the traits of both birds.

I first met David at the hotel the night before the Uluru Convention. He is a tall man who looks at you like a crow does, accurately reading your presence, assessing your thoughts. He has a mischievous wit as well. My first impression was that he is a natural leader. He was spinning a yarn with several members of the Broome delegation, leading the stories and the laughter. He didn't hesitate in introducing himself. He spoke confidently, immediately cracking jokes.

A highlight of the tour with the Uluru Statement from the Heart was my visit to David's father's Ballardong land in April 2018. David picked me up early in the morning with his university student son, Jack Collard. The three of us piled into the car with the Uluru Statement in its cardboard tubes, laying through the middle between us. Talking about basketball and Jack's studies, we began the 90-minute journey to Muresk, deep in the southern West Australian Wheatbelt. We were going to meet the Noongar Ballardong Elders. David works hard to bring the Elders together regularly.

It was a great meeting. I was given the opportunity to tell them about what had transpired in late May 2017, in the heart of Australia, Uluru. I explained the proposals that came from that historical gathering, and how important establishing a Voice would be to the unity of the First Nations people around the country. I answered many questions. Then the Elders endorsed the Uluru Statement. They proudly stood to hold it for photos that would capture the moment forever.

The Noongar Ballardong Elders were lively and spirited. They had serious business to discuss. They were considering various strategies to provide opportunities for their young people, and they were also making plans to learn their language, which had been denied to them in their youth. It was David's plan: teach the Elders so they can teach the children. In these Elders, I sensed a fighting spirit that day. When I interviewed David for this book, he helped me better understand what I felt on golden Wheatbelt cockatoo country.

'My family have been fighters for a long, long time. And I speak in regards to my grandmother, riding around on a horse with a petition as a nine-year-old that her father wrote up, trying to get his children to be allowed to go to school. His name was John Kickett. So that was my great-grandfather.

'We're also fighters – where my grandfather's gone across to France and fought in the trench warfare.'

David's Noongar forefathers fought for Australia in the world wars.

'When war broke out in Gallipoli, they actually went to sign-up and they were told because they had a Black mother that they weren't allowed to,' David explained. 'So in 1914 they didn't go, but a year later, after the disaster of Gallipoli happened, they were allowed to go and sign-up because the big call went out, "We Want You!" They signed up and went across and fought in France. It's interesting to know that in the First World War, we had thirty Noongars actually go and fight at Gallipoli.

'The horrors of war were no different, whether the men were white or black, soldiers were gassed; 127 in one day including my grandfather. He survived – fought in World War Two as well.'

Despite the sacrifices his grandfather had made – David's family still struggled because of his Aboriginal heritage.

'For me personally, I've grown up in the Wheatbelt. I come from the Aboriginal reserves. I remember living in camps; corrugated iron, dirt floor. Going down to the creek, getting water. So I'm one of those kids. I'm also one of those kids that's been passed around family. I've grown up pretty rough and tough, but I have also been smart enough to take advantage of the opportunities that I've been able to make for myself.'

There's Wardong, the crow, I thought. The Wheatbelt in the south-west of Western Australia, near Perth, with its swathes of farmland, would have been a tough place to grow up Black. I asked David about racism.

'Racism binds most of the communities we lived in. Being in

Wheatbelt country, only a couple hours out of Perth, racism was rife so I actually call it, myself, I call it redneck country because it's a place where the 1905 Act actually was still being put in place.

David explained, 'In 1905 it was the Protection Act – "protecting" all the so-called Aboriginal people. A.O. Neville [Chief Protector of Aborigines] was the guy who enacted that. Aboriginal kids were taken away from their families. So the Stolen Generation is part of that policy. But out in the Wheatbelt – and I can still remember a little country town called Pingelly, where Dad was born, worked and we lived – we had to be out of town before the sun went down. It was the Sunset Clause. If you were in town you got locked up. So Noongars were very much aware of how to sneak around town. You had people who wouldn't serve us. You had to wait in another line to get served in shops.

'Things like my dad being born in the hospital, but he was in the little shed down the back of the hospital, which was called the morgue. So that's where Aboriginal people were born. And if you needed medical help from the hospitals, we had Aboriginal people living on reserves, so you had to stay on your reserves. You couldn't go into the hospital. There was no Assimilation Policy back in their day. That came along later.'

The Aborigines Act, 1905 was 'An Act to make provision for the better protection and care of the Aboriginal inhabitants of Western Australia.' The Act created the position of Chief Protector of Aborigines, the legal guardian of every Aboriginal child to the age of sixteen years. He permitted authorities to 'send and detain' Aboriginal children in institutions and in 'service' (work). This legislation empowered a white 'protector' to dictate every aspect of David, his siblings and his parents' lives. It lasted until 1 July 1964 – almost sixty years.

David went on to talk about an example of how his mother's

family survived despite the oppressive Aborigines Act. 'Like on my mum's side … my old grandfather had what we call a farm. They got the land because he behaved for the white man. He cleared the land with his boys. He fenced it. And he used to burn and bag charcoal. He actually dug a well for the family. So the farmer down the road saw this wonderful land up the road and wanted it, and tried to get rid of him.

'Our grandfather made the well, and the well's still there today. I drive back and check; make sure it's all right and it's still got water in it. But this old [neighbouring] farmer came along and decided to poison the well. So he put salt in the well. But our grandfather, him and his boys just built another well next to it. To get around that.

'The reality is that those attitudes were like, "Well, you cleared the land so I wanna take that land off you." But my grandfather didn't let this guy take their land off them.'

I asked the obvious – did this neighbour get away with it?

'Well, yeah. He got away with it [poisoning the well]. But the neighbouring farmer went further. He reported my family, saying the kids weren't going to school and the camp was dirty. So the manatj [Noongar slang for authority or police] drove out one day, as you can probably gather. When you see the movie *Rabbit Proof Fence*, you see the little black car coming out there with the manatj.

'So this is what happened with our family. My old grandfather was a very righteous man, because he grew up and was educated at the mission. So that's why he learned the practice of farming and all that, back in the day. So that's why he got land allocated to him, and he was doing the right thing.

'But anyway, just imagine the manatj driving up the road. They can see him coming. He gets to the camp and he looks at the camp, and the camp's spotless. Because in the summertime usually, and I can still remember the practice, summertime you have your canvas, or your tents, all sitting there and you wet it down. In the morning you sweep all the sand and check for tracks and everything, so you can see whether a snake came into the camp and when it went out. Or if it was still in the camp.

'The manatj pulls up and gets out of his car. He walks over, and he says, "Oh, I had a complaint about you guys not sending your kids to school and this place was dirty." He's looking around and old grandfather's standing there saying to him, "Well I don't think that's true, do you?"

'And of course, when my grandfather walked out he actually had his shotgun cocked over his arm. And while the manatj is talking to him, he puts a couple of shells into both barrels. And then when the manatj is finished and says, "Yeah, I'm pretty happy," my grandfather actually then shut the barrels up and went, "Click." He just said to manatj, "If you ever come back here again," he says, "I'll shoot you. I'll shoot you dead." He said, "I'll put you in your car and I'll dig a hole on the farm here. And I'll bury you inside your car and no one will know you've been here." He says, "So don't ever come back."'

I thought David's grandfather must have been a brave and intimidating man to stand up to the authorities in that way! His next story was about his grandmother. It was just as impressive.

'My grandmother who married him, well her father was the one I was saying who wrote the petitions. John Kickett was one of the instigators of trying to get kids an education in [those parts of] Australia, through the education department. Around 1914, I think, he started writing the letters. They wouldn't allow him to go to the war at first either, 'cause he had Black parents.'

David explained why his grandmother rode around with the petitions for an education.

'[Because the great-grandfather] got into a fight with two white fellas there, and because he got the better of them, those two white farmers went off and reported him to the police. So as a Black fella, you're not supposed to be fighting around, causing disturbances or drinking alcohol. He lost his certificate [to leave the reserve] because of that fight.

'When Grandmother was just nine years old she rode around on horseback with a petition signing the district up to say "We want a school."

'I think, just listening and hearing what my Elders did at that time in WA history, if they didn't do that our family and my family would probably be part of the Stolen Generation. Do you know what I mean? They would've been taken away and all this connection to Country, the history, the stories, their culture, would've been lost.'

Many Noongar children were stolen from their families and they have survived without having learnt about their culture or their language. David told me more about his work re-connecting the Elders who were stolen, or who had their culture denied.

'We *do* still have our language. That's one of the things that I'm working on. I'm trying to share language with everybody else. It's quite a powerful thing.

'We have a walking trail we're developing, a Ballardong heritage trail, taking people back [to sacred sites]. Re-connecting them to our cultural grounds, ochre pits, corrobboree grounds. Our birthing and burial sites. All of it is connected.'

At the time when David and his fellow Noongar people were campaigning for the Uluru Statement from the Heart, they were also in the final stages of enacting the largest Native Title settlement in history, the South West Native Title Settlement, known as 'The Settlement'. The Settlement that is being negotiated is between the Western Australian Government and a collective of Noongar Native Title claimants: Whadjuk, Yued, Gnaarla Karla Boodja, South West Boojarah, Ballardong, Wagyl Kaip and Southern Noongar. It will cover approximately 200,000 square kilometres of land and it will affect an estimated 30,000 Noongar people. David explained why a First Nations Voice enshrined in the Constitution remains an important matter to resolve, in addition to their negotiations with the state.

'The aspirations our mob had for the development of ATSIC in the late '80s was that we were hopefully going to get a Voice, from regional right through to federal level. We wanted a Voice because we wanted issues that were brought up and raised at regional and local level, to actually be looked at and addressed.'

David described what I had heard in the dialogues. The frustration with the bureaucracy; the countless middle men – well-to-do bureaucrats – enjoying a great career on Indigenous suffering.

'The white bureaucrats that sort of led ATSIC at the time didn't really want to accommodate the aspirations of the Black fellas from all over Australia. So, when we considered the Voice proposal, I thought it was ideal because, personally, I could see how it worked. It's unfinished business. We had back then and still have all these bureaucrats in between that are pretty much helping to undermine the whole process for Aboriginal self-determination and self-management. We need to take control.'

Wardong, the crow, adaptable, intelligent. David spent thirty years in Aboriginal affairs, both in the state and federal governments. From his experience, he knows that as great as a local agreement or treaty may be, there will still be state and federal bureaucrats to overcome, and ever-changing ideologies with each election cycle that can undermine progress and outcomes at a legislative whim.

I found it interesting that despite David's many years of involvement in Indigenous affairs, he still seemed to be an optimist.

'When I heard that all the dialogues were happening, and then getting regional delegates together in the same place to seek a unified approach, I thought this is ideal. We haven't done it before like this. And for me, this was like, as old Cedric Wyatt used to call me, "Young Collard", going through Aboriginal affairs, he would have said to me all those years ago when I first started, "This is what we've been asking for, Young Collard."

'I had thirty-odd years in Aboriginal affairs. A First Nations Voice is something that we'd been screaming for back in the day when we were Department of Aboriginal Affairs. So I was really excited about going across to Uluṟu to be able to lead the young people in my group, as the old fella in the group.'

When I asked David to tell me about a special memory from the Uluṟu Convention, he said there were two moments he will never forget. The first was the Welcoming Ceremony, with the law men, the Elders, the kids and the camp dogs – and us. And the second was the making of the Uluṟu Statement from the Heart.

'I thought there was a special energy at the Welcoming Ceremony, especially where we were situated at the time. The sun going down over the rock. It was absolutely powerful. The energy from everybody that came. The expectations people brought with them. But also so many friends that you actually caught up with from other states and territories. It was good to see one, big, happy family getting together, finally.

'And that was one of the most powerful things that I saw, just by sitting at the back, looking at all the people connecting up. I mean, everyone had their differences and everything else, but also everyone, I think, had the same sort of aspirations as we did. Unity at last.

'I can tell you, when the Uluṟu Statement was read for the first time it just touched me. Went straight through me and just touched me. And I just thought, Yes. We finally got to say what we want. And it's powerful. That's how powerful the Statement was. I mean it was hard work bringing it together, but it said everything that was right.

We have to work with what we've got now. We need to use the most powerful tool that we've got, our words and our voice.

'Making the Uluru Statement is one of those things that I'll never ever forget.'

Since that first trip to visit the Noongar with the Uluru Statement, I have been back a few times. David has worked hard to introduce the Uluru Statement to Noongar people north and south of the Swan River. He has been Manatj, the cockatoo, flying in a flock of passionate advocates: Noddy Cole, Doyen Radcliffe, Ezra Jacobs-Smith, Rebecka Fitzgerald, Louise O'Reilly, Kathy Bowie, Deborah Oakley and Gail Beck, among others. They've been a great team that will be vital to winning a referendum to enshrine a First Nations Voice in the Constitution.

Since that first drive to Ballardong Country with David and his son Jack, the younger of the Collard men has excelled in his undergraduate studies in Political Science and International Relations. As a delegate for his university, the University of Western Australia, Jack participated in the eleventh session of the United Nations Expert Mechanism on the Rights of Indigenous Peoples. On the world stage, Jack spoke of the aspirations of his people, the Noongar. Jack has been working to achieve the proposals for Voice, Treaty, Truth in the Uluru Statement from the Heart. I believe Jack will be a leader for his people. Maybe a representative in the First Nations Voice we are fighting for.

David and his family make me confident that we will achieve a representative Voice. We'll achieve it because Jack's great-grandfathers fought for this country, despite being excluded. We will achieve it for Jack's great-grandmother, who, as a child, rode through a community that wanted to dispossess her family of their farm – a second dispossession – defying them and winning the right for an education. We'll achieve it because of the work that David, among others, is doing.

'I said to my son, Jack, "You have to come back and get grounded first." I said to him, "It's good to be educated and being smart, but you gotta also be connected." I told him he needs to know his Country. He's gotta know his people. And he's gotta know the pain and the suffering and what his people have gone through to get him to where he is today. So he understands what he's fighting for. Not just fighting for something because it sounds good. But understanding why we're fighting. He has accepted my challenge.'

David explained why he put this challenge to his son. 'If the young generation are not grounded, they can do damage. Even though they think they're doing good and doing right.' David paused, then with determination, he said 'They must be taught to understand where Noongar come from, and also understand why Noongars feel the way they do.'

'It's important to understand that if you're going to offer people solutions, you must understand where people have come from.'

Manatj, the white cockatoo. Wardong, the black crow.

ON THE WAY: THE HUNGRY MILE

As I walked down the gentle slope toward the Hungry Mile, where the slick office towers now stand at Barangaroo, I thought of the contrast between the wealth of the building I was soon to visit and the poverty of the workers who, in the tough years of the Great Depression, had jostled for a hazardous day's work on the docks. They had been pitted against one another in the 'bull system'. They were violently exploited by the bosses for their desperation during the tough depression years when labour was at a surplus and worker's rights were insufficient.

I admired those workers who turned their fists away from their workmates, and raised them in the air, united, to win permanent jobs. They broke the bull system. Their story is one of triumph. They lifted themselves from their plight with discipline and unity. As I walked through the revolving glass doors of Barangaroo's Tower One, I pondered how workers rights are regressing again. Unions have been under constant unjustified attack. I considered, Will I be damaging the campaign, as a passionate unionist, speaking at the wealthiest of corporations about the Uluru Statement?

I decided that I would stand proud. After all, most of the people I would be speaking to are workers. It may be good for them to hear from a unionist.

In my address to a room that was full of representatives of multinational companies and legal firms, I said, 'The call for a First Nations Voice is a matter for all Australians. It's a matter that goes beyond Left and Right; across the political spectrum and across ideologies. The Uluru Statement invites humanity to shine through the dark veil of ignorance.'

When applause broke out after I read the Uluru Statement from the Heart, I realised that I was right. Australia is ready for justice and healing. All decent people will see the value that a First Nations Voice will bring by guiding our country to a fuller expression of nationhood. Only weeks later, when we rallied at the community action in the federal seat of Wentworth to tell voters of Malcolm Turnbull's dismissal of the Uluru Statement, some of those workers from the shiny Barangaroo tower were there in the crowd, at their first ever rally, with their fists in the air with ours.

Wiradjuri, Yorta Yorta and Gamilaroi,
New South Wales

ALLAN MURRAY

Locals and visitors to Sydney squeeze past each other on the busy footpath beneath Australian Hall's grand old façade at 150 Elizabeth Street. They are oblivious to what transpired there on 26 January 1938. In that place a spirited group of Aboriginal people came together. Side by side they stood, holding placards that stated: 'Aborigine Conference – Day of Mourning – Aborigines Only'. They were incredibly brave women and men, marking the day that the British began a brutal invasion only 150 years ago. They were there defying threats of harsh repercussion for their protests. They were fed up with the harsh treatment of their people on missions and reserves, and fearful that more children would be stolen. In desperation, they took a stand.

Though I knew of the Day of Mourning, I was unaware of the venue until Allan Murray, who I'd met at the Uluru Convention, took me there. Australian Hall is the first non-Aboriginal structure to be recognised in Australia as an Aboriginal heritage site. The building was only saved by protest. A protracted battle was waged to save the Hall because of its significance to the early push for Aboriginal Rights. The Chair of an inquiry into the matter of the Hall's protection, William Simpson, in recognition of the significance of the 1936 protest, stated that the action was 'the first formal and recognised step towards the promotion of the "equality of rights" between Indigenous and other Australians'.

Simpson went on to say: 'It must also be acknowledged as the embryonic assertion of land right claims which have been recognised in the historic and contentious 1992 Mabo decision of the High Court and the subsequent *Native Title Act 1993* … Thus the Day of Mourning conference may properly be regarded as the foundation of contemporary Aboriginal political and civil rights movements and on the evidence is a major Aboriginal event associated with renowned Aboriginal leaders, advancement of civil rights for Aborigines and of great social, structural and cultural significance to the Aboriginal community and to the history of Australia.' (Quoted in the *Dictionary of Sydney*, dictionaryofsydney.org)

The Inquiry recognised the significance of the Hall to Indigenous people, and the recommendations were strongly in favour of its protection. However, although the Hall was registered on the National Estate in 1996, only a year later the New South Wales Minister for Planning granted an exemption to the building's owners to demolish it and leave only its façade. A new campaign began, culminating in a march from Sydney Town Hall to the Australian Hall on the 60th anniversary of the Day of Mourning, in 1998. The struggle led to the Metropolitan Aboriginal Land Council purchasing the Hall with funds from the Indigenous Land Corporation.

Twenty years later, on the 80th anniversary of the Day of Mourning, I joined Allan Murray at Australian Hall to celebrate with his community. The speakers and many in the audience were descendants of the brave men and women who had protested in 1938. The speeches reverberated in that room as if the words were spoken in unison with the spirits of their ancestors – a connection they could not have enjoyed had the spirit of struggle not been passed on through the generations.

When I spoke to Allan, I could hear in his voice the pride he has for his people who survived the brunt of colonisation on Gadigal land. Allan was the former Chair of the Metropolitan Aboriginal Land Council and I met him for our interview at the Land Council offices in Redfern. He began by talking about his parents.

'My father was a Wiradjuri Yorta Yorta man, taken from Cummeragunja at the age of five and then was taken to Kinchela Boys Home up there in Kempsey.' Allan explained how his father eventually moved to Sydney, living on the outskirts of Redfern to work as a postal officer, riding bikes around Glebe. It was in Sydney that his father met Allan's mother, a Gamilaroi woman.

'Mum was a Stolen Generations child. Government policies meant she could be moved from one business to another. Or [from] another home to another home. She had to work in one of those big houses in Rose Bay as a domestic servant.'

Allan explained that at heart he is a Redfern man. 'I was born and bred in Sydney, my community is the Redfern community but also I know that I've Country down at Cummeragunja, Yorta Yorta land, and then also we've got Country in two places, and that's Pilliga scrub and also Wolgal itself.'

When I asked what it means to be a 'Redfern man', Allan said it was about 'strategising'. He shares in the responsibly to create opportunities for the youth of Redfern and importantly, to organise better housing.

When I visit the political heart of the Redfern community, 'The

Block', I don't only see the pride, I can feel it. The community is an artscape of Aboriginal murals, celebrating and commemorating Indigenous history and achievements in Sydney. In Redfern, pride comes from resistance. Resistance against racism and against being pushed out of the community by gentrification. But resistance has been hard. During the final stages of writing this book, The Block was demolished for development.

Redfern was named for the white settler, Surgeon William Redfern. In 1817, the Governor of New South Wales, Lachlan Macquarie, granted him 100 acres of Gadigal land. There was no treaty with the Gadigal people. The lands that came to be called Redfern were the spoils of an unjust frontier war.

Redfern eventually became an industrial hub. Immigrants and Aboriginal people made it their home as more than a hundred factories drove the young Federation's growth. Immigrants from Portugal, Lebanon, China and England found work and made their lives there. For Aboriginal people, moving to Redfern was a means to get away from the damaging control of the Aboriginal Protection Board in the reserves.

In the 1980s, as automation started to replace workers, unemployment began to rise. A combination of the effects of racism, heavy handed policing, and many failed policies, as well as the social issues that always accompany poverty made life extremely hard for many in the community – especially if you were Aboriginal. As the city grew, gentrification of the suburbs around it began to put pressure on many to move out of Redfern. But the community is still fighting back.

In 1992, Prime Minister Paul Keating gave a historic speech at Redfern Park. His words were a breath of fresh air. It was the first time a prime minister had spoken with brutal honesty about how First Nations people were being treated in their own country. They were hard words, but that day in Redfern, they were celebrated because they were the truth: 'We committed the murders. We took the children from their mothers. We practiced discrimination and exclusion. It was our ignorance and our prejudice.'

The Redfern community, the 'Black capital of Australia' as some describe it, has had many wins thanks to their grit and determination. Many of the first Aboriginal-led services were established there, such as the Aboriginal legal services, Aboriginal medical services, and the Aboriginal Housing Company.

Allan is no stranger to representing his community. In the 1980s, he organised Indigenous public servants to stand up for their rights in the workplace. He also helped members of the community to find housing as the opportunities to secure low-rent properties dwindled.

'The houses that we've got are dilapidated, decrepit type houses. There's no renewed infrastructure to bring those properties up. They're still pushing people out.'

I asked Allan to tell me about the regional dialogue that he attended leading to Uluṟu. I wanted to know what motivated him to be there.

'I wanted to have more of an understanding … and given that my father was removed under the protection days, I know that legislation is important. Legislation now has to change in a way that it supports us, and keeps us from being a dying race.'

It was a lesson learnt from his father's youth. Allan's dad was stolen from his family – legally. His community was discriminated against – legally and without repercussions.

'We can't continue to have legislation that disempowers the Aboriginal and Torres Strait Islander people.' We need to change our problems at the root cause. That is, we need the power to affect decision making in Parliament.

When Allan attended the regional dialogue, he didn't support the push for symbolic constitutional recognition. He couldn't see how symbolic words could be important, as compared to stopping what he described as 'the despair and poverty, disregard and disempowerment of our people in this country'.

Allan's view was shared in the constitutional dialogues and the culminating convention at Uluru. Our people want substantive constitutional reform, rather than symbolism. Substantive reform by way of a representative Voice has overwhelming support.

At my prompting, he recalled how he was elected to attend the convention. 'I said to them, "I would like to go to the Uluru Convention and anything that's gleaned from the dialogue will be articulated at the Uluru Convention." I'd like to express their views at the convention.'

Allan leaned forward as he told me about his experience as a delegate to Uluru. He was clearly proud to be elected. With a face that went from solemn to cheeky, Allan spoke about his trip there.

'It was exciting, to pack your bags and you leave your family for a couple of days, knowing you're going to come back. It was good. We were waiting for the plane to arrive, and in the waiting area there was all the masses of other First Nations delegates who had been flown in from South Australia and Queensland. We were all on the one charter service going to Yulara airport.

'I'm sitting there and I'm noticing all these Black fellas gathering and we're getting on the plane, and one of the flight attendants came out and says, "Hey, you mob, we're flying to Yulara." Something along those lines. That sort of cheered everyone up. So we got our tickets and walked in and we were greeted. We were given the seat allocation and I can't think of the flight attendant's name but he was good. The attendants were good and really entertained us and made sure our trip to the middle of Australia was a perfect trip. There was a real buzz and there was excitement.

'On the flight, before we got ready to leave the plane, the flight attendant said, "Thank you very much", but in his croaky voice you could sense that he must have loved our company. You could almost hear the tears in his voice when he said, "Thank you very much for flying with us, dah dah dah, we're proud to deliver you." That was pretty exciting too.

'The gravity of what we were doing didn't hit me until he said that with so much emotion, and then getting off the plane and putting your first feet on red soil. Well, on the bitumen but on the way to Uluṟu. That's when it really made ... Things started to fall in place in terms of where you're going and how important it is.

'On the way down, I was sitting next to Sol Bellear. Sol and me, there's one team that we love, and that's the Redfern All Blacks. We both played for the Redfern All Blacks.'

The Redfern All Blacks are Allan's passion. The local first-grade Rugby League team had won four premierships in a row at the time of the interview. The team was one of Sol's passions too. Allan described Sol: 'He was one of those individuals who fought and campaigned for Aboriginal rights. He was part of the Black Panthers movement in the '60s and '70s – he grew out of that. He became an ATSIC Commissioner and was always a member and chairperson of the Aboriginal Medical Service. In terms of community and sporting clubs, when you hit the gutter and need a hand up he was one of those fighters who you'd look to to pull you back up. He was a director for the South Sydney Rabbitohs at one stage too.'

Sol was a Bundjalung man from Queensland, who moved to Redfern after the 1967 referendum. As a strong young leader in the movement for Aboriginal rights, he strategised, organised, marched and braved the heavy handed authorities with other now well-known and celebrated leaders such as Roberta Sykes, Paul Coe, Kevin Cook, Gary Foley and wharfie Chicka Dixon. Sol is credited as a leader in establishing the first Aboriginal Legal Service and Medical Centre.

I first met Uncle Sol at Uluru. I noticed his hair had the tighter curls of an islander. As I shook his huge hand, I asked if he had Torres Strait Island blood. Sol smiled and explained who his mob were, both Bundjalung and South Sea Islander. We immediately connected. I observed his style – cool and calm, thoughtful and considerate. After Uluru was done, I worked closely with Uncle Sol to bring people together to campaign for the Uluru Statement. He was dedicated to achieving the outcomes from the unique consensus in the heart of Australia. He understood the need for a constitutionally enshrined First Nations Voice because it was an important step for First Nations unity.

Almost every time we spoke, to organise a venue for a meeting or to discuss potential allies, he would comment on the great support he had received from the union movement. Uncle Sol was especially fond of the Teachers Federation. Reflecting on his days of tumultuous protests for land rights, he would often say, 'We need to hit the streets again, Thomas. We need to get our allies around us, and you young people need to lead.'

He was a man that anyone would want on their team. Uncle Sol Bellear, the Redfern All Blacks legendary front rower and premiership winning captain, passed away on 29 November 2017. I made sure the Uluru Statement was there to lead his last march through the streets of Redfern. The Uluru Statement was carried to Redfern Park by young Quondamooka leader Dean Parkin and Wangkumarra friend Sean Gordon. Roy Ah-See, the Chair of the New South Wales Aboriginal Land Council, led the solemn service to say goodbye.

Allan's experience at Uluru was made all that more special for teaming up with Uncle Sol Bellear again.

Allan described the jubilation he felt when the Uluru Statement was endorsed. The ups and downs he experienced. He reminisced about how after the low point following the walk-out, he visited the great Uluru to watch the sun setting as the shadows crept across the desert. He described to me how it brought him peace.

Allan said he went to the last day of the convention feeling positive. He said that when the Uluru Statement from the Heart was endorsed, he 'felt like a burden had been lifted'. He was relieved for others as well, 'because I felt that for some people in the room, it must have been really hard to come to a point in time [when] we're all thinking as one'. He said, 'The burden was lifted to make us stronger and then to move happily out of the room.'

I asked Allan if he wanted to share both a positive and negative issue for his Redfern community. He thought for just a moment, and then used his beloved game, Rugby League, and his beloved team, the Redfern All Blacks, to describe them.

'When I was playing for the Redfern All Blacks and when Sol was playing, we were playing against all types of Australians. Mostly white Australians.

'The reason why a group of Aboriginal men got together and played is that during the week, we get discriminated against. We will train together, wear our guernseys and next minute we're on the football field. We're not on the football field just to play football. We're there because on the field it's different to when we are off the field, being trodden down. On the field we were equals.

'On the football field, you can put your head up high. But we know that tomorrow we still have to feed our families, we've still got to find employment. We know that our opposition teams have a better lifestyle. They can return home and feel very comfortable because they won't be discriminated against when they wake up the next day. And if some of our players are on Centrelink benefits, you know that all their benefits will go on rent. They wouldn't even have two dollars here or there to buy food. But the positive side of playing rugby is, once our mob comes together, they know that we can be competitive. We can be resilient and able to do things.

Allan began to talk about his vision for the future. 'I'm just thinking of a community that is viable, can create its own businesses, can have a market, can have a butcher, can have its own bakery, where they purchase from one another under a community umbrella, like a cooperative. We can do better if Australia says yes to our invitation from Uluru.'

After the interview with Allan, as I walked back through Redfern toward my hotel, I passed several Indigenous brothers. 'Hey, brus,' a casual greeting as we walked by, not a break in our stride. I'd never met the guys before. That doesn't matter. When you see another brother in the big city, the quick gesture says, 'I see you, I got your back.'

The small exchange made me smile as I weaved my way through the crowd. It was twilight and cold, especially for a Darwin bloke. Though I was warmed by my thoughts. All Allan wants for his people is that they can remain living there, stay close, and continue to heal. Allan, the brothers that I passed on the street, the community – they want to hear the sound of their children playing, safe and secure. They want to have the ability to continue to come together to plan for their future, or to fundraise for the mighty Redfern All Blacks. Surely, that isn't too much to ask.

Wiradjuri and Wailwan, New South Wales

TEELA REID

Teela Reid is from Gilgandra in the Central West of New South Wales. It's a small town with a population of approximately 2500. Her grandparents, on both her maternal and paternal sides, were very much affected by the control of the mission managers in the region around Gilgandra. Teela grew up listening to their stories about their families' survival and of hardship, living under the control of the *Aborigines Protection Act 1909 (NSW)*.

These stories and her affinity with her community – family, friends and Country – inspired Teela to pursue a career in Law. She has learnt from an early age how the power of the Law can oppress her people. She is motivated to better understand how it can also be used as a tool to liberate her people from the shackles of government control.

'Fiery and brilliant'. This description of Teela in an article in *The Australian* by Indigenous Affairs writer, Stephen Fitzpatrick, is accurate. She stands her ground and responds to nonsense with the complete opposite – well articulated and carefully considered logic. Teela is young but her journey is already worth following. As a lawyer and an advocate for her people, she has experience practicing in criminal and civil law and is passionate about law reform.

I first met Teela at the trial dialogue in Melbourne, in November 2016. She was easily the youngest of the sixty regional facilitators, and eight years younger than me. I was probably the next youngest in the room.

She was quiet during the trial dialogue. With many revered Elders there, it was a wonderful opportunity for us to listen. Little did I know, Teela would become a powerful spokesperson for the Uluru Statement people's movement. With strength, knowledge and determination, she has been a prominent advocate for the Uluru Statement since famously taking the former prime minister to task in December 2017 on the ABC program, *Q & A*. I learnt that she had chosen this path years before she reached this waypoint to her destination.

At the time that I arranged this interview, Teela was working as a lawyer at Legal Aid NSW in Sydney. Legal Aid provides advice to the most marginalised and poverty stricken people in a community. The people Teela advocates for are vulnerable and often already spinning in a whirlpool of social dysfunction, trying to swim away from the dark vortex of prison.

The legal professionals at Legal Aid don't do it for the money or the glory. They are under-resourced and overworked, which was no doubt part of the reason why it took repeated efforts to convince Teela to be interviewed for this book. When the day arrived, I met Teela and we made our way to Belmore Park, near Central Station, across the road from the Legal Aid NSW office. We found a shady spot on some comfortable grass. I started by asking her who her mob are.

'I'm Wiradjuri and Wailwan, born and raised in Gilgandra in the Central West of New South Wales. Wiradjuri is one of the bigger First Nations in New South Wales. And my mob are kind of Central West plus a bit further north-west, which is Wailwan Country. I'm passionate about my region.

'A lot of my mob were forced onto missions. Growing up, I heard a lot of stories about mission life from my mum and my grandparents. They told me about the regulation of my people's lives. I learnt how they were forced onto missions in Gulargambone, north-west of Gilgandra, and then a little township outside of Gilgandra called Balladooran, but also, back before then, Condobolin, around those areas in New South Wales. That's on my mother's side. On my father's side they were put on missions out in Wellington, like Nanima Mission. They grew up living in humpies.

'My grandparents weren't allowed to leave the mission without permission. They weren't allowed to walk on the same side of the street as white fellas, and my grandparents would tell me how my great-grandparents had to wear dog tags to identify them as Aboriginal. Those were the days when you could apply for an exemption of your Aboriginality. In other words, you could apply to the government to sign away your Aboriginal identity. It was the Aboriginal Protection era, where they had to seek permission to marry, for instance … almost all aspects of their lives were controlled.

'I wish I had recorded my grandfather's stories. He told me how difficult it was just to survive, how their lives were restricted to the mission. My grandparents' stories of survival shaped who I am today.'

Teela was raised by her single mother, a caring, loving and selfless person whom she describes as a 'staunch and witty' woman. Teela's grandparents were also integral to her upbringing. I could feel that she loved them dearly. As I listened to Teela speak of her grandparents' experiences, I noticed that the maltreatment and oppression they had suffered had stoked a fire in her belly. Their accounts of survival were the hearthstones that have kept her grounded and focused.

'My grandfather was really proud of his mother. Her name was Elsie-May, and my name is Teela-May. So, I kind of take on her name.' Teela smiled. 'He told me how she was fierce and really smart and that she was a real fighter, she always stood up for her family. A lot of my family tell me that I remind them of my great-grandmother, Elsie-May.

'My pop was the person who introduced me to the land rights movements in New South Wales. Because I was the eldest grandchild that lived in the same town as my grandparents, my pop would drag me off to Land Council meetings from a very young age, about three years old, I reckon. He introduced me to Black politics.

'My grandparents didn't have the freedom to practice their language – their culture was stolen before they could pass it onto their grandkids. They were punished if they practiced it. They also lived through "Exclusion on Demand", where a Black kid could be expelled from a school, or denied attendance if a white kid's parent demanded it. That was New South Wales education policy, legislated in 1902. It remained in the teacher's handbook until the early '70s.'

Segregation was rife for most of the twentieth century in Australia. It has been estimated that the 'Exclusion on Demand' policy excluded 50,000 Aboriginal children from either white or special Aboriginal schools. Growing up in western New South Wales, Teela experienced the legacy of discriminatory policies early in life.

'An example is that my mum was afraid that us kids would be stolen. When I was in primary school, I remember being really sick and I couldn't go to school. This was is in the mid '90s. The authorities rocked up at our doorstep. I remember seeing the panic in my mum's eyes. She was so afraid. My mum told me to hide because she thought I would get stolen, despite it not happening to my family before. The psychological impact on our people from those policies was evident to me. There is an all too real, constant fear of authority. A fear that your children could just be taken.

'When I was growing up, there was a sense of shame being Black. I know some people that wouldn't wear red, black and yellow. I think about that period of time when I did my schooling, through the Howard era, where the government criticised the truth of our recent past as a "black armband" approach, intentionally whitewashing our history and our stories. I really wanted to reclaim a sense of pride in being Black.'

It was her grandparents' stories, their gifts – lessons from the past and an ingrained community perspective – that would help Teela make the life-changing decision to become a lawyer.

'Because of the stories passed down to me and my own experiences, I always had a strong sense of social justice. But it's surreal to think I am a lawyer. To me I'm just the girl from Gilgandra. I played a lot of sports growing up in my community, so I commenced my career as a high school PE teacher before transitioning to a career in Law.

'When I was a teacher, I had the opportunity to attend the United Nations Permanent Forum on Indigenous Issues (UNPFII) in New York. This was a defining moment for me because it was when I first seriously contemplated the power of the Law and the political system to control Aboriginal people.

'The year I attended the UNPFII, the Northern Territory Intervention was a huge issue on the agenda. People were shocked and furious about the intervention measures. It raised really complex human rights issues. Many were dismayed because the Australian Commonwealth Government had suspended the *Racial Discrimination Act 1975 (Cth)* to implement the Intervention. I thought to myself, That piece of legislation, the Racial Discrimination Act, it's really important. It struck me that politicians can just suspend such important legislation to implement racist laws, unimpeded, while we have little institutional power, not only to stop them from doing it, but also for us as First Nations to influence the creation of laws.'

Teela's experience at the United Nations and coming to realise the limited mechanisms in Australia to hold politicians accountable – 'we have little institutional power' – coalesced with her grandparents' stories and the problems in her community. With a desire for change driving her, Teela decided to go to Law school. She chose the University of NSW in the eastern suburbs of Sydney.

'I had never really considered becoming a lawyer growing up. Though people always said that I should become one, or a politician because I don't mind having an argument.' We laughed. 'I had to consider, What will being a lawyer mean for my people? Could I do it? The experiences I had at the United Nations made me think, Maybe I can be a lawyer? I knew it would also come with a level of responsibility that I don't take lightly. Access to Law school for my people does not come easy, it's a privilege, and I will need to try to use my knowledge to give back in any way I can.'

Teela struggled in Law school. 'A lot of the other students there were quite sheltered from Aboriginal issues. Often, I would be terrified to go to class for fear I would say the wrong thing or read the wrong case. The readings for Law school were intense – for one class, between twenty to one hundred pages, easy. I always second guessed myself, not backing my ideas enough and always having too much self-doubt to feel like I could actually be a lawyer.'

Eventually, Teela established a network of legal professionals through the New South Wales Barristers Indigenous mentoring program. She built strong relationships with many judges, barristers and lawyers while also maintaining her community connections back home in Gilgandra. This proved to be a powerful foundation in developing her confidence.

Anangu performers in Mutitjulu at the Welcoming Ceremony before the Uluru National Constitutional Convention began.

ULURU STATEM

We, gathered at the 2017 Na
all points of the souther

Our Aboriginal and Torres Strait Islander tribes w
sovereign Nations of the Australian continent and
islands, and possessed it under our own laws an
This our ancestors did, according to the recko
culture, from the Creation, according to the comm
'time immemorial', and according to science more
years ago.

This sovereignty is a spiritual notion: the ancestra
the land, or 'mother nature', and the Aboriginal and
Islander peoples who were born therefrom, rema
thereto, and must one day return thither to be ani
ancestors. This link is the basis of the ownership o
better, of sovereignty. It has never been ceded or e
and co-exists with the sovereignty of the Crown.

How could it be otherwise? That peoples possesse
sixty millennia and this sacred link disappears i
history in merely the last two hundred years?

With substantive constitutional change and struct
we believe this ancient sovereignty can shine th
fuller expression of Australia's nationhood.

Proportionally, we are the most incarcerated pe
planet. We are not an innately criminal people. O
are aliened from their families at unprecedented

M THE HEART

Convention, coming from
ment from the heart:

se we have no love for them. And our youth
ntion in obscene numbers. They should be our
re.

s of our crisis tell plainly the structural nature
This is *the torment of our powerlessness*.

tional reforms to empower our people and
lace in our own country. When we have power
our children will flourish. They will walk in
heir culture will be a gift to their country.

tablishment of a First Nations Voice enshrined
on.

culmination of our agenda: *the coming together*
captures our aspirations for a fair and truthful
h the people of Australia and a better future
based on justice and self-determination.

arrata Commission to supervise a process of
ng between governments and First Nations
about our history.

counted, in 2017 we seek to be heard. We leave
art our trek across this vast country. We invite
us in a movement of the Australian people for

The Uluṟu Statement from the Heart

Artwork

1. You can see the tracks of Mala, the Rufous Hare Wallaby people. The track of the rufous hare wallaby shows that the Mala came from the north.

2. From the south-west came the men of the Liru, the poisonous snake people.

3. Kuniya, the carpet snake who was pregnant and about to lay her eggs, came from the east.

4. Kurpalynga, the desert dingo dog, came from the west.

5. Together, the Mala and the Kurpalynga left Uluṟu to the south.

6. In the middle of the painting, where the Uluṟu Statement is, that is where Uluṟu is. The Uluṟu Statement is where all of our different stories come together.

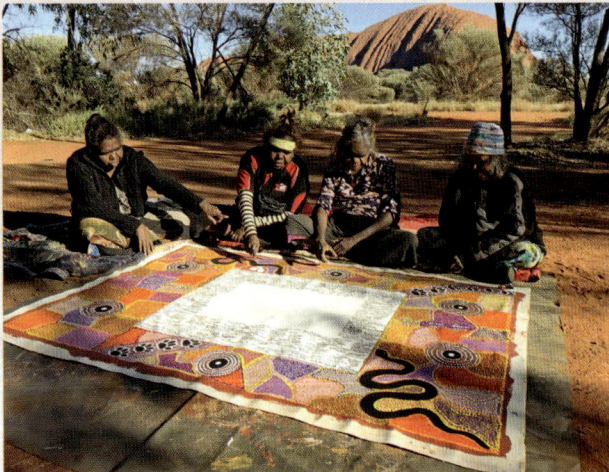

The Uluṟu Statement was spiritually and culturally endorsed in the Aboriginal community of Mutitjulu. The canvas was then painted by Aṉangu law women in the community. Here they explain the meaning of the painting with Uluṟu in the background.

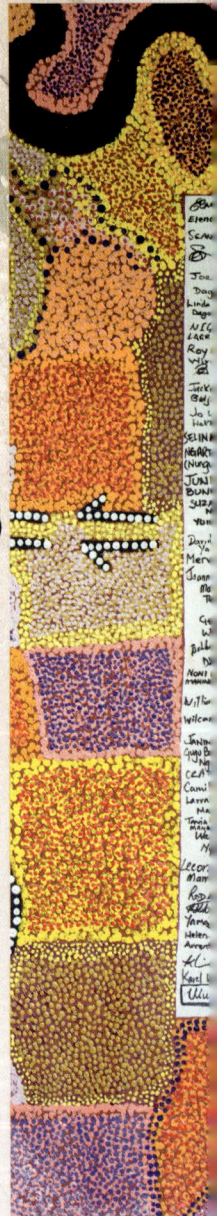

ULURU STATEMENT FROM THE HEART

We, gathered at the 2017 National Constitutional Convention, coming from all points of the southern sky, make this statement from the heart:

Our Aboriginal and Torres Strait Islander tribes were the first sovereign Nations of the Australian continent and its adjacent islands, and possessed it under our own laws and customs. This our ancestors did, according to the reckoning of our culture, from the Creation, according to the common law from 'time immemorial', and according to science more than 60,000 years ago.

This sovereignty is a spiritual notion: the ancestral tie between the land, or 'mother nature', and the Aboriginal and Torres Strait Islander peoples who were born therefrom, remain attached thereto, and must one day return thither to be united with our ancestors. This link is the basis of the ownership of the soil, or better, of sovereignty. It has never been ceded or extinguished, and co-exists with the sovereignty of the Crown.

How could it be otherwise? That peoples possessed a land for sixty millennia and this sacred link disappears from world history in merely the last two hundred years?

With substantive constitutional change and structural reform, we believe this ancient sovereignty can shine through as a fuller expression of Australia's nationhood.

Proportionally, we are the most incarcerated people on the planet. We are not an innately criminal people. Our children are aliened from their families at unprecedented rates. This cannot be because we have no love for them. And our youth languish in detention in obscene numbers. They should be our hope for the future.

These dimensions of our crisis tell plainly the structural nature of our problem. This is *the torment of our powerlessness.*

We seek constitutional reforms to empower our people and take a *rightful place* in our own country. When we have power over our destiny our children will flourish. They will walk in two worlds and their culture will be a gift to their country.

We call for the establishment of a First Nations Voice enshrined in the Constitution.

Makarrata is the culmination of our agenda: *the coming together after a struggle.* It captures our aspirations for a fair and truthful relationship with the people of Australia and a better future for our children based on justice and self-determination.

We seek a Makarrata Commission to supervise a process of agreement-making between governments and First Nations and truth-telling about our history.

In 1967 we were counted, in 2017 we seek to be heard. We leave base camp and start our trek across this vast country. We invite you to walk with us in a movement of the Australian people for a better future.

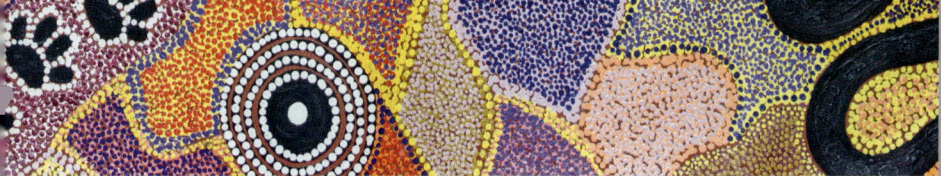

Thomas presents the strategy behind the important sequence of reforms to the Uluṟu National Constitutional Convention on the morning the Uluṟu Statement from the Heart was endorsed.

The jubilant delegates at the Uluṟu National Constitutional Convention soon after endorsing the Uluṟu Statement from the Heart.

Supporters of the Uluṟu Statement engaged with voters in the electorates of prime ministers who refused the call for Voice, Treaty, Truth. This action was in Cronulla Mall in the federal seat of Cook.

This photo was taken at the Yule River Bush Meeting – a place where the First Nations of the Pilbara region have been meeting for many thousands of years. It is one of the first places Thomas took the Uluṟu Statement in its journey around the country.

The March for Winds of Zenadth Cultural Festival procession on Waiben (Thursday Island), in the Torres Strait.

As the procession approached the festival grounds, dancers performed at intervals before the Uluṟu Statement from the Heart.

'I soon realised that someone in the Law school needed to step up to help students like me who struggled. One of the challenges I noticed was that not many Aboriginal students were mooting [mooting is participating in simulated court proceedings, or mock trials]. We weren't getting on our feet; we weren't advocating in courtroom settings. I relied on my teaching background and organising skills to design the UNSW Law First Nations moot. This created a safe space for Black students to moot on issues that were relevant to them. Eventually, Aboriginal students were mooting before judges of the district, federal and supreme courts. It was incredible to see the competition grow to the point that it was hosted by the New South Wales Supreme Court Chief Justice in Banco Court, the highest court in the state.

'With the support of my Black peers, I went on to be elected as Vice- President [Social Justice] of the UNSW Law Society. One of the issues I tackled at the university was this perception some of the non-Indigenous students have that there are no real Aboriginal people in New South Wales. I took non-Indigenous Law students to Central Western New South Wales to meet Elders and listen to young Indigenous people's stories. We made a documentary of the experience called *Yindyamarra*. I was part of a great team at UNSW that did a lot of social justice work.'

Teela's work didn't go unnoticed. In 2014, she was awarded the UNSW Law Spirit Award for her contribution to the Law school, and in 2015, she received the Inaugural Indigenous Barristers' Trust Award for her efforts in increasing participation in advocacy. In 2016, she was appointed to the prestigious role of Tipstaff to the Honourable Justice Lucy McCallum of the New South Wales Supreme Court, and in 2017, Teela was selected to attend the Emerging Leaders Program at Harvard University.

While her legal career was flourishing, still on Teela's mind were the lessons she had learnt at the United Nations. She recognised the damaging flaws in Australia's foundational and most powerful legal document, the Constitution, and she wanted to do more. While she was Tipstaff, the opportunity to participate in the constitutional dialogue process in Melbourne and Sydney presented itself.

'Initially, I thought that amending the Race Power, s 51 (xxvi), was the most important reform. The question of how to remove or replace the word "Race" was interesting, as a lawyer. But my view changed after listening to the mob in the regional dialogue. I listened a lot – especially on the first day – when a lot of frustration was ventilated. There were many contemporary experiences of dispossession and hopelessness shared, and then there were the Elders who told stories about the frontier wars and massacres. Mob were also questioning, "Why are we here again? The government's asking us for solutions but nothing ever changes ..."

'I felt the mob really carried the weight of the entire nation within the constitutional dialogues. To attempt to redefine the nation's narrative through law reform was hard work. How do we assert our sovereignty in a country that still denies we were here first? It was evident that this was going to require sophisticated legal and political reforms. It soon became clear to me that tinkering with the race provisions would not resolve the unfinished business that Australia is yet to settle with First Nations.'

Teela was demonstrating why she is now considered to be an important emerging Indigenous leader. I noticed from her reflections that she listens to others and she remains connected to her community. Her legal work and the lessons from her grandparents are interconnected.

'Growing up, I remember sleeping in the front yard at my grandparents, having a fire, having a yarn and bringing the mattresses out to the garden so Pop would tell ghost stories. But the community is different now. A lot more people are getting locked up because we are not recognising and addressing the trauma that our people have suffered. We are failing to divert our people from the criminal justice system.

'As a lawyer, I see this in the criminal justice system today. I think the system needs to be reformed. The current approach isn't working, more and more of our people are getting locked up, particularly since the Royal Commission into Aboriginal Deaths in Custody. Two main reasons why the Indigenous incarceration rate in New South Wales is soaring is due to people being refused bail and other justice offences such as breaching court orders.

'For example, if you look at Aboriginal women, they're the most likely to be locked up for very minor offences, or they are criminalised when they are victims of crimes. They usually have shorter sentences under six months, which suggests it's a minor offence. Meanwhile, while they serve a custodial sentence, they have likely lost their children and their homes. Aboriginal women are probably the most incarcerated on the planet. I'm more likely to be incarcerated than I am to be healthy.'

Teela helped me understand why it is so important to have Aboriginal legal professionals working in criminal justice. Through our interview, I could also see why she has a passion for law reform. Teela's fire was burning bright. I considered how leaders such as Teela could be even more effective if we had a First Nations Voice backed by the Australian Constitution – the guarantee to be heard and for our words to be acted upon.

We ended the interview with her recollection of her confrontation with the then prime minister on the ABC's *Q & A* program in 2017. The prime minister had just dismissed the Uluru Statement, and Teela wasn't going to let him get away with it.

'When I had the chance to challenge Turnbull on his dismissal of the Uluru Statement from the Heart, I knew I had to push back against his lies. I felt the weight of the mob who had put all that hard work into the constitutional dialogue process. It wasn't easy work and it was a profound moment in the history of our struggle. We can't let another generation of First Nations be voiceless in our own country. We must fight for what's right. Nothing has ever been handed to us on a silver platter, it's time to realise Voice, Treaty and Truth in Australia.'

I agreed with Teela Reid. After all, how could it be otherwise?

GARGU KANAI

Gargu Kanai is an Italaig woman from Moagal (Moa Island) in the Western Island group of the Torres Strait. She is also Ipkai of the Kaurarega, the Torres Strait Islander people closest to the mainland. Her great-grandmother was from the mainland, a Garrawa woman, giving Gargu a mixed heritage of Torres Strait Islander and Aboriginal.

When you say her name, you don't roll the 'r'. Instead, the 'r' is pronounced with a touch of the tongue to the palate. It's a sharp sound. I'm not a linguist, but that's how a wharfie describes how to pronounce Gargu properly.

As I sat with Gargu on the Cairns Esplanade, ready to do the interview, we took a moment to enjoy the fresh sea breeze and the salt-air smell before we began. It was a perfect tropical evening.

Gargu is a busy woman. She was visiting Cairns to attend hearings for a Native Title claim in the Torres Strait Islands. Work on the claim commenced more than twenty years ago. Sadly, such a lengthy process is not unusual. In the time it has taken to settle a

Native Title claim, many Aboriginal and Torres Strait Islanders have moved from youth to Elder. Many have passed on to be with their ancestors, never to see the outcome of their life-long struggle.

In addition to her Native Title work, Gargu is a forty-five year-old mother of five children. Gargu told me about her family. 'My two older ones, they were given to me by traditional adoption, from my niece and sister. I'm a grandmother of fourteen grandchildren, each and every one has slept on my belly.

'I've helped rear all of them, in amongst everything I do. So, my grandchildren never forget me. I've got three children living with me at the moment. I live in Townsville, but I do a lot of work around Native Title, just helping mob. Always just on a voluntary basis.'

Gargu left the Torres Strait when she was three years old. Her father, James Kanai, better known as 'Ponki', needed medical care that was unavailable on his small island home. There was little choice. If he were to survive to see his children grow to be adults, if he were to live to pass on his knowledge, they had to leave. But Ponki was a thinker and a visionary, and from challenge emerged opportunity.

'In the '70s, my father was sick, and needed to go down [to the mainland] for hospital reasons. He moved us all down there [to Townsville] because he wanted us to learn white man's way; white man's language, their written language, so that we could go back and help our people.'

Gargu was to learn about more than the white man's ways, she also learnt about the struggle for land rights. As she grew up in Townsville, she would witness her mother and father's activism, as well as the work done by the great Koiki Mabo. Gargu's mum was closely related to Koiki. Gargu calls him 'Granddad Koiki'. 'In 1976, when we moved down, word had got around that my mother was there.' At the time, Mabo was a janitor at James Cook University. On hearing that his niece, Gargu's mother, had moved to Townsville, he tracked her down to make sure they felt welcomed.

When Gargu talked about 'Granddad Koiki', I could see the pride in her eyes. She was proud to have witnessed the discussions, the comradely debate, and the development of ideas and strategies to improve the lives of their people back at their island homes. They were navigating the place between two worlds, as different as the ocean is to the land, toward a time when they could reclaim their sovereignty over a little island that was theirs since time immemorial. As the child of the men and women who were leaders in the early days of the land rights struggle, Gargu felt the sacrifices that they made.

'Mum and Dad were always writing letters. The Kaurareg push for land rights actually started down there in Townsville, not on the island. My Granddad Koiki helped Dad set up a meeting of the Kaurareg peoples. And that was the same time for Mer [Murray Island]. When Grandad Koiki was doing all his research, he was working at the uni as a janitor.

'It was difficult growing up, Mum and Dad travelled all the time for our people's land rights. Mum and Dad had been following that old minister, Minister Gerry Hand, with letters, seeking to be heard about issues in the community back on the island and our land rights. When he'd visit TI [Thursday Island], Mum and Dad would leave us with the family and they'd go up just to deliver him a letter, because it was very, very hard to get any letters to the minister. So, they waited till they were visiting, and they'd go and hand-deliver the letters themselves.'

Gargu's parents would deliver the letters in person because they had learnt that, otherwise, the letters were likely to be discarded or ignored before they reached the government minister.

'They'd visit all the mayors, advisors, members of Parliament, and department officers in Townsville, fighting to be heard, and we kids would be sitting there and waiting while they'd go inside.'

In addition to the constant letter writing and lobbying, Gargu's parents diligently worked at teaching and sharing their culture. 'They'd travel away just to dance. Just Mum sing and Dad dance. We would do all the family gatherings. This meant that we would always have family come over, and we'd sit and we'd learn, practice our culture, island dancing and everything.

'I never understood why we did that, because even though we'd practice all these dances, make all these headdresses, and all this dancing, we never danced anywhere. It wasn't until now that I realise what it was. It wasn't about learning dances to go and dance; it was about the kinship, how our people were. We were always close, always had that respect. That respect where our family would come and not have to ask for us to babysit. They'll just go and just drop the kids at the front yard and the kids would come in and there were often no questions asked. It was that type of kinship.'

For islanders living on the mainland, family and culture help to maintain a connection to the ancestral homelands. Gargu started to speak more slowly, more measured. I sensed that what she was about to say next was rarely shared, often hidden in her heart.

'I often get told that Townsville's a very racist place, but the funny thing was that I never actually experienced racism. A lot of my friends were white. My best friends, actually, were white, we'd hang out together. But yeah, though I never experienced racism, it was probably more that I didn't realise it was racism.'

Gargu paused, reached in to herself, and continued. 'The teachers would tell us that we would never amount to anything.'

She looked down at her hands, and said, 'I finished school in '89, and, ended up moving back home to Kubin [a village on Moa Island]. With Mum and Dad, we went back home and, because I spoke English fluently, I didn't understand language or broken [Island Kriol]. And all the kids up home, they grew up together, so they were all – they had all their close friend groups. And I was never a part of that because I spoke English. So, I guess, my best friends were my brothers and sisters, because we were the ones who grew up down south. We kind of stuck together. In fact, we still do today. I'm still, now even though I've …'

Gargu began to weep in to her hands. After only a moment or two, she looked up at me, paused, regained her composure, and continued. 'Even while working on Native Title, I would have letters written to me from my own mob telling me, "You know nothing of your culture. You're not from here. You're an interloper. You don't belong." And that was my life going back home. But, regardless, even though that was happening, I had this love that was put in me for my people that I had to help them.'

I understood what Gargu was feeling. Although I had always felt welcome amongst family and other young people when I visited Waiben (Thursday Island), I was still an islander who grew up on Larrakia land without language. I couldn't help but feel different. I thought of how difficult it must also be for people from the islands coming to the mainland. I thought of my father. It must've been hard for Dad when he went to work in the Northern Territory. He was just seventeen years old and spoke little English. He persevered. So did Gargu. She speaks language fluently now.

When I first met Gargu, she told me her name means 'lily pad'. As I learnt her story, I realised that the Elders who named her must have listened to Country – the ancestors knew who she would become. In her life Gargu is the lily pad. She is floating between two worlds; she draws her life and love from both – her foundation from her roots, her strength from her interconnecting structure, and her energy from the sun. She has persevered through the seasons, and sometimes she blooms. Her contribution to the making of the Uluṟu Statement from the Heart was a time when she bloomed.

Gargu was invited to attend one of the early meetings held by the Referendum Council in Broome. Key Indigenous leaders were asked to share their views on how the dialogue process should proceed. 'I saw all these leaders that were our people. I'd seen them on TV! Walking past Stan Grant in the plane I was like, Oh my god! Oh my god, that's Stan Grant! I knew I was a part of something big when I saw them, and I thought, Am I even a leader? But I was there. I knew from day one that I wanted to be involved in this. This is something big for our people. We have to make this work. I thought of my grandfather, who was a part of that 1936 Maritime Strike.'

During the Maritime Strikes, about 400 Torres Strait workers in the pearling industry went on strike for nine months, until they finally gained better working conditions on the pearling luggers. The strike also secured Queensland Government support for a Torres Strait Islander Representative Council, which met for the first time in 1937. (Nonie Sharp writes about the strike in detail in her article, 'Culture clash in the Torres Strait Island: The maritime strike of 1936', *The Journal of the Royal Historical Society of Queensland*, 1981.)

'My mum's dad, my grandfather, his name was Wees Nawia. He was a part of the Maritime Strike. He lived on Kirriri [Hammond Island] in the 1920s. My grandfather was removed from Hammond Island by gunpoint. He tried to help his uncle [who was being threatened by the Protector], and he was pushed and had a gun put to his head. "Get into the boat, you silly boy." It was in the 1920s, and he was standing up to the Protector who was removing the Traditional Owners – the Kaurareg people – off Hammond Island to make room for the church and the non-Indigenous people who wanted to live there. They were removed from Hammond Island and sent to Moa Island at gunpoint.

'I am proud that my grandfather was part of that 1936 Maritime Strike. They secretly organised the strike across all the islands by sending messages under the water. They won that struggle and the government was forced to facilitate a Torres Strait Island Councillors Conference on Masig [Yorke Island] in 1937. Straightaway, when I was in Broome with all those leaders, I was reminded of the 1936 Maritime Strike. I knew this is something that I want to be involved in.'

Gargu's greatest hope was that if she and her fellow participants at Uluru put their best efforts into an intelligent and achievable set of proposals, then those proposals would address the shortcomings her people have struggled with in the area of Native Title.

'Native Title has given us recognition that we are sovereign to our Countries, to our lands, but yet, we are still being kept from having a say on what happens. The laws and policies that are put in place don't suit our people.' Gargu talked about the problems with housing, overcrowding and restrictions on how their land can be used.

Speaking with passion now, Gargu said, 'That's why we need that Voice. We need that Voice because we need to change the legislation. It needs to change so that it would also suit our people's needs. I contact the government all the time, I meet with people from the government and tell them this is what we want. We stress these issues to them. We tell them they need to change the policies. The policies don't suit our people.

'The policies need to accommodate our people. We live in a wealthy country. We could share that wealth. In the Torres Strait, our food costs are high, and we have a high cost of living. Yet there's no jobs. It doesn't need to be that way. We need that Voice to Parliament.'

Gargu went to the convention with a clear understanding of what was needed at home. She also took the opportunity to bring a piece of home to the heart of the mainland. Her people from the

Italaig tribe on Moa were invited to dance on Aṉangu land, and they decided to bring the sacred Baidam (shark) Dance.

'The Baidam Dance hadn't been performed by our people for a long time, it is usually performed by Elders. There're probably fifteen Elders who know the dance that are still alive. All the dancers before had passed on. All our frontline dancers, all the old ones, I said to them, "We've got an opportunity. We can go over to Uluṟu to share and continue this dance. Allow our young people to learn." So, we brought the young and the old together to practice the dance.

'They were so excited, the youngsters. They'd talk about it all the time, because you don't go to Aboriginal Country and dance island dance. It's like it's taboo. You don't do that, unless you're invited.'

The dance troupe were welcomed to Uluṟu before the rest of the convention's participants. 'The Aboriginal leaders from the community took us to the old people's home in Mutitjulu. Our Elders are the kind of people who can see through you. They will see you not as just a person standing there, but see you spiritually. When we went there, the Aṉangu Elders, they were telling their story to us. They came and sat down, and we were introduced to them. They started telling us their story. Their fight. What they'd been through. When we left, we thanked them, shook their hands. They'd hold our hand and the look you'd see in their eyes said, "You need to help us." They wanted this just as much as us, going to Uluṟu. The community members wanted the Uluṟu Statement because they had done so much in their lives and they weren't giving up. So, if they're not giving up, we shouldn't give up too.'

Gargu and the dancers felt a great weight of responsibility to perform well. They were representing the Torres Strait Islands and their community on Moa Island. 'The dancers had to do our dance right. Especially with the Baidam Dance. It's a dance where you cannot stand away from the crowd. The people, you can't have people behind you when you dance that dance. We asked everyone to come forward because that dance is spiritually significant for us. And you can't make a mistake when you dance. It has to be right.'

Talking about the significance of the dance, Gargu explained, 'Our people are seafaring people. We travel by the stars. We travel by the stars, and by the horizon, you see the hills. The stars and the shape of the islands show us which direction we have to go to get home. They show us when it is the right time to go hunting. They show us when it is the right time to plant our gardens.'

Gargu then explained the motions in the dance.

'The Baidam Constellation is seven stars. It is very much about how the stars move. When you look at it, the constellation looks like a shark. When it's standing straight, you know it is going to be finer weather. The way the stars move, they are the actions that the dancers were doing.

'When the Baidam would move, the stars, when they move in the next direction, it tells us the weather will be rough. That is when the dancers were doing that shaking motion with their heads. Because when it moves like that, it'll be rough.

'When it'll be rainy time, the constellation turns, and they turn to the side. Because it turns to Daudai [mainland New Guinea], that's when you know straightaway that the rain's coming. Because when the nor 'wester comes, it is our monsoon time. A storm is coming.'

As Gargu took me through each stage of the dance, my heart swelled, and my skin tingled with excitement. I said that I could now see that the Baidam Dance played out what was to come throughout the days of the convention – the calm, the rough weather and the storm ahead. Then the moment of relief as the storm came and washed over us. A great moment and then calm.

Gargu smiled as I spoke, and said, 'Yeah! I was thinking about that! That this is the story because … we were going to Uluṟu to do this big thing. Everyone from everywhere was now going to be there together, to do this Statement. And this is what our people wanted. And it started off fine. The Baidam stood still. It started off fine. And then ... in the middle, and shake and move, when the Baidam move like this, you know, it's rough. And that was happening throughout that conference. It was rough.

'But it doesn't stop there, because when the Baidam turn, for Daudai ... it hasn't stopped. That rain is coming, that rain is going to fall down, you can't do anything during the monsoon time. But it'll come back again. It'll come fine, so our journey has not stopped.'

We were both talking excitedly now. I said how, in reflection, I could see that the dance had shown us the way through. Gargu summed it up easily. 'We had the rough time, and the storm, then the rain were our tears of joy. And when that last star goes, when the shark lays down again, then it's calm. Peace.'

Peace. The lily pad, on the surface between two worlds, had brought us the stars to guide us to that destination we wish for. Peace.

ELVERINA JOHNSON

Elverina Johnson lives in Yarrabah, a small community in North Queensland with a population of almost 5000 people. She has four sons, and two grandsons. Elverina is a creative person – she designs clothes, paints and performs on stage as a musician. She is proud of her community; I was excited at the prospect of meeting her there.

It was mid-morning when I drove up the steep, winding mountain road, surrounded by lush green jungle. When I reached a crest atop the mountain, before the road meanders down to Yarrabah, the dark emerald vegetation slipped away to reveal a turquoise blue sea. Nearby, in the beautiful waters of North Queensland is a living treasure that is visible from the near reaches of space, the Great Barrier Reef.

I stopped to take some photos of the magnificent view. As I looked around, from the sea to the dense jungle, I thought it curious that the mountain formed an all too convenient barrier between farmlands, settled and inherited mostly by the descendants of colonisers, and a small Aboriginal community called Yarrabah. From atop the mountain, the little town looked like any other tropical paradise. But this one has different laws to others, because of the Indigenous population.

Yarrabah is the largest regional Aboriginal community in the country. When I asked Elverina where we should meet, she simply said, 'Meet me by the church down at the beach.' I agreed without asking for any more details. It can't be too hard to find a church on a beach in a little community, I thought. I was right.

I couldn't have imagined a more beautiful setting for an interview. The little old white church, with a roof as green as the jungle on the mountain, is surrounded by lawn that meets the beach and the sea. After a cup of tea at the small cafe nearby, Elverina took me on a tour of the community. When we returned to the beach, we walked over to a concrete table on the church grounds, and we began.

'I love Yarrabah, it's my home. Because I'm an artist, I have travelled the world using different genres; I'm a performing artist, visual artist. I'm a creator, they say, my art covers all bases. I've also been very passionate as a community leader for social justice. That's always been my passion and that pretty much started at a very young age.'

When I met Elverina at Uluṟu, I didn't know she was a great artist. When I saw her again, it was at the National NAIDOC Awards Ball in 2017 accepting an award – NAIDOC Artist of the Year. She was an extremely popular winner, a crowd favourite.

She explained where her creative mind came from, as well as her inspiration and fighting spirit.

'My grandfather was a trumpet player. So, that's the music side of it. And my grandmother, she was a singer in the choir, she has a soprano voice. The visual arts part of it, I haven't really seen a history of that in my family. But I guess that's something that came from a creative upbringing. That's just an extension of the creativity that was already there.

'My art is inspired by oral histories. I've been inspired by every day living here, like things that I see, fishing, because we're rainforest people, we're saltwater people, my art depicts those everyday things. What we see, the ocean, and what we eat, the bush tucker, the rainforest, all of that.

'Art tells a story, and it is how we keep that knowledge alive. I bring the knowledge from the old people through the art. But also, in song. I've written many songs in my language about Yarrabah, about our Elders, about using language. Song is a non-threatening way for kids to easily pick up the language, through music. So it's just using those different mediums to carry on our culture.

'I guess I got my values from my mother and my grandmother, and from a Christian foundation, as well. They helped me learn about who I am, as a Yarrabah person, as a Gunggandji person. My grandfather was a person in the Church, and he travelled around Australia a lot in the early Church days. He fought for the rights of our people, but in a different kind of format. He used his position, in the Anglican Church, and talked about his community. He was a leader, he united people. The fight for recognition was happening right back then.

'As I was growing up, just seeing the way our people have been treated, I learnt that my people are being treated differently. We had less than those around us who are not Indigenous. I could see the difference between the struggles, I guess. You start to realise that there are things that you have to fight for. You realise the unfairness of how you're treated, so that helps you to formulate your drive for justice and for better outcomes, for a better life, for a better way of living.

'We have housing issues, overcrowding, violence and dysfunction within our community. These issues stem from underlying racism. Racism contributes to the lack of jobs. Racism affects personal development. When our people try to do something for themselves, and move out of the circumstances that they're in, when our young people try to move out of community, or want to get jobs outside, they face this racism. For example, if they apply for a house in Cairns, and people know that they come from Yarrabah, they don't get the house. The stereotypes and the barriers are out there. So, the result is a sense of hopelessness. They think to themselves, What's the point, might as well go back to Yarrabah and do what we do every day. No job, sit around. These kinds of things cause people to just go back drinking and you know, drug addiction and all that kind of stuff.'

Overcrowding is a cause of social dysfunction and health problems in Yarrabah, as it is in most Indigenous communities I have visited. When Elverina took me on the tour of her community, she showed me some homes where families live with their extended families, often with others living there too. She took me to the outskirts of the community as well, where makeshift homes built from pieces of tin and timber clung to the steep slopes that reached down to the sea. 'We've still got people living in the little shacks. We have a lack of housing and accommodation in Yarrabah, so, people are forced to go and build their own little places. Mind you, these shacks are still standing, even through Cyclone Yasi [a category 5 cyclone, with winds that reached 285 kilometres per hour, which hit the north coast between Cairns and Townsville in early 2011].'

Everywhere I looked, the people's resilience was obvious, as was their pride. The homes, built from scavenged hardware, had survived the devastating cyclone that had destroyed many of the old timber colonial homes along the nearby stretch of coast. Yarrabah is a community that is proud of being an outspoken part of the Indigenous Rights struggle. Their Elders were great campaigners for the 1967 referendum. Yet in many ways, Yarrabah is excluded from the mainstream system, perpetuating a cycle of hopelessness, especially among their youth.

As an example, Elverina referred to the sign at the community boundary that boldly proclaims that Yarrabah is an alcohol restricted area. 'The alcohol restriction doesn't stop the problem.' She said, 'People turn to alcohol because of the intergenerational trauma, the feeling of hopelessness. When they try to break that, they come against those barriers.

'So when the hopelessness affects the mental health of our people, they can still go into Cains and have a drink, but they can't bring their alcohol over here. There are instances where people have gone to liquor stores in Cairns or the local towns, bought the alcohol, and once they have bought it, the owners of the shops then ring Yarrabah police and let them know these people from Yarrabah have alcohol. So then, police will wait for them at the bottom of the hill.'

'That's just setting them up!' I exclaimed.

In a matter-of-fact way, Elverina simply replied, 'It's a regular occurrence. All the alcohol management plan has done is set up young people. A young Yarrabah kid, of course, wants to celebrate their eighteenth birthday. They might have their licence, they go to enjoy themselves in Cairns because there isn't that here. They come home, get booked, then have a criminal record already. That's all it's done – just put more of our young people in jail. They've got nowhere to stay in Cairns, so they risk driving home under the influence. Accidents, get booked, you know? Go to jail, then they've got a criminal record that affects their opportunity to find work or find a house to move out. It has a domino effect.

'The community has its own ideas on how to address our problems, without this mandatory ban on alcohol. We have been calling for a local pub in the community, one that is basically family oriented. Where families can go and have meals there and a place for people to go and socialise and basically monitor themselves. Learn how to drink sociably. Part of that is bringing down the domestic violence rate, picking up school attendance. That's part of the reason why the Alcohol Management Plan was developed in the first place, to deal with both issues. But it's just been a really hard fight, I guess. People do feel helpless, they feel like, how much more discrimination can we be under here?'

All Indigenous communities in Queensland are treated the same way, Elverina explained. 'But as soon as you get over that hill, you can go and have a drink anywhere, in a pub or wherever.

'Alcohol abuse, domestic violence, these problems also exist in white communities with unemployment and intergenerational trauma. Yet, they don't have the restrictions.

'How many women have been killed within the last few weeks. There's been like what, seven? Seven women have died within the last few weeks, across Australia through violence. None of those were Aboriginal women and none of those have happened in our community. Where's the restrictions around those little townships because of drug and alcohol affected violence?'

As a traveller and artist, Elverina clearly sees the difference in attitudes towards Indigenous and non-Indigenous communities. When she went to the Cairns Regional Dialogue, she made a compelling speech that saw her elected to go to the Uluru First Nations Constitutional Convention. She said it was an experience she will never forget, but what stood out for her was the sense of achievement when the Uluru Statement was endorsed.

She smiled as she said, 'It was good to be a part of that process because it brought all our different concepts together, bringing our wording together. I felt so proud to be a part of that. There are some words in the Uluru Statement that were part of something that I said. And just having my name on that Statement itself, being a part of such a historical process – it just made me feel good that what we did will go down in history. You know? That will go down in history. My children, great-grandchildren for generations to come will find that as a reference point.

'My great-grandchildren will maybe do a project on that and they'll say, "Oh, my great-grandmother's name on there."

'Non-Indigenous Australians seem to think we're all just anger and all that, but you know, we've got some pretty fluent Black fellas. I am proud to have been in that room then, and you could feel, you could actually feel the elation. I saw that for some, a load was taken off their shoulders and put into that Statement. It's like, okay, now take this back to Parliament. But then I guess the other part of that was when it was rejected.

'When the prime minister dismissed it, I was so angry, like the government put all this money out. Go and do this, go and consult with the people, blah, blah, blah. Bring something back. It's like someone being given all of the tools, the money, and told to go and make something with this. Bring it back. And then they say, "No, that's not good enough."

'It just made me feel like, What's wrong with these people? What do they want? What more can we do? We only have our voices. I don't want my children or grandchildren or great-grandchildren to be fighting this same battle down the track.

'What strikes me the most is that when I was part of that process, I wasn't just doing it for me. I was doing it for my community. I was doing it for the next generation after me. To try and make things better for them, to give hope to our young people.'

The experience at Uluru, and then the slap in the face from the government when the prime minister dismissed the call for a First Nations Voice, have been life changing for Elverina. She pin pointed the moment when she had an epiphany and decided she would fight back.

'I was living in Brisbane, and one day I got really depressed. I got really depressed because I was thinking, Why is it that we're always struggling, as Black fellas? Why is it that we can't seem to get past a certain point, we're always struggling financially, we're always struggling to build a business? We're always struggling for an education. A lot of non-Indigenous people, a lot of them are born into financial inheritance. But here we are, in our own country, as First Nations, we're still struggling to make ends meet in our own communities. Then I realised that we're still living on crumbs. We're still living on crumbs financially in our own country. I thought about something that I had read in the Bible about when the disciples were sitting at the table and they had a meal, and one of the disciples was arguing to Jesus about not having enough. Jesus said to the disciples, "Well, even the dogs feed on the crumbs that are thrown under the table." And that kind of had a really big effect on me when I thought about it. I thought well, I'm basically living off crumbs. When our women face domestic violence, that's crumbs. When we have a lack of housing, that's crumbs. When we face racism every day, that's crumbs. Everything that causes dysfunction in our community, we have inherited those problems because of the impact of colonisation. We are still eating the crumbs.

'I thought, Well, if I'm living off crumbs as an adult, and as a mother, what am I giving my kids? I am splitting my little crumb to give to my kids? I cried, I cried so much. I thought, this has to stop. How can I get out of this rut?'

As she spoke, tears were welling in Elverina's eyes. She paused, wiped her eyes, and went on …

'I realised that we've accepted it, as a race of people, because of hopelessness. We think, Well that's all they're going to give us, we might as well accept it. But something rose up within me and

I thought, No. I don't want to accept crumbs. I want to sit at the table. I want to have a banquet just like everybody else. I want to have the financial success. I want to run a successful business. I want to be able to live in a home that's going to be suitable for me and my kids. I decided I'm not going to take anymore domestic violence. I'm not going to take anymore abuse. I'm going to stand up against the crumbs left to us by racism. I'm going to stand up against injustices that my people are facing and continue to fight. We are the First People, we should be sitting in first place.

'This moment, it led to me starting to build my business. I started rising up. I started speaking out more and started participating and talking about positive outcomes. I have shared this story with a lot of people now, and when I do, it's like, the light comes on for them.

'So, I started to think, how do WE get there? How do WE get from under the table to the banquet? How do WE get to that point? We get there by speaking the truth.

'The truth of it is that my mother's generation, my mother was a domestic slave out on the stations. She never received any of her payments for working out on the station. She was beaten for not working if she was sick. The truth is my grandmother would have her head shaven if she had a boyfriend, or if they spoke in the language or talked or did anything that was contrary to the rules at that time. Or worse, be forced to rake the yard with her bare hands. All of our inheritance has been stolen off us – cultural inheritance, financial inheritance, our position in this country.'

Elverina's story is compelling. She tells the stories of her people in her artwork, such as the story of her grandmother raking the yard with her bare, bloody hands as a child, on her knees in a dusty yard, distraught, soaked from her sweat and tears. And now that you've read her story, you know that Elverina will not take no for an answer – she wants to sit at the table; it is time her voice is heard.

ON THE WAY: ULURU, WE LOOK TO YOU

Andrew McCutcheon

Struck down by motor neurone disease, Andrew McCutcheon felt frustrated. As a former cabinet minister in the Joan Kirner Victorian Government and long-serving Collingwood Council member, Andrew had been inspired and uplifted to hear of the wonderful Uluru Statement from the Heart only months before he was on his death bed. Andrew was saddened and angered by the decision of Prime Minister Turnbull's government to reject the Uluru Statement.

Andrew McCutcheon was well known for his passion, so he wanted to send a message to politicians, and anyone else he could reach, about the importance of the convention and the consensus that had been reached. He inspired his music therapist and family to write a song about the Uluru Statement. He hoped that although his agonising final days would soon pass, the people of Australia would look to Uluru and end the torturous plight of First Nations people. He called the song 'Uluru, We Look to You'.

Before Andrew's final breath, the song was complete and he asked, 'Can we make it go viral?'

I was at Andrew's State funeral where, as Fiona McLeod and I held the Uluru Statement from the Heart canvas, the song was performed by Anneliis Way, Nicholas Seymour, Dan Kelly, Louise

McCutcheon, Kirsten Hoak, Nicola McCutcheon and Olivia Hoak.

Vale Andrew McCutcheon.

I was so touched by Andrew's story, his song and his dying wish that I promised his family I would do all I can to see his wish come true. The song lyrics are included here with the hope that the music, not just these words, will go viral some day soon.

'Uluru, We Look to You' by A. McCutcheon and A. Way
This is the song that was written by Andrew McCutcheon, his music therapist Anneliis Way, and his loving family. You can also listen to the song on YouTube.

> We haven't always seen eye to eye
> There once was a time when the white man denied
> That the black man existed and we tried to hide
>   them away
>
> The white man invaded the black man's terrain
> Pretending they owned the whole southern plain
> Denying a history, spanning thousands and thousands of years
> Thousands and thousands of years
>
> Uluru we look to you
> Show us what we need to do
> Open our eyes so we stand side by side
> Uluru ... guide us to truth
>
> Colonisation, disease and destruction
> A deliberate campaign of extermination
> Black children stolen by misguided hands

The importance of songlines and Dreamtime dismissed
Their languages banned, the subtleties missed
Waterholes poisoned, land was given away
Land was given away

Uluru we look to you
Show us what we need to do
Open our eyes so we stand side by side
Uluru … guide us to truth

We can't change the past, but we can shape the future
Respect the connection to Country and nature
Choose Makarrata, settle together this time

I have a dream that the suffering has ended
Indigenous Australia has been reunited
Come on politicians, listen and learn today
Listen and learn today

Uluru we look to you
Show us what we need to do
Open our eyes so we stand side by side
Uluru … guide us to truth

Gunditjmara, Victoria

JILL GALLAGHER

Jill Gallagher is a Gunditjmara woman who was one of ten children. Her family was often forced to travel, searching for work, mostly in seasonal picking and factories. Jill's father was Irish, and he died when Jill was very young. Her grandmother was from Lake Condah Mission and Framlingham Aboriginal Mission.

Jill was a rebellious child, which was understandable. She knew that untruths were being told about the history of her country, and with her family's seasonal picking work, she had been to nineteen different primary schools before she was eight years old.

She has worked hard from a young age. First, to survive, and then to create and build a career, going from factory work, to the public service and repatriation of her peoples remains, to becoming a pioneer in Aboriginal health and cultural heritage. She is now the first Treaty Advancement Commissioner, guiding her people to what should be a settlement of great historical and generational significance.

I met Jill in her office at the Treaty Advancement Commission in Melbourne to interview her. I didn't know much about her amazing life to begin with, so we started the interview with Jill telling me about growing up in rural Victoria.

'My mob are Gunditjmara, from a little mission called Lake Condah, in western Victoria. That whole area around Lake Condah is Gunditjmara Country. My father was an Irish immigrant, and he died when I was six months old, so I didn't get to learn about that part of my heritage.' Jill only recently learnt exactly how old she was when her father died. 'I just got my father's death certificate, for the first time ever, a couple of weeks ago. Before that, I couldn't trace it. On the back of the death certificate, it listed all his children and their ages. So, my mum was a single mum of seven kids all under the age of nine.'

Her mother went on to have three more children, raising ten children on her own. Jill is one of the middle-born siblings.

'I grew up like most Aboriginal families in the region. I don't know what it was like in other states, but in Victoria, the only source of employment that Aboriginal people could get back then was either in factories or seasonal picking. We did a lot of seasonal picking, and we travelled, mainly throughout Gunai-Kurnai Country, which is Gippsland. It wasn't long ago that I added up every primary school that I went to. I went to nineteen different schools in my primary school years. Nineteen. And that's due to moving around and trying to find employment.

'In primary school I'd work in the bean paddocks, picking beans after school. It was the only source of employment our mob could get, was seasonal picking, whether it be fruit or beans, or onions or veggies.

'For any kid changing schools it's quite traumatic, whether you're Aboriginal or non-Aboriginal. But because there was a lot of us, and we were different ... the racism that our family experienced ... I remember one occasion – we were in my own Country, Gunditjmara Country – my mum took some of us, not all of us, in for a counter meal in a local hotel. I won't mention names ... We were asked to leave because they didn't serve Aboriginal people. I was only about eight at the time, but that was so traumatic that I remember it. I've never forgotten that. People don't fully understand the impact of racism; it has big health implications – mental health implications, depression – a whole range that for some make it difficult to get a job.'

With a mischievous smile, Jill briefly digressed. 'Isn't it strange, Thomas, when you see where I am? I was never one for authority figures. I couldn't understand the system, how it didn't teach our culture or teach the true history of this country. I used to argue with teachers. I'd say that it wasn't Captain Cook that discovered Australia ... Hello! We've been here a lot longer than that! It was being rebellious against the system, so to speak, that led to me leaving school halfway through year seven. I started working in factories in Fitzroy, making fiberglass baths.'

By the time Jill was eighteen, she was a single mother herself. She did some work in women's refuges, supporting women who were suffering from domestic violence, and then she decided she wanted to do more for her own children's future. The timing was good. Labor leader Joan Kirner had won the Victorian state election, becoming the first female state premier. With a Yorta Yorta woman, Lois Peeler, advising the premier, the policy setting changed for the better and Jill had an opportunity to enter the public service. Lois was one of the singers in the group The Sapphires, which was the subject of the acclaimed movie of the same name, released in 2012.

'Back then, they used to have aptitude tests, not only Aboriginal people, but for all people. I failed it twice by the way. But then under

Joan Kirner's leadership, the Victorian Government developed a program, the Aboriginal Employment Program. It allowed Aboriginal people to come in through a different method. I got in under her, Joan Kirner. An amazing woman.

'So, I came in under that policy, and I spent fifteen years in government. In that time, I took every opportunity that government offered to better my education and skills. I did middle management courses, I did computer courses, emotional intelligence training. They had a lot of training programs for Aboriginal people within, and outside of government, and I capitalised on that.

'So, I started out my career not a well-educated person. I left school at year seven. I started to fight the system.'

Jill took on a role at the Museum of Victoria, first as a trainee and then as an employee, where she played an important part in the fight for her people. Under the leadership of fellow Gunditjmara man Jim Berg, Jill worked in the struggle to repatriate thousands of stolen Aboriginal remains.

'Jim Berg was the then CEO of the Victorian Aboriginal Legal Service. He started legal proceedings against Melbourne University to return 800 Aboriginal skeletons, a collection called the Murray Black Collection. It was named for George Murray Black, an amateur collector who collected Aboriginal skeletal remains between the 1920s and 1950s. The remains were from the Maraura, Kureinji, Tati-tati, and Wati Wati peoples.'

Jill remembered the case vividly. 'Jim Berg won his court case because under Victorian law, you had to have a permit to have Aboriginal human skeletal remains. They didn't have a permit. So, they had to hand them over to the Museum of Victoria. I had the task of unpacking the Aboriginal skeletons, which at one stage got a bit spooky. But it was also very emotional because those people actually came from burial grounds right along the Murray River on both sides.'

As Jill told me about the work that she did with Jim Berg, I thought about the men, women and children who had been buried with ceremony and love hundreds or thousands of years ago with their dignity and humanity intact. But they'd been ripped from their places of rest to be experimented on or displayed like trophies. I was deeply affected with sadness and anger. I was also angry that the only reason Jim Berg won the case to repatriate those Maraura, Kureinji, Tati Tati, and Wati Wati remains was because the grave robbers didn't have a permit! As if anyone should ever be granted a permit to steal the bodies of our ancestors. I marvel at the endurance and spirit of Jim Berg and his colleagues, such as Jill, who undertook what must have been tormenting work.

'Most of my career has been working in protecting and returning Aboriginal cultural heritage. I worked for the Victoria Archaeological Survey, and our role was to go around and protect Aboriginal heritage sites in Victoria. I was also involved in setting up the Language Corporation that now exists here. I don't know of any Victorian Aboriginal person who can speak our language fluently. We know bits and pieces, we've developed and published dictionaries. There is so much more work to be done.'

After fifteen years working in the public service, Jill then took up a leadership role in Aboriginal Health before her recent appointment as the Victorian Treaty Commissioner.

'I've heard about Treaty most of my life. Even internationally, but here in Victoria we've had a lot of our advocates, our people demanding Treaty. So, the word "treaty" is not a new thing for me. But what is a new thing for me is that here in Victoria we've got a government that's willing to explore what that can look like.'

On 29 November 2014, the Labor Party was elected to government on a progressive platform that included reconciliation and Indigenous Rights. Dan Andrews's government began delivering on this commitment by holding a Self-Determination Forum in February 2016.

'The government held the Self-Determination Forum because they wanted to ask the mob two things. One was if we supported constitutional recognition. The forum participants rejected symbolic recognition … But they overwhelmingly supported substantive constitutional recognition through the enshrinement of a First Nations Voice to Parliament.

Jill explained the second question that the Victorian Government put to Victorian First Nations: 'They also wanted to ask the mob what self-determination means to us as Aboriginal people, because this government, the Andrews government, has a very strong policy on self-determination for Indigenous communities.' The answer was that Victorian First Nations want treaties.

'So that's where the official call for Treaty came from. The Andrews government didn't dismiss it. They basically said, "Well, you've asked, let's explore how we can do that, or if we can do that."'

Wryly, Jill added, 'Very different to the Turnbull government.'

'Hence, we've been on the road to Treaty. When I heard that, I said, "Oh, my Lord, the government's listening." So, I thought, I've got to be involved, I really must be involved.' And Jill did. She joined the Treaty Work Group.

'Being on the Treaty Work Group wasn't easy because we got kickback from some in our communities. Some people said we are a government-run institute, that we're handpicked by government, we're government lackeys, two-bob Blacks. We got all that. So, the working group said, "We need to be, as much as possible, independent of government." The working group came up with the idea of having a commission, a Treaty commission, and a commissioner with independence from government.'

'We've had three goals since we began the process: we've

established a treaty advancement commission, which is done; next, a piece of legislation that tries to protect the process and commits the government to continue to work and talk to community on treaties, this piece of legislation got through; the third thing was the ARB, Aboriginal Representative Body, also with Treaty authority. That's the direction the working group set for my office. We established a Voice for First Nations in Victoria.

'After meetings in many towns across Victoria and a state-wide forum, we released a proposed model for the Aboriginal Representative Body back in September 2018. There was a period of just over a month to get feedback. And we're now [December 2018] in the middle of analysing all that feedback and adjusting the model to reflect it. Some of it we can, some of it we can't because it's just unrealistic. There were big border issues – how we could deal with the mob along the Murray River because it straddles both Victoria and New South Wales. So, we're now exploring how we can manage that, how we can include the mob across the river, how can we include Aboriginal people who live interstate or overseas, how will they participate if they're from Victoria but living elsewhere.

'That's what we're considering now, and we hope to have an election process up and running by mid next year, where people will go to the polls, our people. We'll set up an electoral roll; we'll set up electoral boundaries, which we've almost done, and next year we'll go to the polls and vote for our representative body. And their role will not be to negotiate treaties, but to negotiate the treaty negotiating framework with the Victorian Government. We also need to focus on capacity development for the negotiation. The government is now getting ready, we need to get ourselves ready too.'

If you are reading about Treaty for the first time, you may notice that it is an incredibly complex process. It is also very different from the treaties you may have heard about in New Zealand, Canada and the United States of America, because generally, those treaties were negotiated at the time when the settlers/colonisers were establishing a new sovereignty. Treaties assisted the colonisers in legitimising that new sovereignty, sometimes against other colonisers who would potentially stake claims. Australia completely lacks this legitimacy. There is no sovereign-to-sovereign agreement. Aboriginal and Torres Strait Islander land was taken by force. As I write this, the conservative side of the Australian Government continues to dismiss calls for Treaty, a crucial point that Jill is conscious of.

Negotiations in Victoria have been a long time coming. The Andrews government's announcement in February 2016 came after more than two hundred years of dispossession, forced destitution, societal exclusion and thorough ignorance, which continues. 'Treaty' was a word that both major parties had taken pains to avoid. The change of attitude came from a long, courageous struggle by Aboriginal people and Torres Strait Islanders, and tens of thousands of progressive non-Indigenous Victorian voters, who have rallied with First Nations people with increasing vigour on the streets of Melbourne. Jill explained why the struggle for constitutional reform is vital to treaty making.

'If we've got a Voice that's enshrined in the Constitution … if we've got a representative body there empowered by the Constitution, to advocate the needs of Aboriginal and Torres Strait Islander peoples in this country – then we can hold the federal government to their obligations to our treaty outcomes with the state of Victoria. The Morrison federal government are scared of us getting Voice, Treaty, Truth. But they shouldn't be, there are treaties in Canada and the Canadian Government hasn't fallen over. The Canadian Government hasn't lost power. They haven't gone broke. Price Waterhouse Cooper did an analysis report of their treaties in British Columbia. What it said was that due to the treaties – the modern-day treaties – they bring $1.75 billion in tourism into the economy.

'I've seen what happened overseas. I've observed that the First Nations in Arizona, the First Nations in America, they have a hook in the Constitution.

'I asked the chief in Arizona, "If you've got one piece of advice for us in Australia, or Victoria, what would it be?" And you know what her comment was? "We have a hook, we have a Voice in the Constitution, America's Constitution. It doesn't rely on government being sympathetic, they must negotiate, according to their Constitution."

'This international experience helped me to understand the importance of the Uluṟu Statement. We need to have that hook in the Constitution that empowers us. That doesn't mean you can take Australia back and send everyone off this continent; that's not what it's about. It's about recognition, empowerment and living together in peace.'

Jill was one of the hundreds of First Nations people at the historic meeting at Uluṟu. She said that the final day, Friday, 26 May 2017, was unforgettable. 'When I heard the Uluṟu Statement from the Heart I remember – Janine [Coombs] was with me – I just cried. We didn't dream that we would achieve something so substantive and yet so simple. We were proud that we were a part of that.'

When I left Jill's office, I felt privileged to have heard her story. The story of an amazing woman who grew up in rural Victoria, back in the days when segregation was so blatant that a single mother and her hungry children could be refused a meal at a hotel. A woman who picked beans after school and who cared for the repatriated bones of hundreds of ancestors. Jill Gallagher, the first ever Australian Treaty Commissioner, understands what must be done next. We need a constitutionally enshrined Voice. We need peace.

Wotjobaluk, Victoria

JANINE COOMBS

Janine Coombs is a Wotjobaluk woman who lives in Melbourne. Wotjobaluk Country is in the western region of Victoria that takes in Antwerp, the small town where her great-great-grandfather was born. Janine laments that her language was almost wiped out. It wasn't passed on to her father's generation and so she and her siblings never had the chance to learn it. Janine's remarkable father, Kevin Coombs – the first Aboriginal person to represent Australia as a Paralympian as a wheelchair basketballer and athlete – told Janine how her grandparents would be physically assaulted for speaking language.

'My dad told me how he, his siblings and his parents were in the church and they were talking to each other in language. The mission manager's wife walked passed and slapped them on the back of the head and said, "You will not speak that heathen language in the House of the Lord."'

Janine hopes that her people's language can be revitalised and introduced to the next generations through the Department of

Education and Training in Victoria. She isn't waiting though, under the Berengi Gadjin Aboriginal Land Council, a language dictionary has been developed and teaching the youth has begun.

Janine has dedicated her working life to her people. She has served as Chair of Barengi Gadjin Land Council, is a member of the Victorian Traditional Owner Settlement Framework Executive Committee and is a member of the National Heritage Trust's Indigenous Advisory Committee. Since 2013 she has been the Chair of the Federation of Victorian Traditional Owner Corporations. Most recently, Janine has been on the Victorian Treaty Working Group, focusing much of her time on the development of a framework and representative structure so that treaty negotiations may advance with the Victorian Labor government.

When I interviewed Janine, we started by talking about her parents.

'Oh my god, he's a cripple!' exclaimed Janine's grandmother.

'Oh my god, and he's black!' observed her grandfather.

When Kevin Coombs met Janine's mother Linda, the relationship was off to a challenging start. But Kevin was not deterred. He said to his young fiancée, Linda, 'It's all good, but I know I've got my work cut out here.' Kevin and Linda have been in an enduring, loving relationship ever since.

'My grandparents absolutely adored my father … after that introduction, they did nothing but treat him with respect and love. That's what anybody would want, respect and love,' Janine said affectionately. 'After Mum and Dad got married, they thought about having kids. The doctor said to Dad, "You've got a better chance of winning Tattersalls." When Mum got pregnant, Dad said to the doctor, "You might want to go out and buy that Tatts ticket, because my wife is pregnant." My father loved a challenge.'

I soon learnt that his daughter, Janine, is a chip off the old block.

Kevin Coombs became a paraplegic at twelve years of age, when he was accidently shot in the back.

'Dad's father would travel getting any work he could. He would send money to the family when he was at work and every six months he would come home with gifts for the kids. The family had moved to Balranald, which is a town that's 50 kilometres north of Swan Hill.

'Dad's mum died when he was only five years old. Welfare came and said, "We're going to take the kids." But some of my grandmother's relations, Uncle Rids and Aunty Tibbs, went to Welfare and said, "No, no, no, no. We'll take the kids on. We live on the Aboriginal mission in Balranald, and they can live with us."

'So, it was while they were living at Uncle Rids and Auntie Tibbs' that the older boys decided that they'd go rabbiting. While they were out, they didn't realise that one of the younger kids had snuck along and was following them. Anyway, Dad sat down on the bank of the Murrumbidgee and put his rifle down. He didn't hear this kid. Next minute he knows, he turns around this young kid has got his rifle and shot him. The kid didn't realise that the gun was loaded. At the time Uncle Rids and Aunty Tibbs had their nephew over who was showing off his second-hand – but polished up to the nth degree – Vauxhall car.

'One of the kids came running back to the house, saying that my dad had been shot and so, this nephew found my dad, threw him in the back seat and drove flat out to the little bush hospital in Balranald. He drove through paddocks, barbwire fences. He didn't stop to open any gates. The mission where the accident happened was on the outskirts of town, and by the time he reached the city limits of downtown Balranald, the engine fell out of the car! The hospital was at the other end of town, so the nephew just ran the rest of the way to the hospital to get somebody to come and grab him. Then, because Dad had lost so much blood, he needed a blood transfusion. It just so happened that the nephew was the same blood type, so he saved his life.

'Once Dad was stabilised, he was flown down to Carlton kids ward. Back then, they had nurses and staff who hadn't seen an Aboriginal person before! Let alone an Aboriginal with a spinal injury. Some of the stories that I have read about the conditions that they left my father in at the hospital just breaks my heart.

'Because of his accident, he couldn't control his bowels or his bladder. The nurses would give him one wash in the morning and then he was left to his own devices. He'd lay there all day [in excrement]. This led to him getting pressure sores, which was normal in those days with a spinal injury, but my dad ended up getting a really bad pressure sore. But Dad makes light of it. He'd say, "I know it must've been bad." I'd say, "Well, how do you know that, Dad?" He said, "Because the young nurse came in one morning, pulled down the sheet to give me a sponge bath and she took one look, turned, then threw up!" He said, "I never knew how bad it was, but I was going by her reaction it must have been pretty bad!"'

Kevin spent twelve months laying on his stomach to recover from the bed sores.

He was moved to a new spinal injuries' unit at the Royal Austin Rehabilitation Hospital in Melbourne, where he was to stay for the next ten years. He was young and a long way from his family. Fortunately, though, it was there that he learnt to play wheelchair basketball, among a variety of other sports. Sport was vital to his rehabilitation. Kevin relished the challenge and cherished the comradery with other people with disabilities. Some of those friendships have lasted a lifetime. Janine explained that while racial bias was very much a harsh reality for her dad, humanity still shone through in Balranald.

'The town of Balranald, the town itself, they actually had a raffle organised by Reggie Tress from the Ford dealership. People donated money and they paid for his first wheelchair. These were non-Aboriginal people with their prejudices but who still had an attitude of looking after your own. It was like, You're a country boy, so we're going to help you out.

'My dad has kept up relationships with his siblings and the community in Balranald since then. My sister and I grew up with summer holidays back at Balranald. Generations of the town's people know who my dad is.'

When Janine said this, I thought, Generations of all Australians should know who your dad is ...

Kevin Coombs OAM excelled at wheelchair basketball. He competed in the first wheelchair basketball national championships in 1960, performing so well that he became the first Indigenous person to represent Australia at either a Paralympic or Olympic competition. He went on to compete in five Paralympics, as both a competitor and as captain and coach. He proudly represented Australia before he was counted as a citizen, and travelled internationally to do so while uncertain if he would be allowed to return. At the 1974 Dunedin Commonwealth Games, he received a silver medal. Kevin Coombs was more than a sportsperson, he was a pioneer for Indigenous health services in Victoria and a role-model and mentor to many, especially his daughter, Janine.

From a young age, Janine chose to work for her people and her community. She recalled her proudest moment, the passing of legislation that secured a treaty process. She was part of a treaty working group that dedicated three years of hard work to achieve legislation that was unprecedented in this country. They travelled to all parts of Victoria, holding forums for First Nations people so that the communities could be informed, and so that the people in those communities who were dealing with the day-to-day issues, could inform the working group, helping them plan the way forward. Janine told me how tough it was, working through the issues with the many Aboriginal people who held a range of different perspectives. They were many people who were not only recovering from but were still dealing with the impact of countless detrimental policy decisions. They worked, listened, considered, negotiated and fought their way to the first step in any collective parties' negotiation process – determining representation.

'When I joined the Treaty Working Group, we set about our work consulting with communities and government to develop options for a representative body and to give advice on the next steps for a treaty-making process. I recalled the concern that First Nations people had about a change of government in the lead up to the Victorian state election. They had seen what happened to the treaty process in South Australia.'

The South Australian Indigenous community had begun a similar process with Jay Weatherall's Labor government. When Labor lost power in the March 2018 state election, the new Liberal premier, Stephen Marshall, ended the South Australian treaty process. Janine and many Indigenous people in Victoria were worried that their hard work for a treaty would end with a change of government.

'I was part of the legislative sub-committee. We developed the preamble and the legislation based on the three years of work in the communities through many forums.' Janine told me how difficult the drafting was but everyone in the working group was determined to get the job done. Janine was in the Victorian Parliament on the day the legislation was voted on.

'I was at Parliament House from ten to nine in the morning until twenty past ten at night when it finally got passed. The first person that I rang was my dad. I called him and I said, "Dad, it passed!" Dad said, "Who passed?" As if someone had passed away ... I said,

"No, Dad. It passed! The legislation passed!" I'll never forget his exact words. He said …'

Janine looked away from me, her eyes quickly filling with tears. 'I still get emotional when I talk about this.' She faced me again and continued. 'Dad said, "When this government came out and said they'd talk to the Aboriginal community about self-determination and Treaty, I thought it was all tokenistic." He said, "But after having a conversation with you, Janine, and you were determined to be sitting at the table to hear what the government had to say, you and the Treaty Working Group did all of this work. You did consultations. You copped a fair whack from the naysayers and the ones who disagree with it. You've stayed the course, you worked hard on the subcommittee for the legislation …" I'll never forget what Dad said to me next – "Don't you ever let anybody say a bad word about the work that you've done, because there is nobody that is prouder of you than me and your mother."' Janine found a tissue in her bag, wiped her eyes and continued. 'It was a deeply emotional moment for us, we never thought it would get this far. We never expected that the legislation would get passed.'

Janine made me think of the Nelson Mandela saying, 'It's always impossible until it is done.'

'For me, that legislation represented the last three years of my life. I couldn't believe what we had achieved when that legislation passed, which is the same with the Uluru Statement. When I told Dad that I would be part of the delegation to Uluru, he asked me to explain it to him. So, I explained it, and I kept him and Mum, and other family, up to date the whole way through. One of the great things about movements like this is that it starts with conversations. What we have been through starts a conversation with my non-Indigenous mum's brothers and their wives and their children. A constant stream of information. A conversation can challenge the stereotypes. My grandmother, for example, didn't realise that as Aboriginal people, we're mentioned in the Constitution of Victoria but in the national Constitution, we don't exist. She was really shocked. She thought I was mistaken. I told her that this is one of the reasons why the Treaty and the Uluru Statement are so important.' Janine paused, then laughed. 'Now my younger cousins message me on Facebook, saying the work I am doing is cool.' Proudly she continued, 'My son Jordan, and daughters Kayla and Kayma, we talk regularly and now they do the same. They go and educate both their Indigenous and non-Indigenous friends.'

Janine then told me about a frustrating conversation she'd recently had.

'I was at a function, and a woman, she looked like she was from that TV show, *Real Housewives*. Anyway, she came to me and she asked me why I was at the function. It struck her that I'm Aboriginal. In a patronising tone that I have heard before in this situation, she said it was wonderful that I am Aboriginal. Next minute from behind me a random white guy says, "I'm sorry, did you just say that you're Aboriginal?" He said, "Can I tell you I am an honorary blood brother of the Navajo Indians." I'm like, Good for you, dude, that's America.

'Anyway, so we got talking about Treaty and the Uluru Statement. I explained how we need a treaty and a constitutionally enshrined Voice. Suddenly, the *Real Housewives* woman asks me, "Do you know any language?" When I said no, she said, "So you're not a real Aboriginal. The real Aboriginals are in the Northern Territory." I said, "You've been listening to Tony Abbott too much!"

'We've had the last two prime ministers say, "If you want to see a real Aboriginal, go to the Territory." Then she said, "I think it's really sad that your Elders have neglected to teach you the language, because in my family, my grandmother teaches me my language."

'I think the woman was Greek or Italian or something. I asked her how her grandmother would go teaching her language if she had seen firsthand her grandparents getting physically assaulted because they spoke it; if it was beat out of your parents and lost through the generations. I asked her, "Do you still think that it's my grandparents' fault?" This woman responded, quite exasperated as if I was silly, "Oh, well, surely there's a book somewhere …" It was a difficult conversation, and hurtful. I had to walk away.'

Janine is resilient. As she continued to tell the story, I was thinking how she and her father are alike. They both love a challenge.

'It's those people that we, as a collective – whether it's here in Melbourne or whether it's in the country – need to have conversations with. The woman came up to me again later. She said, "Look, I apologise if I offended you." Then she said, "I just cannot believe that nobody knows about this. Nobody knows how your language disappeared."

'I said, "Yeah, and nobody knows about the massacres that have happened around the country." She said, "What massacres?" I said, "Exactly." She said, "Well, why don't we read about these? Why isn't this stuff in the newspapers? Did massacres happen here in Victoria?" she asked.'

From one conversation, Janine moved a person from knowing nothing, to suddenly seeing how blind she had been. The truth was always there, in plain sight, but she hadn't seen it.

Janine laughed. 'What was fascinating was that Mr Honorary Navajo dude was just all about, "Let me show you my initiation tats." I said, "No thanks. I've got to go!"'

With time running out for the interview, I asked Janine to tell me about her experience at Uluṟu. She reflected on that life-changing experience. 'I couldn't stop pinching myself at first, because I was with these national leaders and community leaders, and here I am, Janine Coombs, who did nothing but work in community organisations. I raised my three kids, had my trials and tribulations. Suddenly here I was, a part of this convention with these amazing people, their cultures and the languages and the stories.

'We had the information, we were given the space to have the conversations – a culturally safe space. Everybody, whether they agreed or disagreed, was heard. We all came together as a collective and determined a common goal – a Makarrata Commission to do truth-telling around the atrocities that have happened and to establish a national Treaty framework, and a Voice to Parliament.

'I can't find the words to describe the feeling I had when we came together. It's a bit like when you first see Uluru, like there is a vastness that you really can't put into words. It was very similar to that for me.'

I mentioned to Janine later on that I thought she had a great way of describing the moment of consensus at Uluru. Seeing Uluru for the first time is simply indescribable, so immense is the spirituality, majesty and power. Comparatively, it's much easier to describe the immediate hopes and aspirations that we formulated in the heart of the nation, now written, clearly, in the Uluru Statement from the Heart. Janine's bright young eleven-year-old grandson, Carlos, described her work – the collective hopes that came from Uluru – with the honest simplicity of youth after seeing her on TV. Carlos said to Janine, his grandmother, 'Mum explained it to me, and I know what you are doing with all those other people. What you are doing is going to make life better for me and my brother.'

Janine didn't need to say it, I could read it from the pride in her eyes and the reach of her smile, but she told me anyway. 'When Carlos told me that, I thought, well, my job is done … that made the last three years of hard work worth it.'

RODNEY DILLON

Rodney Dillon is a Palawa Aboriginal man who lives near Hobart. He grew up in Nicholls Rivulet near Cygnet, in the south-west of Tasmania. Rod left school after year 7 and briefly worked in the bush as a timber logger before gaining his skills as a carpenter. For more than twenty years he worked in his trade at a zinc refinery, leading his fellow workers as a union delegate, and was then elected as a Commissioner for the Aboriginal and Torres Strait Islander Commission (ATSIC).

Rod has been a fighter his entire life. He has fought to be proud of his identity, and he has fought for the right to fish for his traditional foods. He is most proud of his fight for the reparation of 'the Old People', the remains stolen and shipped overseas as remnants of a race the colonisers thought they had wiped from the face of the earth.

Rod Dillon is a broad, strong looking man. His features are weathered and, at sixty-three years old, his body shows the signs of decades of hard work. When we started talking after I picked him up from his home, I quickly recognised that we spoke the same language – typically blue collar. He swore like a construction worker, as I could swear like a wharfie. I knew we'd have a good day on his homelands.

Rod suggested we should do the interview at Bruny Island. Only a stone's throw from the Tasmanian mainland, the island is significant because it is the birthplace of Truganini, who the colonisers said – somewhat triumphantly – was the last Tasmanian Aborigine. We drove the short journey from his home to the Bruny Island ferry terminal, and in a procession of cars, we rolled aboard to await departure. The ferry's ramp soon lifted, and we made our way towards our destination, blown by a stiff salty sea breeze.

'Just over there, that's where they cut Truganini's fella's hands off. They threw him into the sea and Truganini was forced to watch him drown.'

As he said these words, Rod gestured toward the deep blue waters just beyond the ferry's wake. The brutality of the event Rod described was stunning, but not surprising. The 'fella', Paraweena, was to be Truganini's husband. The vicious European invaders had lured them on to their row boat, promising to take them to Bruny Island from the Tasmanian mainland. After they left Truganini's partner to drown, they raped her repeatedly.

We sat in silence now and I thought about how I felt when I arrived in Tasmania. In a hushed tone I shared my experience with Rod. 'I felt it … when I left the airport. On that first hill, on the way in to Hobart. It's a haunting feeling here. I can feel there's been such an incredible amount of pain.' Rod looked at me with his grey-blue eyes and nodded. He knew how I felt.

Truganini's story is tragic and horrendous. Before she had reached her late twenties, her mother had been stabbed to death by a sailor, her stepmother kidnapped by mutinous convicts, her uncle was shot by a soldier, and her sisters were abducted and forced into sexual slavery by sealers. Her story is an example of the life and death of so many First Nations people in the time of the Tasmanian genocide. With little prospect of a life like that of her forebears, Truganini was coaxed into joining her remaining people on a mission under the 'Chief Protector', George Augustus Robinson, appointed by the governor. Robinson was under instruction to round up the remaining Tasmanian Aboriginals and take them from the mainland to island missions. Disease wrought destruction on the impoverished Aboriginal population of the missions. While the people perished, Robinson profited handsomely. With government support, he found Truganini and took her to the Flinders Island Wybalenna Mission.

Truganini left Wybalenna Mission for a time, searching for remaining family members in the north-west of Tasmania. The search ended in heartbreak, no family was found, and she returned to Flinders Island. Robinson was a prolific ethnographer, and Truganini assisted him in his field studies. She also helped him to convince her remaining people to live on the mission. She was probably concerned that they would come to the same fate as the rest of her family. Despite her contempt for the white settlers, ironically, when Robinson was almost speared by her people, Truganini saved his life, and the act was reported in a Tasmanian newspaper.

When Robinson was appointed as Chief Protector of Aborigines at Port Phillip in Victoria, Truganini and twelve of her people travelled with him. Robinson soon abandoned them, leading to Truganini and several others becoming bushrangers. They raided and robbed settlers, eventually killing two sailors in an altercation. When the posse was captured, two of the Aboriginal men were hanged in Melbourne's first official executions. Robinson came to the rescue though, arguing that the women were totally subject to the men. Truganini was freed from the hangman's noose.

She was then sent back to the Flinders Island mission before being moved again to a new settlement at Oyster Cove, close to where she lived in her much happier youth. There, she was able to revisit her childhood life, diving for shellfish and hunting. By 1869, it was said that Truganini and William Lanney were the last living 'full-blood' Aboriginal people in Tasmania. When Lanney died, his remains were mutilated, causing the aging Truganini concern. She said, 'I know that when I die the museum wants my body.' She made a dying wish, asking that the white establishment allow her to rest in peace. It wasn't to be. Two years after Truganini passed on, the Royal Society of Tasmania exhumed her remains. Her skeleton was displayed behind glass until 1947 – like a trophy of an extinct animal in a Tasmanian museum.

Rod Dillon's life story is connected to Truganini's. Not just because Rod is, like Truganini, a Tasmanian Aboriginal, but because in Truganini's final years – when she had returned to living some aspects of her traditional life – one of her joys was to care for and teach his grannies the ways of traditional life.

'My great great-grandmother, Fanny Cochrane, she used to run around with Truganini. Truganini didn't have any kids, and Fanny Cochrane had twelve kids. Truganini used to take some of the kids and teach them how to hunt and fish down here, to gather food. And she helped Fanny look after the kids. Helped her rear the kids a bit. That's how my family built a relationship with this part of the country. She was like a second mum. We've been there for about five to six generations, I think. I feel very strongly about this area here. It's part of who we are. When I go out to Truganini Lake, you can hear the old girl out there. You know she's there.'

When the ferry docked at Bruny Island, the barge ramp was lowered, and the convoy of cars rolled off. Rod and I drove a short distance to the largest sheep farm on the island, Murray Field, owned

by Weetapoona Aboriginal Corporation through the Indigenous
Land Corporation (ILC). Rod had done the hard yards to convince
the ILC to buy the farm in 2001. Today it's a successful business
that Rod is very proud of, though when it was first purchased, it
got tongues wagging. Overheard in the pub were comments such as,
'Did you hear that the Blacks bought Murray Field?' said in tones
laced with indignation.

When we stopped at the farm, Rod showed me the shearers' shed
and introduced me to Bruce Michaels, the farm manager. We then
drove to a little shack on the farm, nestled on a cliff overlooking a
small beach. On our way Rod joked, 'We're the only Black mob that
employs fourteen thousand white fellas.'

I can be a bit slow sometimes. With my eyebrows raised I asked,
'The farm employs that many people?' Rod laughed, looked at the
flocks of white sheep covering the rolling hills … 'Oh!' I laughed.
'Good one, mate!'

The little shack is shared with any mob that want to use it. I
had a look inside, basic but cozy. Rod said I was welcome to bring
my family to stay there, and I promised I would. Around the shack,
small field flowers were growing amongst the grass that was probably
kept in check by the 'white fella employees', and there was a fire pit,
no doubt essential in the colder weather. The view from the cliff
was amazing. In one direction were more cliffs and the entrance of
a small bay, and then open sea and distant islands, and in the other
direction, in a closely neighbouring bay was a tiny grey beach. To my
eyes, initially, the setting was peaceful, quaint, beautiful. But Rod
made me feel something else.

'You can feel Truganini's strength within this area. She was a
strong woman. It's like when you go out to the George Augustus'
Mission at Missionary Bay [Bruny Island].' Rod pointed across the
bay. 'Where he had our people out there. Our people died. They

died because there was no hope. They were taken off their Country, many weren't on their own land, they were sick, and they just died out there. They died of malnutrition, they died from ... they just had no will to live. White people just don't understand that we need to belong to our land and our waters.'

The disrespect shown by the white invaders extended beyond the mortal lifespan of the tormented Indigenous peoples. Not even the buried bones of the dead could rest on Country; at least, not for long. Many Aboriginal remains were collected for various 'scientific' purposes, or to be mounted and kept as trophies of a bygone era, as they did to Truganini despite her plea. Thousands of remains were shipped by the crate-load to British museums. Rod recalled learning this lesson as a boy, sparking a passion for repatriating the remains of the ancestors.

'When I was little, my mother took me out to Fanny's grave. I remember I was looking down at the grave, and Mum said, "There's a pretty fair chance that Fanny's not in this grave." I asked, "Why not?" She said, "Because these graves were disturbed not long after they were buried." Mum explained to me that the grave might have been robbed, or the boys didn't put her in the hole because they feared that she was going to be robbed, so she might be on the hill somewhere.

'As a kid, that had an effect on me to think that, Jesus, are we that poor that we can't keep our own people in the ground? How can we let people take our ancestors and not do something about it? Not stand and fight to get them back? I suppose, all my life, that's ... it still plays on my mind today. It's why I became passionate about repatriation.'

Rod took a lead role in repatriating Aboriginal remains when he became an elected Commissioner for Tasmania in the Aboriginal and Torres Strait Islander Commission. As the Chair of the Culture, Rights and Justice Committee, he pursued the remains and artefacts of his people, both in Britain and closer to home. Rod had some success – and that is the highlight of his life – but there are 'tens of thousands of stolen remains yet to come home to rest', which Rod bitterly laments.

'When you're bringing the remains home and you've got the Traditional Owners carrying the boxes, and they're sitting on the plane; when you're flying in and the first lights you see are the lights of Bruny, you think, I've helped these Old People and Young People. I've held their hand and helped bring them home. This is the first time they've been home for around a hundred and eighty years … you just feel that you have empowered the spirits to come back to where they belong. But there'll be some that we don't know where they belong. That'll take more work. They still need to come back. A lot will need to come back to Canberra, to a keeping place. A place that we should be running ourselves, not the government. We'll keep them properly.

'I don't think I'm a proper person until we get all our people back. I've felt I have a responsibility of making sure that those Old People come home in my time, and … well I'm sixty-three now, and I've come to the conclusion that they're not all going to come home in my lifetime. So, you've got to make sure that other people will fight to bring them back to the Country where they belong.'

Rod's passion has not dimmed. He identified that the struggle to bring the Old People home must go on and age is catching up with him. With that in mind, Rod hasn't only campaigned to bring the ancestors home to rest, he has been working on our future. In his latest work, through his role as Indigenous Rights Advisor for Amnesty International Australia, Rod has been supporting troubled youth to find their way to a better future. He is also campaigning to raise the age of criminality. In Australia, the age of criminality is only ten years old and Indigenous children are grossly disproportionately represented in the justice system. In the Northern Territory, for example, 100 per cent of the youth who are in incarceration are Indigenous. Rod told me of his frustrations.

'Sometimes I look at little kids in trouble, and I'm the only one there. It's not about me being the only one there, but it's about, they haven't got anyone. They haven't got anyone to represent them. They're by themselves, and it's the system. The system that caused us to go into poverty is now locking them up. They took their people off their land, and took their resources off them, putting them in third world conditions. You're only going to get out of people what you put into them. What better than to change a kid's mindset when they're ten to fourteen years old? That is the most crucial time in their life to change their way of thinking about where they're going, instead of putting them in the jail system with wardens.

'We should not be locking up kids. We're turning kids into criminals. It tears my heart every day to see kids becoming used to being in jail. They can't get decent work. Where do people go in poverty when they've got no money? What do they do? If you've got three kids and you've got no money, what are you going to do to feed them?'

I thought about how difficult it must be, growing up Aboriginal in Tasmania. The colonisation of Van Diemen's Land commenced in 1804 and the hostilities began immediately. By 1828, martial law was declared and by the 1830s, the surviving Indigenous people were rounded up and exiled to missions on Bruny and then Flinders Island, where many died from disease. The invasion and decimation of the Indigenous people inspired the classic 1898 science fiction novel, *The War of the Worlds*, by H. G. Wells.

> *The book was begotten by a remark of my brother Frank. We were walking together through some particularly peaceful*

Surrey scenery. 'Suppose some beings from another planet were to drop out of the sky suddenly,' said he, 'and begin laying about them here!' Perhaps we had been talking of the discovery of Tasmania by the Europeans – a very frightful disaster for the native Tasmanians. (H. G. Wells quoted in *The Strand Magazine*, 1920)

The disaster 'for the native Tasmanians' continued in to modern times. Rod shared an example of what it was like growing up as a Tasmanian Palawa boy. 'Everyone knew that we were Fanny Cochrane's family, so it wasn't about identifying, everyone knew we're Aboriginal. The first time I got on the bus to go to school, a fella said, "Get off the bus, you little black whore," and I looked up at the bus driver and he just grinned. That was my first day on the bus.

'My family have always been proud of being Aboriginal. We often talked about Fanny Cochrane and Truganini, here on Bruny, and … We always talked about it proudly.

'But once you got on the bus and went to school, it was like you had done something wrong, to be Aboriginal. The Christian Brothers, they had no respect for Aboriginal people. They talked about "Thou shall not steal", but they built their houses and their churches on stolen land. I couldn't work out how they could justify it. When I asked them I think they just thought I was a nasty little boy, or trying to blow up their system or something. To them we weren't real Aborigines, because we were light skinned. They said, "We'll bring some real Aborigines down here." *Who are we?* It was hurtful, that dilution of who you are. They weren't Christians, they were heathens, and their treatment of me at school and their behaviour towards me, I thought was really poor.'

For Rod, it was a long journey before he became an ATSIC Commissioner. He told me how he learnt to stand up for himself when he was chastised by the Christian Brothers at school; he wouldn't let them make him feel ashamed of who he was. He was the first in his family to get a trade, as a carpenter. Then as a union delegate, he learnt to stand up for his fellow workers. He led them on a tough, seventeen-day strike where they picketed the road in to the zinc works, fighting for better wages and conditions. On the picket, he learnt about the burden of responsibility that comes with leadership. And he told me how his perseverance has left a legacy – a right to gather traditional food. For many years, Rod fought a bitter battle with fisheries authorities and National Parks for a right to take a share of the resources in the sea. It was a battle with the 'red nosed men' – the white 'privileged men' – who hunted him down, often arresting him.

Rod told me epic stories of chases through the bushes in the fog, with the red nosed men's megaphones blaring, 'Sea Fisheries! Sea Fisheries!' As he spun his yarn, he stood up, excitedly gesturing toward distant bushes along the picturesque coast. It was as if he were ready to spring in to flight.

'They just wanted to get fines and get you wrapped up. They can do that, and they done it, and they gave us hell for years with it. They'd sit and wait, and watch. One time they arrested me off of a video I made of catching abalone, showing people that this is our culture. They actually counted how many abs was in the bag, and there were a few too many, so they arrested me off that, off an ABC report! I made the video, trying to educate judges and show them that this is my culture and I have a right to do it.

'I used to put a permit in every week to go and get fish, and they'd knock it back every week. It was about trying to stop you from practicing your culture. Though we eventually won a right to do it. But it was only because we continually embarrassed them that they ever acknowledged any rights.

'When I see kids doing it now, it makes me so proud. I'm happy.

I know it will keep going and they're not getting chased around or arrested for it. They're doing it legally. I had to fight to keep culture alive, illegally, it was hard. We were always paying fines. And my kids were feeling it at school.'

Rod made great personal sacrifices to make it easier for the youth to enjoy their traditional food, but his family shared his burden. It was later in the day, as Rod and I drove to the ferry terminal, homeward bound, that he told me a little more about the hardship his family experienced. He told me about his brave daughter. We had picked up a bag of the plumpest cherries that I have ever eaten in my life, and as he spoke, tears welled in my eyes and I felt like I had a seed in my throat.

'My daughter Bronwyn was in about grade seven. She just started high school, and the other girls was niggling her and saying, "Oh, your dad's going to jail. Your dad's a poacher and he's going to jail this time." So, she wrote a whole story about her father, that her father was a good man and that her father was providing fish and food for the family, and that this food has always been my dad's food. She got up at assembly and told the story. It was a pretty hard story. It was almost like your daughter was fighting the case for you. Yeah, it was a bit sad at the time.'

On our little journey together to Bruny Island, I learnt about a great man, Rodney Dillon. Typical of great people, Rod told me there's so much more to do. With a few traditional construction-worker expletives thrown into the mix for emphasis, we talked passionately about other issues that must be tackled – local Aboriginal people sharing control of the commercial fishery, creating work for the troubled youth, the discriminatory Community Development Program, water rights, and more about repatriation. Rod identified the issues and reiterated the need for a First Nations Voice enshrined in the Constitution.

'All those issues, our water rights, our sea rights, and repatriation. It's all about our right to negotiate with the government. If the government goes to negotiate with Aboriginals, who do they negotiate with? You? Me? No one? They can negotiate with whoever they like. They select our leaders. We don't. That's the problem.

'We need leaders voted in by *our* people, not just by a few here and there. We are weakened because our other representative bodies haven't been protected by the Constitution, protected by being in the rule book. We cannot let our Voice be wiped out by a vote from John Howard, or at the whim of whichever right-wing politician is in at the time. If it's that vulnerable, it's fucked.'

I agreed with Rod, and said to him, 'I couldn't have put it any better myself.'

ON THE WAY: A POSTAL TUBE

Hardwork, spontaneity, flexibility and opportunism – that is what it took to bring the Uluṟu Statement from the Heart to thousands of people who may otherwise have never seen or heard of it in the early days of the campaign.

I would lug the Uluṟu Statement canvas with me everywhere so that I could keep a close eye on it, and so that the eyes of potential supporters would see it too. The content of the wearied, taped-together postal cylinders was too valuable, too important to our campaign to just sit in my wardrobe at home or in a hotel room. There were several senior politicians who – even with their well-honed body language skills – struggled to hide an eye-roll when I would turn up at yet another event with the Uluṟu Statement in hand.

When parting with the precious cargo at the oversize baggage counter, I would look the airport staff in the eye, as if to say, 'You have my life in your hands.' I'd feel separation anxiety on the flight, and I was always nervous waiting to be reunited with it at my destination.

In more than eighteen months of travel with the Uluṟu Statement, it went on a different flight from me once and got lost and then found amongst baggage in the airport twice.

I almost lost the canvas one afternoon when I sat down in the lobby of my hotel. I urgently needed to send an email before taking the lift up to my room, so I laid the mailing tube down by my side. The email complete, I went up to my room and got dressed for dinner. Walking back through the lobby on the way out, around an hour later, the receptionist called to me, 'Excuse me, Mr Mayor, did you forget something?'

'No,' I said.

'What about that long tube you always carry around?'

My heart dropped. 'Oh shit! *Thank you*! Do you know how valuable that thing is?' was my abashed reply.

It was an honour to be trusted to take the Uluṟu Statement from the Heart – the most sacred document in the nation – to the people of Australia. Each time I rolled the canvas out on an office floor, red dirt or grass; each time I hung it to display at a festival, conference or fair, the people's movement for a First Nations Voice gained momentum.

The Uluṟu Statement's physical presence helped to inspire the beginnings of an unstoppable people's movement. Five years on, the sacred canvas travels much less. With a referendum for a Voice now visible – a light shone on our destination by Prime Minister Albanese – the Statement will be carried in our hearts to other Australians, whom we will ask to vote 'Yes'.

You may choose to memorise the Statement as I have. Saying its words is a powerful way to move people. My hope for the Uluṟu Statement is that it will soon rest, with Voice, Treaty, Truth achieved, by the rock and the families who share its name. Uluṟu will become a place of pilgrimage for all the people who helped Australia find its collective heart.

Moon Bird and Pakana, Tasmania

DARLENE MANSELL

Darlene is a Moon-Bird, Pakana (northern Tasmanian Aboriginal) woman who was born on Flinders Island, a large island in the Furneaux Islands group north of Tasmania. Her family were taken to the Furneaux Islands to live on a mission because they were Aboriginal. When Darlene was four years old, her family moved to the north of Tasmania.

Darlene's father was a great Aboriginal leader, and her mother – a committed, strong and loving woman – was responsible for the establishment of the Aboriginal Elders Council in Launceston. Darlene is a proud mother of two boys, Rory, in his thirties, and Rulla, in his mid-twenties. She gave birth to Rulla on Country in the traditional way, which is just one example of how Darlene has pushed the boundaries throughout her life. She is excited that soon she will be a grandmother for the first time.

Darlene continues to be an activist for Indigenous and women's rights, and she is learning her language, which was denied to her parents by the missionaries.

Short in stature, and tall in pride. This was my first impression of Darlene Mansell as I walked into the Hobart Tasmanian Aboriginal Health Centre to meet her. She immediately embraced me with warmth and solidarity, even though we hadn't met in person before. With a beaming smile, Darlene took me around the health centre, introducing me to the health workers and other staff before we found a quiet space for the interview.

Darlene is of the Moon Bird people. The moon bird is another name for the mutton bird, or the short-tailed shearwater bird. In the Palawa/Pakana language, the bird is called Yolla. Darlene told me about the bird that sustained her people for millennia, before colonisation and up to this very day.

'The moon bird travels an amazing journey, actually, around the world. It's a global cultural icon to us Indigenous peoples. When it leaves our islands it goes to Japan, to the Ainu people, the Aboriginal people of Japan, who harvest it. The bird then goes to the Arctic, where the First Nations people in the Arctic eat it. It comes down the West Coast of America, and it comes across to the Pacific and to Māori country. They love the moon birds too. Really, it's quite culturally significant, the little moon bird.

'We harvest the moon bird on the islands between Tasmania and the mainland. There's lots of rookeries on those islands. Some of those islands have been returned to us by the Government of Tasmania. We manage them. It's still really significant to our culture and our community to go out in the season, for four to six weeks, harvesting our little bird. It brings good tucker, it brings good health, and good stories.'

Darlene's parents were both born at the mission on Cape Barren Island. It was established as much to remove the remaining Aboriginal

Tasmanians from the main colony, as it was to Christianise and assimilate them.

'We were forcibly removed, constantly, from island to island. You could call the missions in them days prison camps. Wybalenna was the mission on Flinders Island established by George Augustus Robinson. He was commissioned to remove our traditional people, the last remaining ones, from the main island of Tasmania, and he did so by lying to them.

'My parents were married on Flinders Island. They lived in a tent to start off with, then a little humpy before my dad built a little wooden house on Flinders Island.'

I shuddered at the thought of how cold it must've been. In the late nineteenth century, many of the Aboriginal people worked hard to establish farms on Flinders and Cape Barren, harvesting the mutton bird to support a meagre existence. They also wanted to buy land, however, they were at a great disadvantage compared with the white farmers. Coin was hard to come by, and the authorities purposely put barriers up to any progress by the Aboriginal people. As the colony expanded and the white settlers bought the more productive and liveable land on Flinders, the Aboriginal population was forced out to other nearby islands. Darlene's parents moved to Cape Barren Island before they moved to the mainland of Tasmania after Darlene was born.

'I was born on Flinders Island, and when I was four, we relocated from the Furneaux. There wasn't a lot of employment for Aboriginal people on Flinders Island at that point. It was a transient time, I guess. So, after the mission was closed down in 1945, a lot of the mob came off, and there was a big exodus down to northern Tasmania and the rest of the Tasmanian mainland.

'We relocated to Launceston. Initially, for a bit of time, Mum and Dad were doing the seasonal fruit picking work. I remember moving to a suburb in northern Tasmania, within Launceston, called Invermay, the swamp. That's where a lot of Aboriginal people went. Very working class. A lot of people made their homes there. I remember those times, when I was four, coming off the islands and living at my dad's parents' place, Granny and Granddad.

'Dad was from a large family of eighteen, and more. Granny had lost some twins. So, when we lived there, there were three generations of people living in a two-bedroom little twin cottage. Not even a cottage, but a little two-bedroom place, a big place for Invermay. So, I had my grandparents, about five uncles. Then there was Mum and Dad and us youngins. We adapted because we had to, us Black fellas. Eventually, Mum and Dad were given a Housing Commission house, so we moved into our own family home. I grew up in Launceston, northern Tasmania. I went to primary and high school there.'

As Darlene told me about her family background, I began to see why she had a reputation for staunchly standing up for her beliefs. Before I travelled to Tasmania to interview her, I had heard that at the Tasmanian Constitutional Regional Dialogue, she had chastised the men when she felt that the women were not being heard.

'My parents brought me up with men and women's business, and mutual respect. I won't stand for misogynistic attitudes from Black men or white men. I think there should be more women up front. On the first day of the dialogue, some of the women weren't speaking up. I was like, no, you brother boys, you've got to stop this. I was saying, "Look, my bottom line is that women should have our voice."'

Darlene backs her words up with action. I learnt that she had recently been in Hobart, down from northern Tasmania, to support her family and the community in a difficult time. Two days before we met, a young Aboriginal girl, only thirteen years old, had been arrested at her cousin's house and detained in the Hobart police station under suspicion of breaking a curfew. The girl was strip searched by police and held in custody overnight until she could appear before the magistrate. After a night in prison, the magistrate ruled that this thirteen-year-old child was not under a curfew, she had been needlessly imprisoned and strip searched, isolated and humiliated, and traumatised from the experience. The girl's grandmother told the media that the girl had initially refused to 'remove her underpants', although she eventually did so when she was given a hospital gown to wear overnight.

Darlene was helping to care for the girl, to keep her from doing something harmful to her own wellbeing. I was angry to hear how the young girl had been treated; I thought that it was likely her harsh treatment was because she is Aboriginal. As we discussed the girl's experience, I could see that Darlene was saddened. She brought her tough and formidable protective barrier down to share her recollection of growing up Aboriginal in Tasmania, as aliens on their own land.

'I think most of us in Tasmania from my generation, we were denied a claim on who we were. It didn't matter what we said. I grew up being called a half-caste, a quarter-caste, a coon, a nigger, an abo, a coco, a gin, a truga. It goes on and on. I could come up with a whole dictionary of words, the way we were verbally treated … and I couldn't work it out, because one minute they're suggesting I'm a descendant, I'm a half-caste. But on the other hand, they're calling me a nigger and a coon and an abo. I'm thinking, I haven't got this confused. I know who I am. I think you mob got this confused. So, I always thought of my teachings from my parents, I guess. They instilled very strong values in us, myself and my siblings.

'So my attitude was, the way to beat them, is join them, in terms of intellect. So as much as I was bullied in the schoolyard, I was as smart as the smartest whitey in the class. That was my way. I thought, no, I'm going to be as smart as you mob reckon you are. That has been my way of fighting back. I can buy a car. I can buy a house. I can do whatever you fellows want to do. Even though you took my land, even though you tried to take my culture … even though you took our language, I'm still resilient enough to sit at the table and hold my ground.'

As Darlene built her confidence, she began to look for ways to help her people. She'd go to community meetings with her parents before leaving high school at the age of fifteen to add her energy to a burgeoning land rights movement.

'Us Black fellas were starting to get together. I think it was in the early '70s. I went from grade nine high school and ended up coming down to Hobart and working at what was called the Aboriginal Information Service. We had just created the Aboriginal Legal Service. I was the first Aboriginal in Tasmania to be a legal secretary. Since then, I have been involved with different groups, organisations, unions. Deep down, I am a Lefty. I could almost say, an extreme Lefty. We need those voices to balance this right-wing, and even the centre, attitude. But we've also got to be strategic about it.'

The '70s must have been an exciting time to be an activist. There came a new-found confidence on the back of an emphatic 1967 referendum win, and there were pockets of Indigenous dissent throughout Australia that – whether successful or not – blazed a path for progress. As Darlene continued, I realised that her view on the way forward has come from her decades of experience.

'I think we are missing a collective energy that we should be aspiring to, as we did back in the day. We've been divided into small groups. We've got to have solidarity, get back to that. I mean, you don't have to be an Aboriginal person to support Aboriginal rights. We're getting some good leverage with non-Aboriginal people really supporting us, from unions and other organisations, all sorts of people who realise we need to right the wrongs. But reconciliation should not be symbolic. It's all right to have a Reconciliation Action Plan and do things like flying the Torres Strait flag and the Aboriginal flag, but really, that's all symbolism, and it's nothing tangible for us.

'I think if we can get more momentum … because we just get caught up in our day-to-day survival. All these movements and campaigns, we lose track of them. But I think the Uluru Statement is inspiring. I've heard media, a lot of white fellas constantly referring to the Uluru Statement. I think that's good. It's moved both Black fellas and white fellas.

'I have the Uluru Statement framed up north at home. I was really stoked when I first heard it. I think getting that outcome was a lot of hard work done by a lot of people up there at Uluru. I really believe in the Uluru Statement and it's gaining momentum, because even white fellas now talk of it. Us Black fellas need to be talking about it more. It's like our mission statement now.

'Like I say to my sons – and Rulla is the youngest one, Rory is the oldest – they're saying, "Mum, we need to know about history and culture." I say I can refer to a lot of documents from deaths in custody. I was involved with that campaign many years ago, with uncles passed and aunties passed. But the Uluru Statement, see what that says, that's your platform now to go further.' Darlene looked me in the eyes and continued, 'I think it's amazing what you've done by taking that Uluru Statement canvas around. I think for social media, for these young ones now, they can grasp on to the Uluru Statement. It's the heart. It's the heart.'

As Darlene finished talking about her sons and the Uluru Statement, I felt a deep admiration for her. Darlene wasn't at Uluru for the First Nations Constitutional Convention, yet she has grabbed hold of the hope that the Uluru Statement provides and has held it up as the guiding light for all of us, Aboriginal or other. She was unsurprised and undeterred when Malcolm Turnbull dismissed the proposal. Rather, Darlene spoke to me about her hopes for a new government, and a leader with the vision of her much-admired former prime minister, Paul Keating. She admired Paul Keating because he 'innately and tangibly wanted to achieve something'.

Before we ended the interview, I asked Darlene, 'If you could say one thing to the Australian people, what would it be?'

'Oh, you've put me on the spot! I want to articulate it properly for the way I feel!' Darlene gave me a mockingly chastising look and laughed. She paused and thought for a moment, and then said confidently, 'Reconciliation must be meaningful. We've got to make something of this opportunity. I want to go into the future – my first grand baby will be born in a couple of months – I want to be telling my grandchild stories about the Uluru Statement. My grandbaby might one day be elected as a Moon Bird Pakana Voice!'

Adnyamathanha and Wangkangurru, South Australia

LAVENE NGATOKORUA

Lavene Ngatokorua is the unpaid CEO of the Davenport Community Council and is a board member for both the South Australian Native Title Services and the Adnyamathanha Traditional Lands Association. She is also the Director of both Umeewarra Aboriginal Media and Vimba Warta Civil and Mining, which was named the 2018 Port Augusta NAIDOC Organisation of the Year.

The theme for NAIDOC in 2018 was 'Because of her we can'. Fittingly, in that year, Lavene was recipient of the Port Augusta NAIDOC Lifetime Achievement Award.

Lavene's Aboriginal name is Marrukanha. She is an Adnyamathanha and Wangkangurru woman. Her father's people, the Adnyamathanha, are of the Flinders Ranges in South Australia. The Wangkangurru people are a First Nation of the Simpson Desert region. Her moiety is Mathere, the south wind.

Lavene explained her moiety. 'We have north and south wind. Dad's moiety is Ararru for the north wind, so when my mother married in, because she isn't from Adnyamathanha Country, she took the opposite moiety from him, Mathere or, south wind.

'I was put in the home when I was about two months old. From what I understand, my parents went shopping and when they came back I was already gone. It was about 1968 when I was put in there.'

The home that Lavene refers to is the Umeewarra Mission Children's Home, which was situated about four kilometres north of Port Augusta in South Australia. The Christian Brothers opened the mission in 1937 as a home and school for Aboriginal children. When Lavene was taken, the government had assumed control of it and renamed it Davenport Reserve. The Umeewarra Mission Children's Home continued to operate within the reserve until it was closed in 1995.

Lavene wasn't a delegate at the Uluru First Nations Constitutional Convention, nor was she a participant in the regional constitutional dialogue in South Australia. However, her nephew, Dwayne Coulthard, was elected from the Adelaide Regional Dialogue and went to the historic Uluru Convention. Dwayne is also an Adnyamathanha man. I had caught up with him at the ALP National Conference in December 2018. He was there seeking support for his people's struggle to stop a nuclear waste dump being built on their Adnyamathanha Country, close to the Flinders Ranges. At a rally for the First Nations Voice I organised during the conference, Dwayne made an inspiring speech in front of 400 supporters. He was an impressive speaker, powerfully expressing the importance of enshrining a First Nations Voice in the Australian Constitution, and relating it to his people's struggle at home. Later that afternoon, the Labor Party officially included a commitment to Voice, Treaty, Truth in the Party Platform.

The first time Lavene and I met was at the National Native Title

Conference in Broome in June 2018. Lavene and the delegation of Traditional Owners from South Australia strongly supported me when I led a debate for a resolution from Native Title holders that stated support for the Uluru Statement from the Heart. With Lavene's encouragement, the resolution was carried.

When we met again to do this interview, I quickly realised that her story was different from any other I had heard before. Although she was stolen, she was moved to a mission in the same community as where her mother and father lived. This caused some confusion for little Lavene, especially as other children were returned to their family or sent for adoption.

'I grew up at the "home", Umeewarra. But what's unique about this place, is that the children's home was in the middle of the Aboriginal reserve [Davenport]. I was stolen, but to me, I was just another kid. So I didn't know that terminology. There was a lot of confusion. I sort of considered myself throughout the time as the "forgotten people", because I'd seen other children getting returned back to their families.

'Kids can be cruel. I remember I was sitting on the trampoline, it was about six metres by probably five metres, it was huge. I remember sitting on the bar and looking over and I saw these two people looking across the football field. This fellow was waving his hand in the air and he was pointing over and I can hear him saying, "McWilliams, you're not gonna own my kids!" McWilliams, we called him Mr Mac, he was just a missionary. Then one of the kids goes, "That's your father!" "That's not my father!" Cause it was just two drunken fellows walking home across the oval. What did "mother" and "father" mean to me? We just had missionaries. We didn't have mothers and fathers. We just had brothers and sisters. To even say it like that, it caused confusion for me. What's a mother? What's a father anyway? I don't know what that is. At five or six years old, and living in the mission since the age of two months, they are just words. That stayed in my mind, like it's imprinted on your brain. But that's all I knew in terms of family, I knew I had a sister and that we came from the same parents.'

Her voice was sombre as Lavene described her childhood.

'I have seven other siblings. Six of my siblings were given back to the family, me and my sister were left in the home. That's why I say we were "forgotten", because the welfare had come and given them back. Families took them but not us.'

I asked Lavene, 'Do you know if your mum or your dad tried to get you back?'

'I did ask my mum when I was about twenty-four years old. I said to her, "I want to know, Mum, I need to know. Not to judge you, Mum, it's not about that. But I want to hear from you. I know the welfare story because I hold those records [as CEO of the local council]. But I want to hear your story. Not their version, your version." She said, "I don't want to talk about it." This was her first reaction to me. It was while I was pregnant with my son. I said to Mum, "As a mother, I'm asking you as my mother to tell me your story." She said, "Lavene, I knew every day where you were, and I knew you were safe." I never questioned her after that.'

Lavene told me about how, as she grew older, she didn't know anything different to mission life. She feared being given back. 'The welfare people started to get back involved, saying now you're going to go back with your parents. But my parents were strangers. This is all we've known in the children's home. You're going to uproot me now and take me this way, you want to give us to strangers. We don't know these people!

'We were the opposite of children hiding from being stolen by white welfare workers. Every time the welfare car would come to the mission, us kids would scatter into the sand-hills and run away, because we didn't want to leave, the mission was our home. We were also scared that they were going to put us with families that we don't even know. I remember going out to families, but I ran back to the mission. I escaped about five times from different families. Escaping and going back into the mission. So they left me there.'

Lavene told me that her personal experience at the 'home' wasn't a bad one, though she thought this wasn't common. 'I can only talk about my experience. There were a lot of other people that had bad experiences. I can't tell their story though, it's not my story to tell.' She looked up and smiled as she started to talk about a much fonder memory – a visit from an Adnyamathanha law man, her grandfather.

'I remember my grandfather coming up, and that's my dad's father. He'd come up and bring chips and cool drinks and lollies for me and my younger sister, and he'd also bring extra lollies.' Lavene laughed. 'He'd say, "That packet is for the other kids. But they mustn't share yours. This is for you."

'My grandfather would sit there and tell stories, and to me at that time they weren't significant. I was probably about six or seven. Though I fondly remember he would be pointing towards the hills, and he'd say to me, "You know, this is not your home. Your home is over there in those hills." At that time, I didn't know how important that was to me. Now, I know what he meant, but back then, all I knew was that it was important to him. I would look over there as a five or six-year-old and think, I'm going to get there one day ... I remember saying it to the other kids, "That's my home over there. See those hills? That's where I've come from." I didn't really know what that meant. But that gave me a sense of ... it sewed a seed into me. That's all I remember of my grandfather. Later in life, I learnt that he was a senior law man, he was the holder of Adnyamathanha law visiting two of his grandchildren. We weren't forgotten. He came out to see us. We were a big family, he had fourteen children. It was like he was there to tell us, "You're still one of us. The system's not going to control you." But I didn't know the importance of that then.'

Lavene loves going back to Country and enjoys creative photography. Her photography is a means to remember significant moments in her past and also a way of making political statements. We stopped talking for a moment as she searched her phone for some examples of her work. When I looked at the photos I could see why she was proud. The images were clear and crisp, and the stories that they depicted were easy to understand and powerful. We chatted about how she ingeniously created some of the effects, and we laughed at the weird and wonderful antics that happen behind the scenes. Her assistants, for example, will hurl and pour and fan the elements across a picture to create a compelling and dramatic effect. Then she told me about a photo she produced in memory of her grandfather.

'I wanted to recreate the memory of my grandfather's visit. I got my father to be the stand-in for my grandfather and my niece and my other two nieces, my brother's kids, to stand in for my siblings and me. I asked my father to point to the hills, like my grandfather did when he would visit. I wasn't looking at my dad as I was working, setting the scene. My dad's eighty years old. He's frail and shakes, he can't stand on one leg too long.'

Lavene's face softened and she frowned. Her voice hushed slightly and she said, 'As I was working, my father in a really quiet voice said, "You know girl, we never forgot you ... I never forgot you." He said, "I always worried. I always wanted to come and get you, but welfare were coming in and saying I wasn't right, I wasn't fit." He said, "A lot of the drinking I did was as a result of all my kids being taken ..." I didn't look up at him ... Later, as we were packing and walking away, he was talking, he said, "You know, it broke us as your mother and father. We'd be laying down talking, 'We had all our kids and then there's nothing.'" He said, "There's not a day that goes by that we don't …" He said, "We love each and every one of you."'

Lavene took a deep breath, shook off the frown, and continued. 'It was like my dad having his time to tell me his side of the story, and to be okay with telling it. Back when I left the home, I never called them Mum and Dad. I would just start a conversation because I thought they hadn't earned the title. So why give it? That was what I was thinking. So, I had to practice calling them Mum and Dad in front of a mirror. It was strange on my lips. I have a good relationship with my dad, I love my dad, and I had a good relationship with my mum in a short time there.' Lavene's mother passed away soon after they had reconnected.

Lavene has been an activist for most of her life. She has been a dedicated spokesperson and leader for her community, not only leading from the streets, but also from within the Davenport Council as a volunteer CEO (the Abbott government, in their sweeping funding cuts to Aboriginal communities, stopped funding to the Davenport Council). She told me how from within the system, she has fought the 'seagulls'. 'Seagulls' is her label for the comfortable bureaucracy from the cities, and the non-Indigenous contractors who fatten their bank accounts with profit – sometimes by dubious means.

She also talked about the work she did outside the system, leading protests and being someone the community turns to as an organiser of effective public dissent against detrimental government decisions. Lavene found out much later in her life that her father was also an activist. She sat taller as she told me about him.

'My dad was a big fellow. Like a real big stand tall fella with a lot of big curly hair. Big curly hair!' She laughed. 'There's a picture in the Davenport Council office where I work. It's a photo of a group of fellas who went to Canberra on a delegation from the Davenport Reserve. It was about 1965. I remember Dad talking about it a long time ago. In it is Charlie Perkins. So I said, "Hey, Dad, all this time I was doing all the freedom fighting, and you were the first one going to Canberra, meeting with the Minister, fighting for Aboriginal Rights! Back then!" That shocked me.'

Lavene had always thought her father was too quiet to be an activist. With pride in her eyes, she described how he was quietly political.

'My father, if you walked into his house – even in the afternoon – he watches Question Time in Parliament. He watches everything about the government, he makes notes. He knew that the demise of the Aboriginal and Torres Strait Islander Commission [ATSIC] was coming. He said to his brothers who were running the community back then, he said, "Mark my word, they're gonna get rid of ATSIC." He said, "There's been different questions coming in and you need to set the community up in case it happens." One of his brothers who worked for the regional council said, "No, no, no, it's not gonna happen." Sure enough, ATSIC went down.'

Lavene told me how today, her father is talking about another change coming. He talks of constitutional change. With the lessons from the past in mind, I asked Lavene to digress to a story she had told me earlier that evening. A story about an old man she'd met when she worked at an old people's home. Like her father, he'd also used the tools of the colonisers to advance his people.

'When I was fifteen, I worked at Wami Kata old folks home. I used to want to hear the stories from the old people. But them old people just thought me as a nuisance! The massacres were in their life time. So within that conversation, we're talking about massacres that's not a long way back. Those old people were witness to the waterholes being poisoned, and they're telling the story … like the story of the person on the chair in that photo.'

Lavene referred to one of her photos she had showed me on her phone. It was of a man whose parents were in the old black-and-white photos, with chains around their neck.

'My grandmother had told me the story about his parents. She saw them walking with the chains around their neck. I remember one old man there, he was a survivor of a massacre. He used to limp around. What happened was, when he was hiding under the dead bodies [during the massacre], he got speared in the leg because the white fellas used the spears to stab everybody, to make sure they were dead.

'Before I met that old man, when I was about fifteen years old, I asked one of the missionaries, "Mr Mac, why some white fellas stopped our people from talking language?" He said, "I can't talk about anyone else, but we didn't stop anybody talking language." This Mr Mac, he was being taught law by the Elders. He came to the mission when he was twenty-six, I think. So he was a young fellow and the old Aboriginal men were teaching him. Mr Mac said that those old men said to him, "You are in charge of our kids. Whenever they talk the language, you stop them. They need to learn English in order for them to understand how the white people are working. Because once they learn that, then they will be able to make change. But if they don't learn, they're not going to be moved."

'When I heard that, I was a bit thrown in two ways – conflicted. Because, one, the language stopped, and the connection, but on the other hand, he's saying you learn, because this big movement that's happening, it's going to be here one day. Our kids need to learn to live by that. This was back in the 1960s, that was when that conversation was happening [between the old man and the missionary]. The old fellow was talking about what it is we've been talking about today. We need to learn how – by educating ourselves – to be more strategic. I think that's what our old men were saying. Learn the ways. Learn the ways and that way you will know what to do. You will understand them. For me he's telling us – things are going to change, and you need to be able to understand in order to make changes for yourself to live in this world. To coexist. Even back then, in the '60s they saw it.'

Like Lavene's father said, 'Change is coming.' Though as her father learnt, change doesn't come easy.

Lavene's dedication to her community and her people has taken its toll on her family. She lamented how she has missed much of her son's early years. When her son Drey turned twenty-one, she said she looked at him with fresh eyes and thought, There's no longer this little boy, there's a man standing in front of me. When did this happen? How did you grow up?

She said, 'We think our family will always be there. I come back home and I'm exhausted. I go to bed, I'm up early, I'm going to work. I kiss my son on the head, or he's lying in the bed with me, and suddenly that time is gone?'

Lavene reflected on her life of service and activism and her faltering relationship with her husband. She was frowning again and her sadness began to well in her eyes. 'I can remember always standing in front of people, advocating for this or that – meeting with government people here, ministers over there. But what's happened in my life? I was married for twenty years. Fighting for the community took a toll on my marriage.'

Lavene's voice began to falter. 'The family, we go our separate ways and … I became so consumed in the fight for community that I didn't even fight for my own family. I've got to say that my ex-husband and son have always been there. They've always been in the background. And my sister … It's like I used them. My sister will often say to me, "If only the community knew how much tears you've cried for them …"' As Lavene spoke of the tears that she had cried for her people, it was as though she had unwillingly summoned them forth. I reached out to comfort her. She didn't look down but held her head up, as if she were staring down her emotions. With determination, she continued with a powerful summation.

'I think there's a complacency amongst us. Where's this voice? We are working too much as an individual unit or groups. We are working individually and not coming together and creating a united voice. When I went to the Native Title Conference in Broome, it's like our people are frightened that if they speak up, we're going to lose this or lose that from the government. We're in a trance. It's like we need to get a couple of big dynamites in there. Not blow us up!' She laughed. 'We need a good kick! Jump start, maybe I should say that!

'I remember when you were talking for the Uluru Statement motion of support. There were some people that got up, they really got the fight from what you were saying. And then there were other people who said, "Ay, that's a bit of trouble making."

'Not trouble making!' she said quickly. 'They need to understand the stories! That's the problem I think that we have, Thomas. We're becoming so complacent and numb to what is going on around us and we need to get out of that. It's like we've been given an ether to keep us asleep. We need to break out of that trance and become more voiceful. The sleeping ether, the main ingredient of that was getting rid of ATSIC. We're still in that effect.

'When they took away ATSIC, they then got rid of a lot of Aboriginal organisations. They got rid of a lot of them and they gave the funding and control to the non-Indigenous organisations. So they were giving the money to them, which killed off a lot of Aboriginal organisations that spoke up at a political level. The Howard government silenced them.

'What you said at the Native Title Conference caused a stir amongst the people, it caused conversation. There were people talking about it after, and then in some of our circles, people were saying, "So what do you think?" People were talking about their own opinions. That was good. I said, "Well, that's where it all starts!"

'We need to get together. That waking up from that slumber. It needs to come and it needs to come quicker. Because I believe something – we haven't got a large window of opportunity as Aboriginal people while there is support in the wider community – and we need that wider community to be supportive of us in the lead up into a referendum. We need that talk, we need people to get behind us and that's not always going to be there. We can't do the "Should of, could of, would of". That tribe is bigger than anybody else. Where's the "doers"? The "doers" are only small in number. But the "Should of, could of, would of" is huge.

'There's a raging bush fire that has been imposed on us, but we're all getting tired fighting our individual spot fires. When you look at the Country Fire Service who fight the big bushfires, they work together. We need to be strategic, like the firemen. They create firebreaks, they change the course of the fire. We need to do that. We need to work together.

'You know what, although I'm tired. The fight, I've been in this fight, marching and doing all that since I was nineteen. I just turned fifty-one yesterday. But you know what? Would I change what I've done? No. I love my community. I love what I've done, I love where I work. The experience of life has taught me not to be selfish, but to honour the people. I'm honouring my father, my grandfather, my great-grandfathers and mothers who fought for us to be here. I have a real respect and I don't know, sometimes, I can't even get the word right. I don't even know what the word is for it? For what they have done to give me place? Legacy? I will continue their legacy.'

Before we went our own way that night, I gave Lavene a big hug. I quietly replied to her question about the word she was searching for, 'Lavene, I think you got the word exactly right – "legacy". You are continuing their legacy.'

ON THE WAY:
SACRED HEART

Thrumm! Thrumm! The deep, reverberating island warup (drums) sounded through the chorus of voices as three pairs of young men entered the open-air circle shaped by an excited crowd. Decorated in their island skirts of calico and zha-zhi (palm fronds), they moved with practiced rhythm, mimicking the seabirds celebrated in the dance with precise steps, springing and leaping.

The dhari (headdresses), edged with brilliant white feathers, hypnotised the audience as they flicked from side to side with the sharp head movements of the dancers. The dhari is a symbol of our culture. I sat amongst hundreds of fellow islanders with connections to all nineteen Torres Strait Island communities. The Winds of Zenadth Cultural Festival was in full swing – four days of song, dance and feasting.

I stepped away to take a call from a friend, Harriet Dorante, phoning from her workplace at the Sacred Heart Primary School. Harriet had arranged for me to bring the Uluru Statement to a special school assembly organised just for the occasion.

I had met Harriet on Gurindji Country in late 2017. She was at the Freedom Day Festival, celebrating fifty-one years since the Gurindji people walked off Lord Vestey's Wave Hill Station, sparking a nine-year strike for fair wages and conditions and land rights. She was participating in a leadership course run by the Australian Rural Leadership Foundation. When she saw the Uluṟu Statement, she was eager for me to come to Thursday Island to show the children. My attendance at the Winds of Zenadth Cultural Festival provided that opportunity.

With Harriet's summons, I quickly rolled up the Uluṟu Statement and briskly walked to the school. On my way, I managed to get a hold of Rhanna Collins, a producer and executive editor for National Indigenous Television (NITV), which was covering the festival. I thought it would be a good opportunity for NITV to film some of the Thursday Island kids with the Uluṟu Statement, and I suggested they come along.

After a cup of tea with the principal, and hasty checks for parental authority for filming and photos, the children gathered with excitement in the little assembly area. With impeccable timing, the NITV stars rolled in to join us. Actor Aaron Fa'aoso had the kids laughing and presenter JP Janke began reporting. I was thinking, *How am I going to make constitutional reform interesting for primary school students?*

While Harriet's ten-year-old daughter, Beka Lily, held the canvas, I kept the explanation brief and simple. The children sat quietly and listened intently. When the talking was done, they gathered around, touched the artwork, asked questions and pointed out familiar names and First Nations. As I have learnt since, children quickly understand why Indigenous peoples should have a Voice in the 'rule book'. They wonder why it hasn't happened already.

A highlight of the tour came next. A brave little girl, Ahliyah Jia, volunteered to interview me one-on-one for NITV. Their guest reporter! After only one practice run, and with the instructions to ask whatever came to mind, she absolutely nailed the interview. NITV had discovered a future star finding her sparkle on Thursday Island.

Wagedagam Kabuai, Torres Strait

GABRIEL BANI

Gabriel Bani is a Torres Strait Islander. His island is Mabuiag in the Western Island group. His tribe is named for the north-west wind, Wagedagam Kabuai (major tribe) and he is from a direct line of chiefs. Gabriel's totem is the Koedal, the crocodile.

At one end of the Ken Brown Memorial Oval, the home of Rugby League on Waiben (Thursday Island), the green grass ends immediately after the dead ball zone with a bitumen road. On the other side of the road is the beach, where golden sand meets the turquoise waters of the Torres Strait. The beautiful setting is fitting for the well-loved sport of Rugby League. In the Torres Strait, entire teams, their support staff and fans will pile in to small dinghies, whatever the weather, to congregate for the numerous Rugby League competitions.

In 2018, the Ken Brown Oval hosted the only competition that surpasses the vigour and excitement generated by island-style Rugby

League – the competition of island dance at the Winds of Zenadth Cultural Festival. The festival is held on Thursday Island every two years. While the island dancers are competitive, ultimately it's all about a celebration of culture and the coming together of families and friends from across the region. In 2018, the theme was, 'Stand Strong: Culture is our Foundation'. Nineteen dance troupes from all parts of the Torres Strait and the North Peninsula (Cape York) took part.

Attending the festival is an amazing experience. The array of dancers, the colours and varieties of dress, and the incredible dancing props that depict the constellations, weaponry, cloud formations, and modern-day interactions with patrol boats and pearling luggers – the list goes on – are all designed with flourish, flair and ingenious gadgetry. Stalls sell the artwork and jewellery of the Torres Strait along with traditional foods that are special to a region that became a melting pot of nationalities during the pearling era – ancient island dishes infused with Asian deliciousness.

The Winds of Zenadth Cultural Festival was first held on 8 May in 1987. Since the inaugural event, the participation and perfecting of performances have made the festival an incredible experience. It is now held in September to coincide with the transition from Sager (south-east trade winds, dry season) to Nager (north-east wind, highest heat and humidity). The decision to move to this time of year was culturally significant. The shifting wind signals initiation time for young men and a traditional time for reinforcing social relationships and engaging in trade.

The festival kicks off with a colourful opening procession, where the entourage of brightly decorated dancers and their support groups stop marching every now and then to break into spontaneous dance and song. When the procession reaches the festival, they are led on to the field by Kaurareg warriors, the traditional custodians of the islands around Thursday Island.

The dancing and festivities run from the morning and into the night for four days. Community leaders sit on the stage to watch each performance, and with around ten to thirteen groups performing each day, it must be extremely tiring for dancers and community leaders alike. Gabriel Bani is an elected councillor for the Torres Shire Council and he is one of those community leaders. During the festival, Gabriel was extra busy; he was responsible for formally announcing and welcoming each dance group in turn.

A tall well-built man, he exudes strength, and he is an Elder at fifty-four years old. I watched him during the first days of the festival, and I noticed that he was always calm and statesmanlike. He handles himself like a chief.

On his chest he wears a magnificent pearl shell in the shape of the dhari, the headdress that is held sacred by the tribes and different language groups across the Torres Strait. The dhari symbolises the people's commonality, and for this reason it is in the centre of the green and blue Torres Strait Island flag.

Gabriel was finishing an interview with NITV's Natalie Ah Mat as I approached. His big smile would be beamed across the country to the predominantly Indigenous audience. I could see his great pride in knowing that his culture would be showcased around the nation. He spotted me, and waved.

Weaving our way through the crowd to a quiet spot, Gabriel stopped to greet every second person, pausing to answer questions, or to inquire about the health of someone's family member. As we settled into a comparatively quiet spot at the festival, I thanked him for his time and proposed to get the interview underway.

'Okay, you want me to speak in my native language Kalaw Lagaw Ya, or just English?'

I thought, I wish I could interview in Kalaw Lagaw Ya, my language, but I said, 'English please, if that's okay?'

Gabriel described his connection to Country – he is of the Western Island Group, from Mabuiag Island. His totem is the crocodile, or Koedal. His wind is the north-west wind, or Kuki. His language is Kalaw Lagaw Ya. His constellation is Baidam, the shark constellation that was the subject of the dance at Uluṟu.

'That's where we come from. The tribe connects everyone in the Torres Strait.'

I commented on how well he knows his ancestry, but it didn't come as a surprise. Gabriel's late father, Ephraim Bani, was the founder of the Winds of Zenadth Cultural Festival and the Gab Titui Cultural Centre on Thursday Island.

'My cultural knowledge was passed down to me, obviously, by my father, and was passed down to him by his father. My father went through the full process of initiation with his maternal uncles. So with all the knowledge that my father had, he made sure that he documented everything and he spent time with us, he spoke to us, and he passed on the knowledge.

'We value very highly our traditional knowledge, our genealogies, and our connections with the environment and everything else. My father was actually the cultural ambassador for the Torres Strait, and he was also a linguist. He developed the orthography of Western Island Language that people use today.

'But he saw our culture was eroding, so he did everything he could to inform us as his family but also to achieve his vision for the cultural festival, the Gab Titui Cultural Centre, and the language centre, everything that he was the founder of.'

I had watched documentaries and read about Ephraim Bani. He is one of the most celebrated Torres Strait Islanders. Admired for his foresight, he dedicated his life to stopping the erosion of cultural knowledge. His work ethic and commitment to his vision are legendary, though, the challenges were great.

'For Dad, in the '60s and early '70s, he was always confronted with cross-cultural barriers, stratification in society, the groups, the discrimination, everything. So he had to make a very big effort in trying to work in that world. Just thinking of all the other [Indigenous] leaders throughout the nation who stood up for us, it must've been very challenging. The difficulty he had was getting the support from the communities.

'Think about what Uncle Koiki Mabo also went through, because people have their colonised thinking. Our mindsets, our strongholds at the moment, we value and see things according to the western world views. That's where the challenges are in trying to do the cultural work.'

I asked Gabriel how that affected him, as a son. Having a father who was ahead of his time must have had personal challenges.

'I recall that sometimes he would come home drunk. People saw him as some sort of, not an outcast, but just, "What are you trying to do?" sort of a thing. "Don't rock the boat." That sort of a thing, you know? "We're happy with how things are." But he was determined to … to restore, to revitalise. Especially language that was stopped from speaking in schools. Dancing, that was stopped. The history of our culture.'

Gabriel said this with a wry smile. He clearly loved and was fond of his father. I commented on how strong his father was, to be ahead of his time and still persevere. Gabriel continued, noticeably more sombre now.

'Yes, he was, yeah. And I've been using that term lately, that he was "a father before his time". His last years found him, not in a negative way; I couldn't understand it at first, but he was always drinking now, getting drunk. It wasn't until my uncle told me that, "Don't be angry with Dad …"'

Gabriel, still looking at me, suddenly seemed lost for words.

Perhaps that's not right – not lost for words. I could see it was more how you feel when you experience such sorrow, it is as though your heart swells, blocking your throat so you cannot speak. We sat in silence for a long moment. The deep thrumming of the warrup (drum) could be felt and heard in the near distance, like a heartbeat laden with emotion. Gabriel looked down at the ground between his feet and recomposed himself.

'My uncle said, "Don't be angry with Dad, because the world is not ready for him yet." So … and then he passed away.'

Gabriel's demeanour lifted as he spoke about how his father's vision has been realised, and importantly, appreciated. 'People started to look then. That's when I came into the picture and my big brother,' Gabriel begins to laugh as he talks now, 'People starting to come to us. They would say, "Well Daddy was right!"'

Gabriel said that he wasn't tired from the work he does for his community because his father's spirit carries him.

'If anything my father's legacy makes me stronger to continue that work in the communities now. There's a lot of challenges with the western influence. People look to government for answers. People look to government to lead. But my work now is going out saying that, no, this is not the real issue. The real leadership is here, going back to the clans, the tribes and our traditional thinking.'

I asked Gabriel about the old structures of representation – how we resolved issues for the community before colonisation.

'Our old structures were very strong – not only for solutions for any issues or any problems in the communities, but also to prevent stuff from happening. Everything around our lore – L-O-R-E – the educational part. All the uncles and the young men. The aunties and the young women. They learnt and practiced culture proper. When there was a breakdown, the structure was in place to resolve our differences. We just need to practice it again.

'If we pass on those values, we actually prepare our young people to be in this world. And it reminds me of a saying, "You don't prepare the path for the child, you prepare the child for the path."

'Our culture is thousands of years old, we've got it right. We knew how to have an ordered society.'

Gabriel reminded me of one of the things Bruce Pascoe raised in his book, *Dark Emu*. Bruce wrote about the emerging findings that indicate that we are not only the oldest living culture on earth, but this was possible because of the complex structure and system of laws connecting the people to their Country.

This ancient custodianship made Aboriginal and Torres Strait Islanders the most peaceful culture with unsurpassed longevity.

Gabriel is a leader in search of a better future, and he has built his knowledge and wisdom partly by looking to the past. I asked him about his involvement in the Torres Strait Island Regional Dialogue and being elected to go to Uluru.

'Well, I wasn't really sure at first. I'd heard about [the dialogues on constitutional recognition], and we'd discussed it. I had just come into the council in the last two, three years. And, as you know, Dalassa Yorkston was involved with the team here. [Dalassa was an Indigenous member of the Referendum Council from the Torres Strait Islands.] But when the dialogue actually came up here, I learnt a lot from all the presentations and the speeches.

'At the opening ceremony for the Winds of Zenadth Cultural Festival yesterday I said of the Uluru Statement that we need better representation at all levels. Representation from where we are – the foundational grass roots, street level of the people organising this – but also involved at the highest decision making level to make a stand for our people there. Decisions are made in Canberra and we need to be able to affect them.'

I mentioned to Gabriel how I also learnt about the Constitution and the importance of layers of representation from both the regional dialogue and from my experience as an activist on the street.

'Yeah. Wow. A whole new learning experience,' he said. He then spoke about the 1936 Torres Strait Maritime Strike when Islanders demanded and won the right to establish a Torres Strait Regional Council. He said it was a historic moment that he relied on to guide him on constitutional reform.

'When we came to vote on who would go to Uluṟu and we had to speak about why we should go, I brought up the 1937 councils gathering on Masig [York Island] on August 23 when all the councils first met.

'My grandfather, my dad's dad, was one of the councillors. When we were deciding on who would go to Uluṟu, I said that my grandfather may not have been aware of what was to come when he went on that boat to travel to Masig for the first council meeting. But they all went, even though the weather was really rough – we have songs about how rough it was – they risked their lives to get there. My grandfather composed songs for that gathering and choreographed dances on the boat as they were sailing to Masig.

'When they got there, that meeting that night, with feasting and supper, they danced those dances. They still dance those dances today, as you know. That's our form of recording our history.

'I thought of my grandfather. I was doing as he did, with the dialogue and to go to the Uluṟu Convention. I thought, I don't know what's there, but I'm going.'

Gabriel was elected by his people, and as he travelled to Uluṟu, he was conscious that he was travelling to the heart of Australia for the very first time.

'I had mixed feelings, uncertainty, a bit of fear as well because first time heading that way. But I've been to Alice Springs. I've been to Darwin, Perth, all around the coast, but not really to the heart.'

Gabriel did more than travel to the heart, he touched it as well.

'The amazing thing was that I was to present [an exchange of cultural greetings and gifts] on behalf of all the Torres Strait people to the Elders there. I didn't expect that! At the Welcoming Ceremony, I took the mat [a sitting mat traditionally woven with coconut leaf] and I spoke in my language. I thanked the Elders from there, explaining that the mat signifies life from birth to death, from cradle to grave, that the mat has everything to do with our initiations, our marriages, our ceremonies. I briefly explained the language and told them that we came here, we give you our heart and our life.' The giving of gifts was reciprocated. 'The Anangu Elders gave us the spear and the boomerang. It was a spiritual experience.'

The journey to the sacred Anangu grounds in the heart of Australia was a highlight for Gabriel. The spiritual welcoming and the exchange of gifts were unforgettable. When some of the delegates walked away from the work to reach a consensus, Gabriel explained that he didn't walk out because he was there for our children; it is okay and normal for some to disagree in forums. Though, he said that the walk-out did make him think deeply about what was right. 'It kind of made me think, are we right? If they're saying this, they're also saying that what we're doing is wrong. I was at a bit of a crossroads there at that point in time. But then, well, I stayed because this is what I shared with the group, the ones who went over there: "I'm not here because I want to be here. My people asked me to come, and that's why I stayed." Those people who walked out, they were heard. And that helped them too.'

I agreed with Gabriel. We all had a right to be heard; collectively we made sure of that.

Gabriel said that when he first heard the Uluru Statement, 'I saw hope. My spirit just lit up – or jumped within me. It captured everything. It captured, regardless of where … I'm from Mabuiag, you know? But it captured Murray Island, it captured Saibai Island, it captured Lockhart River, it captured Yarrabah. That Statement just captured everything – that's our heart, you know? That's our position, that's who we are. And that's where we want to go.'

ON THE WAY: OLD T. I.

There are four Celestino Mayors in my family including my father and son, and three men in the family called Thomas. When we are all back on Thursday Island, we get a photo taken together and it always shows a group filled with laughter and love. When I step off the ferry at Thursday Island, I visit my Grandma first, Sheila Mayor (nee Ah Wang). She lives in a little unit complex, a short walk from the small jetty. Everything is walking distance on Thursday Island.

When I sit with Grandma, she is always smiling, asking how Dad is, and commenting on how cranky he is, giving an adorable giggle that only elderly grandmothers have. Her small living room brings back many memories. Not just because the walls are covered with photos of her children, grandchildren and great-grandchildren, but because there's also a feeling of nostalgia in the place itself. The living-room floor where around a dozen of us, brothers, sisters and cousins, slept shoulder to shoulder as children; the tiny porch where Grandma helped me sneak back in to the unit in the dark hours of the morning, after happily being led astray by my cousins. Of all the places in the country, Thursday Island is where I long to be.

I carried the Uluru Statement with me to Grandma's. I carried it all over Thursday Island. At the Winds of Zenadth Cultural Festival in 2018, Pedro Stephen and I carried the Uluru Statement from the Heart at the front of the opening procession. As an Island man who grew up far away on Larrakia land, leading that procession was the proudest moment in all my travels. With every step in that procession, with every voice that sung and every beat of the drums, my heart swelled. I was home.

My Grandma has since passed on. Our matriarch is now at rest, though her legacy lives with us still. I'll whisper her name as I cast my vote in the Voice referendum, and I'll hear her whisper back that she is proud of me.

Ugaramle, Torres Strait

PEDRO STEPHEN

Pedro Stephen is from Ugaramle, or Stephen Island, situated in the eastern island group of the Torres Strait. He credits his lineage from both the eastern and the western islands as the 'powerful rod that keeps me aligned, with a balanced view of where I'm going, especially as a leader'. His father was the first Chair of Tamwoy Indigenous Council on Thursday Island in the 1960s, inspiring Pedro to run for mayor; and he served as the Mayor of the Torres Shire for twenty-five years, an incredible achievement. When he was replaced by the first female mayor in the Torres Strait in 2016, Vonda Malone, Pedro took on a new role as the Chair of the Torres Strait Regional Authority.

The islands of the Torres Strait are connected through family, culture and song; and through thousands of years of trade and stories. One such story is about Gelam, a skilful young hunter. His story is of the creation of the Torres Strait, passed on from one generation to the next.

The young man, Gelam, upset at his mother's trickery, decided to leave his home island of Moa. He began carving dugongs out of trees, sending them to the nearby islands. When he was satisfied with his final carving, he became a dugong himself and to his mother's agony, he swam to the east, stopping at islands in the central group, before settling in the eastern group on Mer (Murray Island) with the soil and the bounty of food that he carried from Moa.

Of course, this is a very brief description of this story. There are twists and turns that I have not included here, each with the purpose of teaching lessons to the next generation, ensuring that the past is never forgotten.

Pedro Stephen began our interview by referring to this story. He has lineage from across the Torres Strait and he described the connections between the islands as a strength. He said, 'Although we are many, we are one.'

I felt this connection as I marched at the front of the Winds of Zenadth Cultural Festival opening procession. Pedro, who went to school with my father on Thursday Island, held one end of the Uluru Statement while I held the other. In the procession were perhaps a thousand people from every island in the Torres Strait. There were many different songs and dances spontaneously rising up to the blue sky, swirling like the clouds before raining upon us in a single, exquisite chorus. When Pedro looked over at me as we marched, I'm sure he knew what I was feeling – an overwhelming pride and connection with my island home that I had yearned for my entire life.

When we reached the grounds, we were escorted by the proud young warriors of the Kaurareg Nation through gates made for the festival from the fronds of coconut trees. The Kaurareg are the custodians of the islands in the south-west Torres Strait, including Thursday Island. The morning was capped off for me when Pedro, as the Chair of the Torres Strait Regional Authority, in his speech to open the festival, asked that I stand. I awkwardly stood up and Pedro thanked me for bringing the Uluru Statement from the Heart to the Torres Strait Islands. He described the Uluru Statement as a journey that connected the voices of many mainland First Nations with ours in the Torres Strait.

Later that day, Pedro and I found a place to sit and conduct the interview. We sat amongst the Erub (Darnley Island) art display in a little side stall that was shaded by a simple roof made of thatched coconut palms. Sitting down on plastic chairs, we paid little mind to the noisy kids who ran through the shack. Chasing each other, they darted around us and back out again in a flash, dodging groups of brightly dressed island women who carried themselves with calm poise – the complete opposite to the chaotic play of the kids.

Pedro began our interview by telling me about his family's journey from his home island, Ugar (Stephen Island), to Waiben (Thursday Island).

'I was born in 1955 and my dad made the decision to move to Thursday Island. Like many other islanders, we moved for the education and employment opportunities, especially when the fisheries declined because of plastics and other pressures.' Technology and foreign exploiters of the island fisheries had taken their toll.

Pedro digressed to explain how the modern times are in stark contrast to the old ways on the islands – the old ways that maintained a balance in people's lives over countless generations. He told me how the Elders passed on the knowledge of the seasons through song, dance and sage advice – advice that was respected by the youth. He explained, 'The moon phase was the management – so we knew what you can fish, when to garden, and all of that. Our culture was a way to balance our existence with nature.

'When I came to school here on Thursday Island, we were in the Black school. Only "natives" went to the school. I think in my father's time they went to grade three. And then us, we went to grade seven. This was leading up to 1967, which is when our people were talking about citizenship rights. While everybody else took for granted that they were equal, we were denied the right to vote until 1965 in Queensland, even while we maintained our responsibility as custodians of the land and protectors of our villages. We worked in the pearling industry, the marine industry, on the railways, and we didn't think twice about taking up arms to fight for Australia with fellow Australians. Through all that our people didn't have a right to vote, and we weren't even recognised as Australian.'

'I think that from the white man's records, they can really identify or articulate that in our history, we rebelled to make the big changes. The Maritime Strike in 1936 flowed into the guys that served in the army. Our people didn't accept that we should be treated less, paid less, compared to the white soldiers. We went on strike in the army too, and when you rebel in the army, you get called a deserter. They used that sort of terminology in branding us to try and force us back to work. But we are a proud people, because we knew how to stand up and fight back – like in 1936. The army still refused to pay us the same as the white soldiers, but when we stood together; we came close to equal pay.

'Us Torres Strait Islanders, when we marched for the 1967 referendum, we weren't even asking for any more or any less than what should be our rights as First Nations, let alone as Australians. We need to continue to push, even though it's like we are always going against the tide.'

Though branded as rebellious, in each of the struggles Pedro described we were simply seeking a respectful relationship. We want a better, more united future. A future where our people can speak for ourselves. That is what Pedro hopes for with the Uluru Statement from the Heart. He said, 'I've been involved in the Reconciliation

Council from when it began, because I believed in reconciliation. I believe that on our journey, when you walk, you must take others with you. My concept in leadership has always been that we must lift while we climb. So, when we press on for our aspirations, we must take others with us.

'But respect must be given, because it hasn't been coming from governments. If I go to your place, I recognise that's your house. I can't walk in there and start moving your furniture around without you getting disturbed. And telling you what to do in your home place. That's the most practical thing, even a child would understand ...'

'In Malo law, "Malo tag mauki mauki, Teter mauki mauki –Your hands and feet can't touch and walk on places that are not yours."' Pedro was talking about the ancient law of Mer.

The Torres Strait was spared some of the harsher impacts of colonisation, at least compared to the mainland colonial centres. The region was mostly left alone until the 1860s when the pearling lords flocked to the islands, seeking their fortune from pearl shell.

'The pearl industry was set up by Captain Banner at Warrior Reef and island [in the central island group], because that's where the pearl shell was discovered, in the shallows. A lot of pearl lords came from Melbourne and Sydney and there was an influx of foreigners, mainly people seeking their fortune. The magistrate had to be moved much closer to the Torres Strait, so they moved him to Thursday Island. So, Thursday Island was set up, first and foremost, for the protection of the pearling industry.'

At this point, I remembered something I had learnt about my own family. I told Pedro about how I read a book that my wife's grandma, Marie Grimmett, had lent me in 2016, just before I became involved in the constitutional dialogues. The book was *The Pearl Frontier* by Adrian Vickers and Julia Martinez. When I turned to page 162, I had no idea that I was about to learn a missing part of our family history. The section was about the attitude and control that the authorities had over the lives of both the islanders and the indentured Asian workers in the Torres Strait pearling industry.

> *Indonesian-Indigenous families were prominent in Thursday Island life, but throughout this period officials described such relationships as illegitimate. An official 1930 report spoke of 'Malays' as 'indolent and … in nearly every case … living clandestinely with coloured women'. If the relationships were viewed as illegitimate, it was because the government had denied permission for mixed marriages. Ahwang Dai, a Dayak from Borneo (but it is not clear whether from the Dutch or British side), came from Singapore to the Torres Straits in the 1880s and in 1891 married Annie, a Badu Island girl with whom he had eleven children.*

Ahwang Dai and Annie Savage are my great great-grandparents. I knew that Annie Savage came from Barbadian, Pacific Islander (Niue), Badulag and Kaurareg heritage. What I didn't know, until I read *The Pearl Frontier*, is that Ahwang Dai was from Borneo, and a native of Borneo, Dayak, as well. I had been to Sibu, in Borneo, not long before making this discovery to inspect a ship as part of my MUA work. I remembered marvelling at the dense green jungle, spread as far as the eye could see across the third largest island in the world. I had no idea that it was once the home of my great-great-grandfather.

His countrymen were second-class citizens in Australia. The native women they married weren't citizens or even considered human. To avoid being classed as a 'native', and therefore under the harsh, overbearing control of the white 'protector', half-caste families were required to move to Thursday Island and completely disassociate with their 'full-blood' families. Pedro told me about the days of segregation.

'I think that when a census was developed by the churches, this instance was after 1871, they counted how many Black people there were. The authorities used the Church to bring some "colonial order" into these communities. They recognised the traditional kinship, the clan groups, and they said no, the better one is actually what we will introduce.' He was describing assimilation policies and apartheid. Pedro spoke of how Torres Strait Islanders overcame segregation and assimilation tactics, instead forging greater unity amongst themselves.

'The Department of Native Affairs wanted greater control, so they established a chairman, like a local government type regime on the islands. They wanted more islanders to work in the government departments. They brought us to live on the reserve at Tamwoy in 1957 so as to control us, but they actually united us when all the natives lived in one suburb.

'It allowed a person from Boigu Island to live next to a person from Stephen Island. They brought the outer islands together. They didn't know then that instead of making us like them, we practiced [culture] and started intermarriage. And then, bang! It united us even more. That's why today, they name Tamwoy Town, "Migi" Torres Strait, meaning that it's actually the "small" Torres Strait.'

The rebellious spirit, the Maritime Strike, the adaptation to new ways of living, and the luck of geographic location has resulted in a unique autonomy in the Torres Strait, through the Torres Strait Regional Authority (TSRA). The TSRA is a Commonwealth Statutory Authority that was established on 1 July 1994 under the *Aboriginal and Torres Strait Islander Commission Act 1989 (Cth)*, now known as the *Aboriginal and Torres Strait Islander Act 2005 (Cth)*. It is the leading Commonwealth representative body for Torres Strait Islander and Aboriginal people living in the Torres Strait, including two mainland communities, Bamaga and Seisia, in the Northern Area Peninsula of Cape York.

'[The TSRA] helps us bring our regional power together.' It's beneficial for us, and also the government – good for all of us.'

'That's really interesting,' I said to Pedro, 'because when I think about the First Nations representative voice, the Uluṟu Statement, what we're actually doing is uniting the First Nations.'

Pedro agreed. This was the journey he had talked about that morning at the festival when he acknowledged the presence of the Uluṟu Statement canvas.

'I believe that we are on a journey, not just as Torres Strait Islanders now,' he said. 'We all walked as the First Nations people of this land, this country. And we all went back to the heart of this country. Aboriginal and Torres Strait Islanders were gathered from the four winds. The winds are significant for us and also for Aboriginal people. For us, the winds are important for how we sail to the next place.'

Once he'd said this, my mind buzzed with the similarity between Pedro's words and the four song lines depicted so beautifully on the Uluṟu Statement canvas, interconnecting in the heart of the nation.

Pedro, always taking care to inform others, said 'The winds identify when we travel. They are part of our management plan; when we fish, what type of fish we catch, how we engage in the fisheries; what type of crops that we plant in our garden. It is in the winds as well. Same as the Aboriginal people, they watch the winds and the phases of the moon.

'That's why a lot of the old fellas, they'll sit on the beach for a long time. Because just the wind touching their face is better than the medicine that they take from the doctors.'

'When the Constitutional Regional Dialogue was here, I believed that the timing was right because we in the Torres Strait had already embarked on the assembly movement. When the Torres Strait Regional Authority was created there was to be a transition to a model more representative of the communities on the islands. We would use the very instrument of government that was given to control us, in reverse. There are various models for representation in the world – the Inuit model, a Canadian model, an American model; no, this is our model. We're not just talking about representation, but we're talking about the legislative policy. We are capable of overseeing health service delivery, for example, we can manage it on a policy level. This is important because at the moment, when you enter remote areas, everything is done as one size fits all. But in the Torres Strait we have a standard. We can manage the balance between LORE and LAW. So, what we're doing is reintroducing our value system. We don't want wasteful services that can't deliver, which is why the dialogue was good timing. For us, we weren't focusing on claiming our sovereignty, we already have sovereignty. It's about us controlling the system.'

For Pedro, the First Nations Voice is about local decision-making, but on a national scale. He believed that we should 'take our Voice right into the heart of the people who make the decisions'.

'The most positive thing about what we did at Uluṟu was that the outcome tells us that we are on the right path here in the Torres Strait,' he said. 'I think that eyes were opened, we could see that it's not only us on this journey. It's time that we, both Aboriginal and Torres Strait Islander leaders, stop competing against each other. It's time we share our strength. So, when we stood up and made that Statement, I had to hold in my pride. I had tears in my eyes because …'

For the first time in the interview, I saw the seasoned leader become emotional.

'I saw that my … my dad was all about, politics. I actually witnessed him coming home and take out his frustration with my mum and us, because he couldn't get through. And because my dad only went to grade three. My mum was a South Sea Islander, or "half-cast". She was able to write all of my dad's correspondence, because my dad couldn't actually write. Standing there endorsing the Uluṟu Statement, it was a feeling of satisfaction. And also, a sense of awesome responsibility. I've witnessed the journey that my father went on, it was his journey that helped get my people to where we are. I thought, now, what I'm doing here in the heart of the country, will take my son's generation forward.' Pedro paused. Contemplated. Continued.

'When I lined up and held the pen to sign the Uluṟu Statement, I felt like I wanted to drop the pen and put my thumbprint in ink. Although I can write, I can do that, but … I wanted to actually drop everything that is foreign, even the pen. To go back to my thumbprint. Because it's not my thumbprint, it's my grandfather's thumbprint. It's my father's thumbprint … It's my son's thumbprint, and it's my great-great-grandchild's thumbprint.'

I thanked Pedro, 'Eso Uncle Pedro.' Then I asked him one last question. 'The prime minister and others have said that the Australian people won't support enshrining a First Nations Voice in the Constitution. What would you say to the Australian people about that?'

Pedro simply said, 'With the same spirit that had called everyone together in 1967, when the referendum goes forward for our First Nations Voice, it will be the same spirit that will actually guide your hands to the pen to vote YES.'

Kaytetye, Arrernte, Warlpiri and Warumungu,
Northern Territory

BARBARA SHAW

Flying home to Darwin after interviewing Barbara Shaw, all I can think about is her crew – the women of the Tangentyere Women's Family Safety Group – the warm welcome they gave me, their solidarity and their strength.

That was my second meeting with the Tangentyere Women's Family Safety Group. The first time I visited them was in May 2018, when – in a very tight schedule of meetings in Alice Springs – I promised to drop in to the Tangentyere Council office to show the group the Uluṟu Statement. Barbara wanted to make sure that I delivered on my promise, calling me as my flight departure time drew closer. I told her I was worried I was running out of time. 'I might miss my flight!'

'You have time to come see us, Thomas. You'll still make your flight!' she declared.

I arrived at the Tangentyere offices, panting from running down the street, but I was determined that I wouldn't let Barbara down. I paused to catch my breath, and walked in to the office where eleven members of the Family Safety Group were having a break from a domestic violence campaign meeting.

After I rolled out the Uluru Statement from the Heart canvas, Barbara and I told the group about where the Uluru Statement came from and what it called for. We talked about what it could mean to the women's communities. Then, we huddled together for a photo with the canvas.

As I was about to leave, they excitedly told me to wait. 'One more photo with our Tangentyere Statement this time!' They unrolled a smaller canvas with dot-painting patterns like flowers blooming on the desert sand. In purple hues were circles representing a harmonious community, men and women, with footprints between – the circles of life. In large letters in the center, amongst the circles, were the words, 'STAND WITH US'.

On my next visit to Alice Springs to interview Barbara, I timed it so that I could meet the Family Safety Group again. Eleven big smiles greeted me. The women suspended their agenda – they were planning the next phase of their latest program, 'Mums can, Dads can' – and introduced me again to each member of the group. After I gave them an update on the Uluru Statement campaign, we had a great discussion about what a referendum is and how difficult it may be to win. Before Barbara and I left to find a quiet space to talk, Shirleen Campbell, a young co-coordinator for the Women's Safety Group, who exuded courage and strength, made a fist and said, 'We need to be strong and united, and we can win this! You can count on us here!'

Is it any wonder that hours later, this inspiring group of women were still on my mind? They are strong leaders in a community that has felt the worst of failed government policies. They are the

people who have it harder than any other demographic in Australia –
Aboriginal women living in a 'town camp' in the Northern Territory.
Barbara is a leader amongst them, and she is a character like no other.
She is a straight talker. Think 'street wise', with a cheeky sense of
humour. Barbara always speaks up, loud and clear, although her
sharp style is softened with tender motherliness. I was right to think
I would enjoy interviewing her.

"My father is Kaytetye and Arrernte, and my mother is Warlpiri
and Warumungu. My dad had three wives. His second wife was my
[biological] mother. She is still living in Tennant Creek because that's
Warumungu Country up there. But it's his third wife that I call my
mum. Her name is Eileen Hussan. She raised me from when I was
two years old. She's Yunkunytjatjara and also part Afghan. I don't like
saying "stepmother", I'd say the mother that grew me up.'

Barbara told me that her biological mother had three husbands,
and so Barbara has many brothers and sisters. As with the mother
that 'grew her up', it didn't matter if the other siblings were from a
different mother or father. They're all family to Barbara. 'Our way,'
she said.

'I live here in Alice Springs. I'm a fourth-generation town camper.
I've lived in a town camp all my life.' Barbara explained to me what
an Alice Springs town camp is. 'Way back when, before they even
started building houses for Aboriginal people, we lived in tents in
little pockets of dwellings on the outskirts of town. A lot of our
camps that sit around Alice Springs were spread out, based on where
the white fellas who needed them for their labour were. We were
living in whatever materials that we could find to make shelter. There
was a six o'clock curfew. No Aboriginal could be in town after dark,
otherwise, they get locked up.'

Barbara's family has lived in the Mount Nancy town camp for
generations. It was her great-grandmother who first moved to Mount

Nancy with her grandmother in tow. Barbara's great-grandmother must've been an amazing woman. A survivor of a frontier war and slavery.

'We were fortunate to grow up with our great-grandmother before she passed.

'I wouldn't say that I remember a lot about her, but we spent a lot of time with her. She was one of them old Aboriginal women who would work on cattle stations looking after non-Aboriginal kids. Basically, housemaid and nanny. She was only paid rations. But even though she was paid in rations and stuff, she managed to look after station owners' kids and a lot of other kids as well, like Aboriginal parents that couldn't take their kids to stations; they'd be left with her. This included my grandmother in her young days. So my great-grandmother lived on a lot of cattle stations.

'Back then, Aboriginals didn't have names like now. They just had their skin names or "bush" names and the white fellas didn't bother to get to know that. She was given Myrtle Ryan but died Margaret Baker. That's because of, I guess having different owner, white ownership.

'It's like when you look at movies about slavery in America. It's like that. It's horrible to think about those kind of movies that are set back in the cotton-picking days, I guess. But my great-grandmother was owned by a cattleman and moved around a bit for her work. It's horrible to think like that, but … She did end up coming back home to Alice Springs eventually.'

Barbara has fond memories of her great-grandmother, counting herself lucky to have those memories to cherish. 'The town camp I live in, it's on the banks of the Charles River. I remember as a child, we would go up the hill, go down into the dry creek. My great-grandmother would tell us kids to climb up in the gum trees and just bounce on the branches. All the little white – I don't know what the

Aboriginal word is for it – back then we used to call it sugar lolly that grow on the gumleaf, they would just fall off and we would eat them. So that was bush-tucker for sweets. I still do that with kids today, just go walking around once we know that it's all on the trees.

'Where we were on the banks of the creek, there were no acacia trees to get witchety grub. But there's another trick of getting the little purple witchety grubs out of the gum tree.

'You find a hole in the trunk, poke it with a little stick. You just wiggle it around and slowly pull that purple witchety grub out, which is just as good as digging in the acacia root. So there was bush food in the creek.'

I noticed Barbara's eyes as she reminisced. They were like windows to a place full of sun, river sand and beautiful Arrernte flora and fauna. Bliss carried on every word as she revisited carefree times with her Elders. 'Another thing I could remember is going up into the hills near our town camp. We used to go walking around in the hills looking for bush-tucker in the vegetation, or killing a euro [wallaby], looking for echidnas and stuff. I remember my dad telling us that our great-grandmother and our grandfather were cooking up carpet snake for us to eat. I reckon that's the best thing I loved about growing up with our old people, is that my mum and dad, they'd just dump us with the old people – dump us in a good way, like, "Oh, yeah you can go there for the weekend, I want a quiet house." And we'd just live off the land for two or three days, which is good. We'd sit around the fire, telling stories, and all the old people would be telling us about our culture. We'd listen to the stories of when they grew up, and how it was when they first met the white man and stuff like that.'

Barbara's father, Geoffrey Shaw, was born near his people's sacred Dreaming site, west of Barrow Creek Hotel, in 1945. His father was a stockman and his mother would go bush with him.

As a boy, Geoffrey would move between family groups in the

different town camps, speaking the various languages of the many people who were brought to Alice Springs. They were used as labour in the town and in the welfare outpost that was called the 'Bungalow', which is where he first went to school.

'When he was eighteen, Dad joined the army and he did two tours of Vietnam, one in Borneo and another in Malaysia. While he was in the jungle, there was a referendum to get us counted in the census. He went away not being counted as a citizen, but when he came back into the country, he was then counted as a citizen. But he still had to fight for seven years for his pension and all the while he was suffering from the effects of war [PTSD].'

Barbara's father continued to fight, and also to build. She proudly went on, 'Dad's really, really big on Aboriginal issues and that's probably where I get my bite, because of him. He's always had that fire in the belly. He started some of the first Aboriginal organisations here in Central Australia. He was the General Manager of the Tangentyere Council for about twenty-one years. Prior to becoming a general manager, he was also part of setting other organisations up, like the IAD, which is the Institute of Aboriginal Development. He also helped to establish Congress, which is a Central Australian Aboriginal medical centre.

'Dad led by example for us. He was always around, even though he was very busy. He was a single father of three for a long time in what was one of the first houses in the town camp. He lived in that house with his grandmother, my great-grandmother, his younger siblings, as well as us. It's a house that's only a year younger than me.'

In Barbara's community – a town camp that started as a collection of tents and tin shacks – the state of the homes and the meagre facilities are poor. The living conditions are a far cry from the standards expected by most Australians. The conditions are not how Aboriginal people choose to live, they are a reflection of attempted genocide, slavery, exploitation, and then policy failure after policy failure – all resulting in disproportionate social dysfunction. Barbara explained a sense of belonging in each camp – the camps are based on language groups. 'We are proud of our communities.'

In 2007, the Howard government mobilised the Australian Army in an act of racist political bastardry. He imposed the Northern Territory Emergency Response measures against all Aboriginal people living in communities in the Northern Territory, including Barbara's. It was the infamous 'Intervention'.

'Before the Intervention, all town camps in Alice Springs had housing managed by association. We also had our land tenure in perpetuity under special-purpose leases. The Intervention come along and changed the land-tenure system. Now lands are handed over to governments, both federal and Territory; it was with the federal, but they gave control to the Northern Territory Government. The outcome is we sublease the land from the Northern Territory Government. In place of our local association, there is now an Executive Director of Township Leases who is employed by Canberra and is located in Darwin.'

During the Intervention, more numerous than the soldiers and the populations of the small communities combined were the waves of bureaucrats coming from interstate. They knew better, or at least, they knew a career could be made from Black disempowerment.

'We were effectively disempowered. The well-paid executive officer who took over control of the community, he don't know us, and we don't know him. One of their excuses they were saying to convince us it was good was they said that in the past, they couldn't do anything in our town camps or our communities because it was owned by the community. They said they wanted to come in and upgrade infrastructure, build new homes, and then wanted to basically have control to do those things.' I asked if anything changed. Barbara thought for a moment, and tentatively said, 'Yes, in some parts of the town camps they built new homes, they put in guttering, new street names, new house numbers. Then you got all the camps that got no housing. The money that the government started allocating back when was $75,000 for emergency repairs. Rebuilds, like knock down and build, that was $240,000. And I think it was $400,000 for a brand-new house. We actually got a say on what kind of houses were built for each family.

'For my house, I had to move out while they did all the renos. When I came back in, I said, "What's this?" This is not $70,000 worth of repairs.

'We could've managed it better ourselves when we had a housing association. Our housing association used to pick up rent we paid, and we would pay just a little extra on top just in case of a need for repairs and maintenance. When we had enough in the budget, we'd maybe build a new park or playground. A lot of people chucked in through rent and they paid extra. We can't do that now because we've come under Territory housing. The changes made it even more of a cost to the taxpayer and it's less efficient then when we did it ourselves.

'The reality is the opposite from what everybody complains about. People would say, "Oh Aboriginal people, we're putting all this money to them." But really we've gone backwards. The money isn't going to what we need.

'Non-Aboriginal people don't know enough about our mob and what goes on in our lives, especially when it comes to money. We have a whole lot of money sitting in federal Treasury; the Aboriginal Benefits Account. It's only for people in the Northern Territory to access because it's coming out of mining royalties. With that money in the bank, in federal Treasury, well that's building up interest too. That money isn't actually getting out to where it's supposed to go, to the people who need it in the community. It's needed for infrastructure in communities and for out-stations and it's needed for our organisations. It is also needed by Aboriginal people that want to go into business in their area. But it is an Indigenous Affairs minister in Canberra that controls the ABA. I sit on the ABA Board. The way it works is, Aboriginal people will come in with applications, the Department goes through them, then we go through it, we discuss it, we say "yes" or "no" to applications and then it goes back to the minister. The minster will go, "Yeah, yeah. No, yeah, yeah, no." He or she, at the end of the day, has got the final decision on our applications. It could be an application like, for example, Johnny up there living on his homeland, all he wants is a tractor to grade it from his house to the highway. So when it's raining it's not so boggy or that kind of stuff.'

'But Johnny misses out! The minister gave ABA money to the Amateur Fishing Association, an organisation that opposed Native Title claims! It's an absolute disgrace that so much money that is supposed to be spent for the benefit of Aboriginal people in the Northern Territory actually goes to organisations with other interests, or is spent in the capital, Darwin.

'Yeah, another example is where, when Mal Brough was the Indigenous Affairs Minister, he goes and puts money into a festival near Brisbane where he comes from. Nothing to do with Aboriginals where it was meant to be spent.

'What he also did when he was in power was he gave money to the Alice Springs town council for the new aquatic centre which again, wasn't really to the benefit of Aboriginal people. The money should have been spent on pools in remote communities. When I was an engagement officer on the Royal Commission [into the Protection and Detention of Children in the Northern Territory] in 2017, we went to a lot of communities and people are asking: "We want a water park for our kids or we want a pool for our kids." It's extremely hot out there, power isn't always on, houses are in disrepair; those communities desperately needed something like that. Something for kids to do too. Simple things like that. People were asking, "Like, why can't we have a theatre where we can show movies for the community?" They can come and sit down and watch pictures out of the heat. That kind of stuff.'

Listening to Barbara, I was disgusted at how Indigenous Affairs ministers, over many years, have controlled millions of dollars of Aboriginal money, yet achieved next to nothing in closing the gaps in life expectancy, incarceration rates, homelessness, and education between Indigenous and non-Indigenous people. Barbara said that, 'The Intervention may have cost billions of dollars, yet it knocked many Indigenous communities to their knees. Elements of the Intervention continue. But who's listening? Not the politicians.' Barbara wants to change this with a First Nations Voice.

'When I went to the Uluṟu First Nations Constitutional Convention, I wanted to do something that could make sure nothing like the Northern Territory Intervention could ever happen again.

'I'm interested in protecting our rights against discrimination. In the Northern Territory, the Commonwealth Government suspended the Racial Discrimination Act so that they could discriminate against us with the Intervention. And we know now that what they did didn't benefit us, it hurt us, disempowered us, caused more social issues. That was my main thought with having a Voice.'

I would like to have written much more about Barbara. There's so much more to tell about what her people have experienced during the awful Intervention. Stories that could have come from apartheid-era South Africa. Stories that are disgracefully from here, Australia. I'd also like to write more about her work with kids. She is a mother to many. She works hard to keep kids off the street and out of prison.

I'm amazed at her patience and her compassion.

The last question I asked Barbara was about the referendum that we both hope for. A referendum to enshrine a First Nations Voice in the Constitution. With characteristic vigour she said, 'I got a lot of good will people who are willing to drop everything and just come walk with us. They just want to know when and where we start campaigning.'

I said, 'I can't wait to start campaigning with you mob for the referendum!'

Barb laughed, 'Me too! I'm dragging all my family out for it!'

Actor and Humanitarian

DANNY GLOVER

My parents were union activists as postal workers, and deeply committed to securing full rights for African Americans. I learned from them that change required activism and protest. We believed that we could forge a better future, so, we got organized. We protested, but more than that, with great leadership from people such as Martin Luther King, Medgar Evers and A. Phillip Randolph we also put specific, tangible positions forward on what change should look like.

I have always been an advocate for human rights, starting from when I was young. My acting has been a platform to reach the rest of the world, supporting the broad struggle for social justice. The civil rights movement that I witnessed in my youth keeps me grounded, as does the union movement. The struggle of the working class and the struggle for social justice are linked internationally, and though we have achieved great change, too often our problems remain the same. It's a constant struggle to defend the ground that we gain and in recent times, we regress.

I have had the privilege of assisting social justice movements in many countries around the world and the good fortune of being able to practice my craft of acting in nearly one hundred movies over nearly forty years. Many of these films have social justice themes, such as *Places in the Heart* and *The Color Purple*. Beyond that, my acting has given me the opportunity to add my voice to the cause of ending discrimination. Unfortunately my own country hasn't come to terms with its treatment of Native Americans and African Americans held in slavery. Like the United States, Australia needs to confront and understand past injustices done to Indigenous Australians in order to build a fair and democratic society.

I first met Thomas in Sydney in June 2018, during the first anniversary of the Uluru Statement from the Heart. Twenty-two years previous, I had travelled to Australia and during that visit, I remember visiting incarcerated men and women. I always visit the people in prisons because you can tell the temperature of the country you go to by the people inhabiting the prisons. The people inhabiting the prisons were First Nations people, far disproportionate to their population outside. My return to Australia, twenty-two years on, made my heart ache because nothing has changed for the Aboriginal and Torres Strait Islander people in that time.

The Uluru Statement from the Heart and the movement that it has inspired in Australia made me reflect upon my childhood. I sensed in that room with Thomas and those First Nations Elders and their youth mixed in with working-class people, an enthusiasm that is one of the vital ingredients to making change. When I listened and heard the Uluru Statement read out loud, I recognized the other vital ingredient for change: a clearly articulated, tangible destination, and how to get there. A representative body in the Constitution is a powerful proposal. It is a vehicle to get organized. Organized first so that a collective can achieve *truth*, *justice* and finally *peace*.

Before I signed the petition supporting the Uluru Statement, I referred the audience to the late great James Baldwin, who said, 'People are trapped in history, and history is trapped in them.' I said these words because I believe they are the most important words for Australia to consider. Australia must turn and look at the people they have wronged and excluded. Australia must face the truth. The truth is the key to freedom.

Quandamooka

DEAN PARKIN

Dean Parkin is a Quandamooka man of Minjerribah (North Stradbroke Island) in Queensland. As one of the original signatories, he was integral to the process that led to the historic Uluṟu Statement from the Heart, attending all regional dialogues and the convention where it was made. Dean is now the Campaign Director of From the Heart – the leading campaign body for the Yes vote in the coming Voice referendum.

※

There is a genius to the Uluṟu Statement from the Heart that is not well understood. Much has been made of the three key proposals – Voice, Treaty, Truth – and the invitation from Aboriginal and Torres Strait Islander people to all Australians to '*walk with us in a movement of the Australian people for a better future*'. However, people who are inspired by the Uluṟu Statement know there is something much deeper that exists between and beyond the words on that beautiful canvas.

It is the power of the people who created it.

I know this because I felt that power directly. At every Referendum Council regional dialogue, I stood at the front of the room, marker in hand and whiteboard before me. My job was to capture the words that people spoke – live on the whiteboard – and then replay those words back to the room to ensure that they had been heard properly. Attendees at the dialogues often commented on the technique I used to capture their words, which is known as 'mind-mapping' and 'spider-diagramming'. What looks like a very messy mass of scribbles is actually a means by which words can be transformed into something like a mental picture that is far easier to recall than script. Or to think about it more simply: we imagine, dream and remember meaning in pictures, not words; to capture greater meaning, we need more than dot points and sentences.

These techniques mean nothing without the ability to listen with your whole, present being. This is the hard part that cannot be taught in a facilitators' training because it involves a deeply personal bond with the speaker to the exclusion of all else: other noise and movement in the room, your own judgement of the relevance or quality of the speaker's words, the time left for this agenda item and what you might eat for lunch. It is just you and them.

As each delegate prepared to speak, I did three things. First, I looked at them and asked them their name so I could report back what 'Aunty Helen' said at the end, to make sure she and everyone else held me to account for my accuracy in capturing her words and meaning. As she started speaking, I would turn to the whiteboard, my back facing the room, clear my own mind and wait. At one level, I was hearing her through my ears but at a more basic level, I was *feeling* her words through my gut. It was not the words but the changes in volume, tone, timing and most of all, the silent pauses between and beyond the words. This was most obvious when I heard older people talk about their young people, as they did so often around the country. It was visceral, the words merely the shareable output of emotions that ranged from soaring hope to ravening fear for the futures of their young ones. That was where their meaning was and that was when I put pen to board.

My great hope is that people now and into the future are aware of the generosity, conviction, bravery and grace that our people demonstrated throughout the process that led to the Uluru Statement from the Heart. It is the power of our people that sits between and beyond the words on the canvas and it is that power that will realise the momentous vision of the Uluru Statement.

My role in the creation of the Uluru Statement was a small one and one that I was privileged to play. Even now, years after hearing it for the first time, every time I read or hear it read, I can see and feel those people in the room and remember those many moments of silence that stopped rooms full of people in their tracks more than the loud, crashing debate and agreement. One of the challenges of feeling these moments through your gut is that it sticks with you far more than mere words alone. It took me some time after the Uluru Statement was delivered to realise that I carry fragments of those soaring and ravening moments with me and will do so for the rest of my life. In truth, that could become a burden, but I choose to take it as a privilege and a reminder of where the Uluru Statement came from and what it truly promises, between and beyond.

Anthropologist,
Yiman and Pitjara, Queensland

PROFESSOR MARCIA LANGTON AM

When I saw the Uluṟu Statement from the Heart for the first time, glowing amid the artworks at the Darwin Indigenous Art Fair, I was struck by its beauty and simplicity. It was clear to me then that the Uluṟu Statement was a powerful document that would take its place in the history of our petitions, such as the Yirrkala Bark Petitions, presented to the Australian Parliament in 1963, and the Barunga Statement, presented to Prime Minister Bob Hawke and Minister Gerry Hand in 1988. These are also painted petitions presenting powerful words with sacred and iconic designs of the ancestors to indicate their great importance.

Others quickly joined me and during the art fair, people from around Australia and the world read the words that drew us together in unity. I realised that the source of its power was this – as a political statement addressing the brutal ugliness of racism and the historic disempowerment of the First Australians, it did so in the language of the ancient artistic traditions of the Anangu people. When it is explained to people, whether Indigenous or not, who want to know what it means, the message never fails to impress them.

I knew that day at the art fair that this Statement would win over Australians because our nation needs a vision that recognises 65,000 years of our history.

Each year in late July and early August, I visit Gulkula to attend the Garma Festival in north-east Arnhem Land, hosted by the Yothu Yindi Foundation. It was established in the 1990s by the late Yolŋu leader, Dr M. Yunupingu, as a vehicle for sharing Yolŋu culture and philosophy with the world. The foundation is led by clan heads and other leaders. Their vision of a bush university, as set out in the original constitution as the Garma Institute, has come to fruition in a number of ways. Since its inception in 1999, the festival has become the major event for sharing Indigenous culture and ideas. My role as a volunteer has been to contribute to the Key Forum by developing a program and organising speakers. This role has become less critical over the last two decades as more and more Yolŋu people, young and old, design and deliver a truly Yolŋu vision of intellectual sharing and a venue for discussing and debating the most pressing issues facing Indigenous people.

In 2017, the key issue discussed at the forum was the Uluru Statement from the Heart.

I was one of hundreds of people at the festival to hear Dr Galarrwuy Yunupingu AM welcome us to his land and learn why he had gifted the term 'Makarrata' to the nation as one of the key proposals in the Uluru Statement.

The day after the official opening, I was walking away from the forum feeling inspired and optimistic after several speakers had addressed the Uluru Statement from the Heart and its potential to bring the nation together by making a place for us in the Constitution. As I walked along the pathway, I ran into Thomas Mayor who had just spoken, and told him that I thought what he had said was very important – he had talked about the need to build a people's movement to move the politicians and to win a referendum. In passing, he told me that he wanted to take the Uluru Statement that had been set in a painting by the women of Uluru to the people of Australia. He wanted to tell people about it and its message. That, I thought, is the magic of the Garma Festival at work. I said that he must do this and tell Australians why the Uluru Statement is right and just.

Thomas was true to his word and sought to collect the Uluru Statement canvas in Darwin after it was shown at Garma and the Darwin Indigenous Art Fair. As luck would have it, my colleague and friend, cultural heritage warrior Dr Lyndon Ormond-Parker was heading that way after Garma and was happy to make the delivery. Thomas was able to collect it from the Museum and Art Gallery of Northern Territory and take it to Daguragu for the Gurindji people's celebration of the first handover of land by a federal government to Vincent Lingiari by Prime Minister Gough Whitlam, on 16 August 1975. From that special place, Thomas took it to thousands more First Nations people and the Australian public – he took it to the people, rolled up in a taped cardboard tube bought from a post office.

I wondered how the clan leaders who painted the Yirrkala Bark Petitions transported their petitions to Canberra. What did they wrap them in? Did they take them on the plane? Who held these precious objects with the ancient clan designs painted on them? I did not see the Barunga Statement painted at Barunga, but I did see it unfurled at that great gathering with dancers surrounding Hawke and Hand in the traditional way.

Since the day that Thomas picked up the Uluru Statement at

the museum in Darwin, momentum has grown. I have been to several events at The University of Melbourne and Trinity College in Melbourne, where Thomas has been invited to speak and present the Uluṟu Statement from the Heart. Audiences are thrilled that there is a clear answer to the question: What can we do to help? The answer is you can take any action possible to move the politicians from their comfortable status quo, and when the time comes, you can vote 'Yes' to the referendum question on the Voice to Parliament.

It is my strongly held view, based on a great deal of evidence, that only Indigenous people can pull the levers of the policy machine that fails us over and over again, resulting in huge waste with a death toll to match. Indigenous people who are able to participate in these roles feel a great accountability to those who are not thriving in our communities. The bureaucratic machine, left to its own devices, is a failed model. It's time for Australians to face that truth and empower us to fix the system. It has been fifteen years since ATSIC was abolished and the pig-headed refusal to allow an Indigenous Voice in matters that affect our ability to live a full, healthy life has continued to be nothing more than the arrogant assertion of a false superiority; and in the face of accelerating suicide and incarceration rates, the infectious disease epidemics taking lives across our communities and the despair amongst the poorest and least powerful Australians. It makes no sense; it costs too much money; and it causes more damage. We have reached the stage when Indigenous Australians simply no longer trust governments and expect Indigenous leadership in these affairs.

If there were a constitutionally enshrined First Nations Voice – a commission authorised by a constitutional power to advise Parliament, just as the Productivity Commission, the Australia Council and many other bodies do, the absurd policies that have ruined lives for generations would not exist. Every Indigenous person says these same things in slightly different ways. Every statement, from the Yirrkala

Petitions to the Uluṟu Statement from the Heart, says the same things in slightly different ways. How can they all be ignored?

My own experience of speaking to thousands of non-Indigenous Australians has led me to conclude that they want an end to this charade too. They want to live in a nation in which we are treated with respect. They want a release from the terrible guilt that they cannot ignore once they understand what happened in our history. They want us to have dignity, and they will approve of the Uluṟu Statement from the Heart referendum question when the politicians in Canberra finally put it to the people.

Three years on from the first publication of this book, now in its second edition, I remain convinced that the Australian people will vote 'Yes' to guaranteeing Indigenous people a say when decisions are made about us.

The campaign for the Uluṟu Statement hasn't been easy. There were many questions about the detail behind a First Nations Voice. And they needed to be answered. When the former Minister for Indigenous Australians, Ken Wyatt, invited me to chair a Senior Advisory Group on designing the Voice, I accepted. With Professor Tom Calma, Chancellor of the University of Canberra, and fifty Indigenous and non-Indigenous people, we did this work, considering the local, regional and national layers of representation.

In October 2020, we presented the Indigenous Voice Co-design Process Interim Report to the Australian Government, and following an intense period of consultation and meetings with hundreds of Australians and having received submissions from over 10,000 more, we presented our Final Report to the government in July 2021.

We recommended an Indigenous Voice to the Australian Parliament and Government and:

a strong, resilient and flexible system in which Aboriginal and Torres Strait Islander peoples and our communities will be part of genuine shared decision-making with governments at the local and regional level and have our voices heard by the Australian Parliament and Government in policy and law making.

We said:

Now, what lies before us could be the most significant reform in Aboriginal and Torres Strait Islander affairs for generations. We heard in chorus – from our own people, along with non-Indigenous Australians – how much it would mean for Aboriginal and Torres Strait Islander peoples to have our voices heard. The importance of what we propose cannot be understated. There was also strong feedback that an Indigenous Voice must be secure and enduring, and appropriately protected ... we were not surprised by the growing support for constitutional enshrinement that was particularly evident in submissions.

We heard many practical and principled reasons why supporting the enshrinement of an Indigenous Voice in the Australian Constitution, including that it would be the best way to protect an Indigenous Voice against abolition, will enhance its effectiveness and recognise the unique place of Aboriginal and Torres Strait Islander peoples in our nation.

Our report has widespread support and will give all Australians confidence in voting 'Yes' for an Indigenous Voice when they go to the polls in the referendum. There is no need for further enquiry. Every question has been answered in the many reports on the matter. There are, however, many lies and dire warnings from those who oppose our right to a Voice in the matters that affect us. I urge Australians to understand the justice and nation-building import of the Voice. Read the reports if you need to. All roads lead to the nation voting 'Yes'.

Anangu, Northern Territory

SAMMY WILSON, TJAMA ULURU

When I flew to Uluru in late May 2017 for the Uluru First Nations Constitutional Convention, I was on a journey with hundreds of other Aboriginal and Torres Strait Islander people. We were coming together to discuss the Australian Constitution, so I spent the short time in the air reading it.

Almost two years later, I travelled to Uluru again. This time, I was alone. My journey to the centre of Australia was to meet with one man, for the final interview for this book – a man named Sammy Wilson. He is Uluru.

On the short flight between Alice Springs and Uluru, I leant my head against the plane's window to gaze on the country below. I looked down at the patterns of spinifex covering ancient sand dunes. The dunes looked small, so far down below, like ripples on a beach. Intermittently, rocky outcrops and sparse desert flora dotted the landscape, and I realised I was looking at a living Anangu painting. It dawned on me that what I was seeing from high above in the small plane was Anangu law – song lines, creation stories – Tjukurrpa. It struck me that, like my flight in 2017, I was passing my time looking at sections of a nation's constitution.

This time though, I thought, I am looking at the original and continuing constitution. A constitution that has existed, according to the common law, since time immemorial.

It was early afternoon when we landed at Uluru. As I stepped from the controlled cool air of the plane's cabin, a hot dry wind licked my face. The warmth felt pleasant at first. Though not for long. The short walk across the tarmac was all it took for the shade of the terminal to be a welcome comfort. Seeing the familiar airport immediately brought back pleasant memories from 2017. Memories that became more intense and heartfelt when I arrived at the Yulara Resort, the place where around 270 of us stayed and convened the Uluru First Nations Constitutional Convention. I checked in, took my bags to my room, then went for a walk to revisit more memories.

First, I walked to the Uluru Meeting Place. The large convention room where – between massive Aboriginal and Torres Strait Islander flags – we shared our regional dialogue outcomes and conducted debate, before achieving a constitutional moment by endorsing the Uluru Statement from the Heart. Thinking about the positive vibe of that third and final morning brought on goose bumps. Afterwards, I had joined the excited throng of delegates lining up to put our names on a blank canvas. We were still congratulating each other, there were more hugs – some of us with swollen eyes from crying. I recalled how my face was aching from smiling.

I laughed quietly as I walked past the bar where many of us celebrated our success until daylight the following morning. I tried to be inconspicuous as I took a photo of the quiet little corner where the guitar players had sat strumming, with the rest of us crowded around singing. The corner may have been empty as I stood reminiscing, but I could hear the revelry still echoing off the walls two years on. I smiled at that fondest of memories.

Next, I stopped at the break-out room where I first met the late Sol Bellear. I bowed my head for a moment, remembering that giant of a man. Sol and other giants of his time, in Redfern, Sydney, spearheaded the Black Power and Land Rights movements, and then established the first Aboriginal health and legal centres in Australia. He never stopped fighting for his people. In his last weeks before joining his ancestors in the stars, he worked tirelessly on the Uluru Statement campaign.

My final destination was to see the magnificent and sacred Uluru. Both the rock and the man, Sammy Wilson. In the way of the Anangu, Sammy is the custodian of Uluru because he is the eldest grandson of the late Paddy Uluru. The grandfather and grandson relationship (tjamu) is one of the most significant relationships in Anangu life. It is his relationship with his grandfather that gives Sammy his real name, Tjama Uluru.

Sammy lives in the small community of Mutitjulu, the closest community to Uluru. He is a leader of his people in two systems of law, both on the boards and councils that affect his community, and in Anangu Tjukurrpa (Anangu law).

The Anangu lands around Uluru and Kata Tjuta were mostly unsuitable to the invading white people's interests. In 1920, the area was declared part of a larger system of Aboriginal reserves. Though, as with almost all Aboriginal reserves, some of the lands were eventually excised for mining interests. Then in 1948, a dirt road was built to bring tourists to Uluru. By the 1950s, miners and tourists were consistently occupying and interrupting Anangu life.

Sammy's father was a man of Scottish descent who wasn't around for long. His skin colour is light, so in his youth, this caused his connection to family and Country to be precarious. He and other light-skinned Aboriginal children were a popular target for child-stealing government authorities. The book *I am Uluru*, written about the Ulu̲ru family by author Jen Cowley with the Ulu̲ru Family, said of Sammy:

> *Sammy Wilson (nephew of Reggie and Cassidy and grandson of Paddy Ulu̲ru) was a child of mixed race and was himself at times on the radar of authorities but was saved from removal by family members on various occasions. Sammy – who, as Paddy's eldest grandson is nominal 'head' of the family – is acutely aware of the dreadful and generations-long impact of forced removal on his family and A̲nangu society as a whole.*

Though the authorities had tried, they didn't manage to steal Sammy. In his youth he walked the song lines and learnt from his grandfather and other Elders in accordance with the Tjukurrpa (A̲nangu law). He takes the custodianship of his family's knowledge very seriously. The decision to give the name 'Ulu̲ru', to the Ulu̲ru Statement from the Heart was made by Sammy and his family, for both spiritual and practical purpose. Sammy wants the power of Ulu̲ru to help achieve change. For this reason, I felt there was no more fitting person than Sammy, Tjama Ulu̲ru, to give the final interview for this book.

On the drive from Yulara to Ulu̲ru to interview Sammy, I took my time to enjoy the incredible landscape. Ulu̲ru is famous for its captivating display of brilliant red at the height of the day, and infinite shades of purple as the sun descends. The rock dramatically changes appearance depending on which of the 360 degrees of circumference it is viewed from. Photographers love Ulu̲ru for the trillions of possible ways that a camera may capture the rock's pose and performance. Sammy wanted to show me a new perspective – a perspective that cannot be captured in a photograph.

'I'll take you for a walk, at Mutitjulu Waterhole, show you the story of Kuniya and Liru and explain some things.'

I was excited to walk to the site of an epic creation story with Sammy Wilson. And, because he is a very busy man, I was lucky. He is Chair of both the Mutitjulu Aboriginal Corporation and the Uluru and Kata Tjuta Park boards; more recently he has been elected as the Chair of the Central Land Council. On the day I met him, he was between meetings for various of these roles.

We picked up some water and hit the road. 'I was born over there [he pointed], near the Stuart Highway. I don't know where the border, but I was born on the land. Not in a hospital and not far from here. Near De Rose Hill Station.' In Central Australia, 400 kilometres isn't far between communities. 'I grew up here on my grandfather's and great-grandfather's Country here. This place. I went to school little bit everywhere. But my school was the land and the language, and my Elders.

'And a lot of my school was from tourism,' Sammy said, and laughed. 'I teach them about my land, and they teach me too.'

Sammy told me how he uses the analogy of a person's bedroom to explain sacred sites to tourists. 'I say to them, when I welcome you to visit my house, you can sit at the table with me, sit on my couch in my living room. But you don't go into my bedroom? Wiya! [No!] That's not good! That's my private place.'

Uluru loomed ahead; a brilliant, bright red. 'When I went to school – in the late '60s, early '70s maybe – my name was Tjama Uluru. I changed it to Sammy because I was scared of this place, Uluru, when I was a young boy. When they asked me what my last name, I got upset and went home. Mum said to me, "What you doing here? You should be in school." I said, "These mob there, they're asking me a lot of questions." I didn't want my Uluṟu name. It's a powerful place, you know. My stepfather is Wilson. He said, "You want to be Wilson?" I said, "Well, yeah." He said, "Okay then."' Sammy laughed. 'I was a bit happy! But I'm still Uluṟu. I know now that this rock is a really special place. It's who I am.'

When we stopped at the Mutitjulu car park, Sammy checked that I had my water and we began walking. We casually talked about what had transpired in that special place, both recently and in the Creation.

'In the '30s, my grandfather Paddy Uluṟu and his brother, there was four of them including one young fella – they was hiding from policemen here because something happened this way [pointing southward]. They speared one cow. They thought it was a monster with its big horns when it came to them at night. Piranpa [white fella] found the wounded cow. So the policemen chased them. They came here, hiding in the rock here, and one of them was shot by the policeman.' It was Paddy's brother, killed by the piranpa's bullet.

As Sammy spoke, he pointed to the crevices in the great rock where his grandfather had hidden, and one of the men had died. It was an eerie feeling, standing where the blood was spilt for colonial 'justice'. I imagined red dust in the unsettled wake of desperate, scrambling men. Indiscriminately fired bullets ricocheting off the smooth rock walls of the shelter, where a man who had played in that place as a child was about to lose his life because an alien, milking cow had been wounded.

'When night time come, they escaped. One went west and the other two, my grandfather, went South Australia near Ernabella. My grandfather never came back until the '50s. He walked back from Mimili with my two uncles, Reggie and Cassidy, who are still living here. The family walked with one camel – something like 350 kilometres they walked. When they got here they found that everything is changing. There were tourists everywhere going in to everything, doing whatever they want. And we had no rights.'

Sammy and I continued down the track toward the waterhole, and excited throngs of tourists chattered loudly as they passed by. They were oblivious to the importance of the man named for the place they'd come to see. I mentioned to Sammy that when I stopped at the waterhole earlier on, I had what felt like a full fifteen minutes sitting in the shade by myself, with no tourists around me. He laughed and said that I was lucky.

Stopping at a bush to pick some small black berries, he told me, 'You can eat this one, arnguli. They call it bush plum too.' Sammy put a plum to his mouth and carefully bit into its flesh. 'Be careful, he got seed inside.' I took one from his hand and tasted it. It was a little sweet and a little bitter at the same time, but nice.

The path now led along the base of Uluru. I commented on the shape of the base of the rock – it was as though a massive python metres long with a body much bigger than me had slithered by, indenting its shape in the hard, red surface. Sammy smiled. 'Uwa! [Yes!] That's her! That's her now, Kuniya the woma python, she come from the east. She had a bad feeling.' Sammy rubbed his belly. 'She was wondering, Why I feel like this? The feeling was because her nephew needed help. A war party, the Liru snake men, had followed him from the west.'

Kuniya's impression in the rock led to the Mutitjulu Waterhole. The waterhole is small, tucked in to a deep bay in the rock. In the afternoon, this little place by the waterhole is cool and shady, and serene if you are lucky enough to have more than a moment alone.

Sammy told me how saddened his grandfather was when he returned to see the careless desecration of deeply sacred sites on and around Uluru. The tourism operators and park rangers paid little regard to the old Aboriginal man. The Anangu people had become outcasts, etching out a meagre living making artefacts and selling them to tourists.

Sammy's uncles, Reggie and Cassidy, who were only boys when they returned to Uluru with their father, recalled those times with other members of the Uluru family in the book *I am Uluru*. Reggie said:

> *He (the park ranger Bill Harney) wasn't very welcoming. He said, 'What are you doing here? This is not your country.' And my father said, 'No, I AM Uluru. This is my Country.'*
>
> *Cassidy too recalls an overtly cool reception: 'I remember when I was little, I was kicked out of the tourist area at Uluru. They didn't want me playing around where the tourists were. That used to happen quite a bit.'*
>
> *Other family members recount that in the early days there were complaints from tourists about Aboriginal people, 'lazy blacks', intruding on their holiday experience, so Anangu were often hunted away from Uluru and Kata Tjuta.*

Sammy cited the 1967 referendum for Aboriginal citizenship rights as the catalyst for change. 'Then in 1967, everything changed after that referendum. Some people wanted to find my grandfather to talk about this place. They wanted to know about his story to help us get the land rights. Remember Sir Doug Nicholls? He was in the government in Adelaide. He was in Parliament. He played for Fitzroy.' Sammy laughed and said, 'Sometimes when I tell people from Victoria or Adelaide, they say, "Yeah, he used to play with my grandfather!" Because Sir Doug Nicholls used to play AFL! I got this old photo where he is talking to my grandfather in Mimili South Australia.'

Sammy's grandfather with other strong Anangu Elders worked

tirelessly to change attitudes toward their custodianship, and, when the *Aboriginal Land Rights Act (NT) 1976* was enacted, they sought to reclaim their land. The Northern Territory Government, pastoralists and the tourism industry fought tooth and nail against any land claim. But in 1983, much to the antagonists' disappointment, the newly elected Prime Minister Bob Hawke announced his government would amend the Aboriginal Land Rights Act to return the title for Uluru-Kata Tjuta National Park to the Traditional Owners. Sadly, Sammy's beloved grandfather Paddy, had passed away by then.

As we walked back to the car, Sammy pointed out another part of the Kuniya Liru Tjukurrpa. 'That's her again, coming from the other side. When she found out her bad feeling was the Liru snake men had speared the woma python, her nephew, she performed a special ritual to give herself power. Here, have a look at them marks. At the bottom of the rock there, that's where she knelt down in the sand. She is kneeling and covering herself with the sand. It's part of a ritual. That's why it is Muti. Muti means "knee"; tjunu means "put down". Muti-tjunu is "kneel down". Mutijulu. When she kneel down, that's her knees. These holes here, when it rains, the other holes change colours, but these ones always the same.' We walked a little further, and he pointed to marks high up on the rock wall to the west of the waterhole. 'Up there, look, you see her war-club marks. You can see where Kuniya hit the snake man, Liru.'

Sammy guided me down another path, to a small cave with artwork that is probably tens of thousands of years old. He explained that the drawings – circles within circles, arches and familiar shapes – are more than art. 'It's not an art. It's a written language. Before all these letters come, this was part of our communication. The circles and lines show where the waterhole is, or for hunting and gathering.'

Walking back from the cave, Sammy stopped me and pointed back at it. 'The aunty and the nephew became one as the rainbow serpent. You look there at the rocks, that's her. She is there curled up, Kuniya. This is where part of her stayed.

'Long time ago, there was no water here. Anangu people come, they put meat, Kuka. They sing out to the water guardian, the rainbow serpent here – *whoosh* – and the water come then. And they leave the meat.'

Suddenly a fresh wind gust blew. It felt odd. I had goose bumps.

Sammy laughed. He said, 'Same as when Oprah Winfrey came here! The wind blew like this. She said, "Oi, I can feel it! Something is here!"'

Back at the ranger station, I sat with Sammy before his next meeting. An elderly Anangu man, also there for the meeting, came and sat with us. We chatted about the ceremony in Mutitjulu for the Uluru First Nations Constitutional Convention, the 'inma' (ceremony), where the Torres Strait Islanders and Yolŋu danced on the same grounds as his people. We also talked fondly about the moment when we endorsed the Uluru Statement – as Sammy said, 'We were all crying.'

In between my questions and Sammy's answers, he and the elderly Anangu man spoke in Pitjantjatjara Yankunytjatjara. I thought perhaps Sammy was translating our conversation. I could pick up the occasional word. I heard 'Tjukurrpa' and 'Voice' mentioned several times.

Without a pause in their conversation, and before I realised it, Sammy was talking to me again. 'You see where I'm living here? There's a rock here, hmm? And we live in a hard place … We're between a rock and a hard place! You like that?' He laughed. Then he said seriously, 'When all the [Aboriginal and Torres Strait Islander] peoples came here, whether they from here or another Country – Victoria or Tasmania or South Australia or wherever – we came together to get our voices in there to the government, or we'll be fighting and arguing with each other while the government is laughing at us.

'We all came together as one,' Sammy said to me. 'Tjungu, means one people, together, with the one Voice. A<u>n</u>angu gotta be in Canberra together with other First Nations – stronger – doesn't matter different language, different culture, but one Tjukurrpa, one story, One Voice,' said Ulu<u>r</u>u.

NOW WALK WITH US

Conclusion

The people in this book – our Voices – have generously shared our many perspectives, stories and experiences because we care about our country and our future. We have done this work because we want you to understand why the Uluṟu Statement from the Heart invites you to walk with us.

If you have truly listened, you will have learnt that our culture – a sharing, proud, resilient, sophisticated and ancient culture – is what makes Australia unique. Our Aboriginal and Torres Strait Islander heritage is the heart of the nation.

Australia has nothing to lose and everything to gain from guaranteeing First Nations voices are heard in the centre of decision making. The establishment of a representative body is how we have chosen to be recognised. Our Voice – speaking for our people rather than our individual intersests, a political party or a mostly non-Indigenous electorate – will enhance and improve Australian democracy.

As the Uluṟu Statment says:

> *When we have power over our destiny, our children will flourish, they will walk in two worlds and their culture will be a gift to their country.*

This gift is for all of us. Centring our culture in Australia's birth certificate will see our 'young' nation mature – a coming of age. It is a practical gift. As the challenges of climate change, wealth inequality and global conflicts mount, the wisdom of the longest surviving people on earth – the custodians of this land and our environment; the masters of dispute resolution, or Makarrata; with our sharing, collective ways and kinships – will be a guiding light for the Australian Parliament.

In the first edition of this book, published in 2019, I wrote that the first barrier to finding the heart of the nation would be the politicians in the Federal Parliament. This has proven to be true. Through this book and throughout my travels I asked tens of thousands of Australian people, who have brought in hundreds of thousands more, to help us move a majority of politicians to support a First Nations Voice referendum. The Scott Morrison government could not be convinced, and so, they have paid the price. On 21 May 2022, almost five years on from the political feat we achieved at Uluru, the Australian people elected a new prime minister. When Prime Minister Anthony Albanese accepted victory that night, he was as passionate about the Uluru Statement as we are. He has made the firm promise: 'There will be a First Nations Voice referendum in this term of Parliament.' When he reaffirmed that commitment, I literally jumped for joy – we now have a leader with the courage to let the people decide.

We mustn't take this for granted – this support in Parliament. Politicians have only been convinced to support a First Nations Voice referendum because we refused to take no for an answer. We have worked hard, with you, to convince enough of them that we can win. As you have read in these pages, from the voices themselves, from the history of our struggle we know that politicians can be fickle. Promises are broken when the political cost seems too high.

As Indigenous leaders negotiate the terms of a referendum with the government, politicians of all persuasions will need to see and hear your loud, proud and public expressions of support.

As I write, the proposal for a Voice referendum is yet to secure bi-partisanship. The Peter Dutton led Coalition Opposition have declared they are open to supporting a referendum, but they remain unconvinced. I want you to help us bring the Coalition on side, though the government and the Australian people should not wait, as if bi-partisanship is a precondition for success. If the Dutton Coalition choose to be on the wrong side of history again; if they fail to grasp the nation building reform that this is – a matter that is beyond Left and Right politics – let them knock themselves out. We will win without them.

I want you to grasp the rarity of this opporutnity. I want you to realise this chance to constitutionally recognise Indigenous peoples – in a way that we have determined we wish to be recognised – will be the last for generations to come. Fail, and we know the gap will not close. Fail, and we know meaningful treaties will take generations longer to reach. Fail, and we know that those who oppose the truth will continue their lies and harmful acts unabated, without repercussion and accountability.

If we fail, there is a real human cost – we are more than statistics in the Closing the Gap reports. Many lives depend on our success. Because in a democracy, nothing is more practical, more lifesaving, than the power to be heard.

So, what can you do to help?

If you are reading this and the Australian Constitution has not yet enshrined a First Nations Voice to Parliament, then the Uluṟu Statement from the Heart remains a live political document, and this book remains a call to action.

There are many actions you can take to help us. None too big.

None too small. Every action to the best of your capability and capacity will help.

Whether you are in a suburb, in a city, or in a small town, please join a Voice Yes campaign group. If there isn't a group already established, please start one to develop initiatives that will educate and activate other members of your community, and maintain pressure on your Member of Parliament.

Encourage organisations you are affiliated with – union, corporate, religious, schools, social, local government council, political party, sporting or NGO – to commit to supporting a 'Yes' vote in the First Nations Voice referendum. It is your obligation – not First Nations people's alone – to ensure that everyone in your street, your suburb, your book club or sporting club, your workplace and your family gatherings have all pledged to vote 'Yes'.

Finally, though importantly, register your support on the website www.fromtheheart.com.au, so when campaign messaging, actions and toolkits are developed and updated, you will be right beside us as we find the heart of the nation.

Below is the QR Code to Thomas Mayor's website where you can find links to his social media accounts and other books, as well as essays and articles he has written.

It was Christmas time, 2018. Travelling to share the message of the Uluṟu Statement, hotels and motels across the country were more familiar than home for me that year, though unlike the year before, I was in a more positive mood. Momentum was building.

I'd warned my family that this Christmas break I would need to be writing. I was still unsure if I were capable of writing this book, but I knew that if I were to succeed, I would need to write as much as I could, as soon as I could.

On the morning before Christmas Eve, my seven-year old son, William, came to my side carrying his favourite novel, *Hot Dog!* by Anh Do. William is one of the best readers in his class, far ahead of his age group. He makes me incredibly proud.

'Dad, what will the name of the book be?' he asked.

I closed my laptop, turned to him, and said, 'What would you call my book?'

'Ummm ...' He smiled a devilish grin and with practiced precision, he put his hand under his armpit and responded with a series of armpit farts.

We laughed, both childishly. I love kids at this age when the smallest things are still funny.

I said to him, 'The name of the book will be "Finding the Heart of the Nation".'

William looked at me, somewhat puzzled. '"Finding the heart of the nation ... Where is the heart of the nation?'

I pulled my son close. I looked him in the eyes and smiled. I put my hand on his heart and said, 'The heart of the nation is here.'

VISIT IF WELCOME, RESPECT ALWAYS, AND LEARN!

Throughout my journey, the people I connected with shared more than stories. They also enthusiastically told me about places and events that fill them with pride. They asked me to encourage you to learn about Aboriginal and Torres Strait Islander Australia. They want you to see and feel Country.

On your own journey, when you head off to find a new track, be aware that Indigenous lands are sacred. Our millennia-old laws and customs, though violated since colonisation, remain intact. Therefore, there are some places where you won't be welcome, Indigenous or not. As a Torres Strait Islander, I am forbidden from some sacred places on Yolŋu land, for example, just like anyone else.

How will you know where you can go and what you can do on Aboriginal land? The answer is RESPECT.

Foremost, respect that all lands and waters were never ceded – they were never given to the colonisers by the Traditional Owners. Our ownership is far more than 'Traditional'. It continues.

Always pay respect to the ongoing connection of the First Nations people and their Country, wherever that may be. Whether you are in the spiritual heart at Uluṟu, or at the Convention Centre in Darling

Harbour, both places are on Aboriginal land. Darling Harbour is as much Gadigal of the Eora Nation, as Uluru is Pitjantjatjara of the Anangu. Wherever you go, always acknowledge the First Nations people.

When on Country, show respect by listening, observing and following instructions. Respect signs or a guide's directions, especially if they forbid entry or photography. Would you let tourists take photos in your bedroom unannounced? The laws and customs may be different from yours, but no less sacred. Don't complain because you can no longer climb Uluru.

When planning a trip, do your research, call ahead, ask permission, and learn the protocols where you can.

Land councils are a good place to start your research. There is a wealth of information online too. To find out who the Traditional Owners are, the AIATSIS Map of Indigenous Australia is helpful. See: aiatsis.gov.au/explore/articles/aiatsis-map-indigenous-australia

I recommend Marcia Langton's book, *Welcome to Country*, as a comprehensive guide to travel throughout Indigenous Australia.

Respect that Indigenous languages are many, questions are handled differently by Indigenous people, and an understanding of English or your slang may be incomprehensible. And you might not be told that this is the case. Questions might be answered by example, or answers are not given in an obvious way. The western perception of time is also different. Don't forget that we are not homogenous.

The First Nations of Australia are truly generous with culture. Across Indigenous Australia, there is so much to see, touch, learn, embrace and feel. You can go on a journey as I did. Start now. Don't wait. Go and find the heart of the nation! Spread the word about the Uluru Statement campaign while you are at it!

FURTHER READING

If this book has moved you, please buy a copy for your friends and family (all author royalties go to the campaign). I have also published two childrens books about the Uluru Statement:

Finding Our Heart, a book about the Uluru Statement for young Australians; and,

Freedom Day: Vincent Lingiari and the story of the Wave Hill Walk-off (co-author, Rosie Smiler, Vincent Lingiari's grand-daughter).

I ask that you help us put these books into children's hands, because we know they'll go forth and teach the adults in their lives about the importance of the Uluru Statement from the Heart.

Thomas's other books and essays

Thomas Mayor, *Finding Our Heart*, Hardie Grant Travel, Melbourne, 2020

Thomas Mayor and Rosie Smiler, *Freedom Day,* Bright Light Books (Hardie Grant Publishing), Melbourne 2021

Thomas Mayor (editor and contributor), *Dear Son: Letters and reflections from First Nations fathers and sons,* Hardie Grant Publishing, Melbourne 2021

Thomas Mayor, 'A dream that cannot be denied: On the road to Freedom Day', 2020, griffithreview.com

'When the heart speaks: Learning the language of listening in Australia'. Opening chapter in: Ashley Hay (editor), 'Generosities of Spirit', *Griffith Review 70*, 2020

'Where truths collide: Challenging Australia's shaky foundations'. Opening chapter in: Ashley Hay (editor) with Teela Reid (curator), 'Acts of Reckoning', *Griffith Review 76*, 2020, griffithreview.com

'Time to heal: Uluṟu healing the people and the land' chapter in: Emma Dawson, Janet McCalman (editors), *What Happens Next? Reconstructing Australia after COVID-19*, MUP, Melbourne, 2020

Publications to look out for

Sam Faulkner (editor), *Growing up Torres Strait Islander in Australia,* Black Inc Books, 2024

Thomas Mayor and Bernadette Foley, *Yes Campaign Handbook: How to win a Voice referendum*, Broadcast Books, 2023

Thomas Mayor and Bernard Namok Jr, *All about the Torreş Strait Islander Flag*, Magabala Books, 2023

Books and articles

Hal Alexander and Phil Griffiths (editors), *A Few Rough Reds: Stories of rank and file organising*, Australian Society for the Study of Labour History, Canberra, 2003

Libby Connors, *Warrior: A legendary leader's dramatic life and violent death on the colonial frontier*, Allen & Unwin, Sydney, 2015

Kevin Cook and Heather Goodall, *Making Change Happen: Black and white activists talk to Kevin Cook about Aboriginal, union and liberation politics*, ANU E Press, Canberra, 2013

Jen Cowley, *I am Uluṟu: A family's story*, Kungja Kutjara Aboriginal Corporation, Uluṟu, Northern Territory, 2018

Megan Davis, 'The Republic is an Aboriginal Issue', *The Monthly*, April 2018, themonthly.com.au

Megan Davis, 'Voice Treaty Truth', *The Monthly*, July 2018, themonthly.com.au

Bruce Elder, *Blood on the Wattle: Massacres and maltreatment of Australian*

Aborigines since 1788, Child & Associates, Frenchs Forest, NSW, 1988

Sean Flood, *Mabo: A symbol of struggle the unfinished quest for Voice Treaty Truth*, Sean Flood, Castlecrag, NSW, 2019

Billy Griffiths, *Deep Time Dreaming: Uncovering ancient Australia*, Black Inc., Melbourne, 2018

Yidumduma Bill Harney as told to Jan Wositzky, *Born under the Paperbark Tree: A man's life*, ABC Books, Sydney, 1996

Anita Heiss, *Growing up Aboriginal in Australia*, Black Inc., Melbourne, 2018

Marcia Langton, *Welcome to Country: A travel guide to Indigenous Australia*, 2nd edition, Hardie Grant Explore, Melbourne, 2021

Marcia Langton, *Welcome to Country youth edition: An Introduction to our First Peoples for Young Australians*, Hardie Grant Explore, Melbourne, 2019

Shane Maloney and Chris Gros, 'Truganini and George Augustus Robinson', *The Monthly*, May 2012, themonthly.com.au

John Maynard, *Fight for Liberty and Freedom: The origins of Australian Aboriginal activism*, Aboriginal Studies Press, Canberra, 2007

Charlie McAdam as told to Elizabeth Tregenza, *Boundary Lines: A family's story of winning against the odds*, McPhee Gribble Publishers, Melbourne, 1995

Tom McDonald, *Dare to dream: The memoires of Tom and Audrey McDonald*, 2016, daretodreammemoirs.com.au

Sally McManus, *On Fairness*, Melbourne University Press, Melbourne, 2019

Bruce Pascoe, *Dark Emu: Black seeds: agriculture or accident?*, Magabala Books, Broome, 2014

Teela Reid, '2020: The year of reckoning, not reconciliation', *Griffith Review*, February 2020, griffithreview.com

Teela Reid, 'The heart of seeding First Nations sovereignty', 2020, griffithreview.com

Nonie Sharp, 'Culture clash in the Torres Strait Island: The Maritime Strike of 1936', *Journal of the Royal Historical Society of Queensland*, vol. 11, no. 3, 1981, pp 107–126

Nonie Sharp, *Stars of Tagai: The Torres Strait Islanders*, AIATSIS, ACT, 1993

Irynej Skira, '"I hope you will be my friend": Tasmanian Aborigines in the Furneaux Group in the nineteenth century – population and land tenure', *Aboriginal History*, vol. 21, 1997, press-files.anu.edu.au

Jeff Sparrow, *No Way but This: In search of Paul Robeson*, Scribe, Melbourne, 2017

Adrian Vickers and Julia Martinez, *The Pearl Frontier: Indonesian labour and Indigenous encounters in Australia's northern trading network*, University of Hawai'i Press, Honolulu, 2015

Charlie Ward, *A Handful of Sand: The Gurindji Struggle, after the Walk-off*, Monash University Publishing, Clayton, Victoria, 2016

M. J. Warren, *Unsettled Settlers: Fear and White Victimhood in New South Wales and Van Diemen's Land*, 1788–1838, University of Sydney, Sydney, PhD Doctorate, 2017

Dr Galarrwuy Yunupingu, 'Rom Watangu: An Indigenous leader reflects on a lifetime following the law of the land', *The Monthly*, July 2016, themonthly.com.au

Anna Krien, 'The death of Kumanjayi Walker: On the shooting in Yuendumu and the trial of Northern Territory Policeman Zachary Rolfe', *The Monthly*, May 2022

Sarah Schulman, *Conflict is not abuse: Overstating harm, community responsibility, and the duty of repair*, Arsenal Pulp Press, Vancouver, 2016

Useful links

Australian Hall: dictionaryofsydney.org/entry/australian_hall

Blackfulla Bookclub: instagram.com/blackfulla_bookclub

Final Report of the Referendum Council 30 June 2017: referendumcouncil.org.au/sites/default/files/report_attachments/Referendum_Council_Final_Report.pdf

Milirrpum v Nabalco Pty Ltd (1971) court case: alrc.gov.au/publications/ native-title-its-historical-context

Torres Strait Regional Authority (TSRA), for further information on the TSRA: tsra.gov.au

Torres Strait local government: statements.qld.gov.au/Statement/2017/8/23/ torres-strait-celebrates-80-years-of-local-government

Trugernanner (Truganini) (1812–1876): adb.anu.edu.au/biography/ trugernanner-truganini-4752

ABOUT THE AUTHOR

Thomas Mayor is a Kaurareg Aboriginal, and Kalkalgal and Erubamle Torres Strait Islander man born on Larrakia Country in Darwin. As an Islander growing up on the mainland, he learned to hunt traditional foods with his father and to island dance from the Darwin community of Torres Strait Islanders. In high school, Thomas's English teacher suggested he should become a writer. He didn't think then that he would become one of the first Torres Strait Islander authors to have books published for the general trade.

Instead, he became a wharf labourer from the age of seventeen, until he became a union official for the Maritime Union of Australia in his early thirties. Quietly spoken, Thomas found his voice on the wharves. As he gained the skills of negotiation and organising in the union movement, he applied those skills to advancing the rights of Indigenous peoples, becoming a signatory to the Uluru Statement from the Heart and a tireless campaigner.

Following the Uluru Convention, Thomas was entrusted to carry the sacred canvas of the Uluru Statement from the Heart. He then embarked on an eighteen-month journey around the country to garner support for a constitutionally enshrined First Nations Voice and a Makarrata Commission for truth-telling and agreement-making or treaties.

Thomas's journey continues, both in person and through the pages of this book. He is the father of five children, and has published multiple books including books for children, essays in the *Griffith Review* and anthologies, and articles with the *Sydney Morning Herald*, *The Saturday Paper*, *The Guardian*, *Crikey* and *The Conversation*, among others.

This book is Thomas's gift to the campaign for Voice, Treaty and Truth. Like the Uluṟu Statement from the Heart, he hopes that all Australians will accept it.

ACKNOWLEDGEMENTS

First and foremost, I thank my wife Melanie Mayor and my children, Shayla, Tiah, Celestino, William and Ruby Mayor, for supporting me to do what I believe in. There is nothing more valuable than the time we have together, and we lost many precious moments while I have done this work. My time away from family has worried my mum, Liz Mayor, and my dad, Celestino Mayor, more than anyone else. Thank you for your love and for always supporting me.

I thank my union, the Construction Forestry Maritime Mining and Energy Union. Thank you to Michael O'Connor, Tony Maher, Dave Noonan and all the officials, rank and file, and in particular the Maritime Division – the Maritime Union of Australia; Paddy Crumlin, Will Tracey, Ian Bray, Warren Smith, Jamie Newlyn, Mich-Elle Myers, Andy Burford, and all of my MUA comrades. Thank you for your solidarity and your vision.

I thank the union movement – the two amazing women who are leading us, Sally McManus and Michelle O'Neil – and every single member, their families, the Elders such as Freddy Moore, Tom and Audrey McDonald, Uncle Kevin Tory and Uncle Bob Anderson; and the comrades who are now at rest. As Australian unionists you've done more than further your own wages and conditions, you've also lifted the standards of living for all. You've won our universal health care (Medicare), the standard eight-hour day, annual leave, personal leave, and the opportunity to retire with dignity, among other standards that are far too many to simply take for granted. You've consistently stood with First Nations people. Union members are not thugs. McManus is right, laws that stop workers from fighting for a fair go and a share of the wealth that they produce were made to be broken. Unions are the backbone of a fair and equal society and it is time for us to grow again.

To the twenty Aboriginal and Torres Strait Islanders who gave me their time and opened their hearts, sharing their struggles, heartbreak, aspirations and successes, thank you. During my travels, I met so many more wonderful people than I have been able to mention in this book. A quick note to you all – from Yule River in the far west, to the big hearted people around Byron Bay in the east, and including the brothers and sisters of the Puyallup and Squamish in the Northern Hemisphere – I wanted to interview many more than twenty First Nations people. I wanted to tell more of your stories and I hope they will be told soon. My respect and appreciation to you all.

Thank you to Aunty Pat Anderson, Professor Megan Davis and Noel Pearson for your hard work and brave leadership. The regional dialogues and the Uluru Convention couldn't have happened without your dedication, vision, and your commitment to genuinely listening to people across many diverse communities.

A special thanks to Teela Reid for reading the draft manuscript and providing helpful support and advice along the way. I thank Rita Mallia, Denise and Sean Bowden, Peter Manning, Stephen Fitzpatrick, Gabrielle Appleby, Clive Scollay and Charlie Ward, who read some of my early drafts and provided honest feedback. I also thank the generous photographers who donated some of the beautiful photos reproduced in this book. Thank you, Jessica Micalleff, for your administrative support. Danny Glover, thank you for sharing your international experience and your solidarity.

I thank Melissa Kayser, Astrid Browne and everyone at Hardie

Grant for giving a wharfie a shot at being an author, Tristan Schultz for the great design work, and Bernadette Foley for your great editorial professionalism; you've been a comrade as I found my way.

Shayla Mayor, my daughter who at a last-minute request produced the beautiful Torres Strait Island-style art for this book, thank you. You have a great talent. I am proud of you.

Last but not least, my deepest gratitude to Marcia Langton for giving me the confidence and connections to complete this work. Your advice has been invaluable, and your kindness encouraging.

ARTWORK BY SHAYLA MAYOR

The artwork in this book displays the Torres Strait style, patterns and images that have meaning in Shayla and her father Thomas's lives.

Shovel-nose shark (kaigas) and pearl shell: On the left side of the artwork is an image of Thomas's totem, kaigas (shovel-nose shark). It symbolises the beginning of Thomas's journey. On the right side of the artwork is an image of a mother of pearl shell. It symbolises Thomas's mixed heritage of indentured Asian pearl industry workers and the Zenadth Kes (Torres Strait).

Turtle (waru) and dugong (dhangal): The turtle and dugong are traditional foods for Torres Strait Islanders. Hunting is always done sustainably and with the greatest respect to the animals that have nourished Islander people for thousands of years. Between the turtle and the dugong are images of waps (harpoons used to capture turtles and dugongs). These images symbolise maintaining traditions as well as a coming of age.

Dhari and ship: On the left side of the artwork is a traditional headdress, the dhari, worn in ceremonies across the Torres Strait. The dhari is featured in the centre of the Torres Strait Islander flag. In the artwork it symbolises the connection to culture, and passing on this culture to the next generation. On the right side of the artwork is an offshore supply vessel. It symbolises Thomas's connection to the maritime industry and the Maritime Union of Australia.

The heart of the nation: This artwork simply symbolises Australia's heart. It is the last artwork in the series. This final piece was created in the hope that we find it.

Shayla also drew the dinkus used between paragraphs and the line drawings opposite the chapter-opening pages. As a proud Torres Strait Islander woman, they are inspired by her culture and Country.

'Aboriginal people are not asking
to live in a perfect world. All we
are asking for is not to be ignored.
You like a bit of a challenge in life,
so being perfect would be boring.
But we can make Australia a
better place by learning from
our history.'

~ Robert Roy